Cows I Have
By William E. Gil

With illustrations by Sarah E. Gillespie

Table of Contents

Prologue

As I walked down the dusty cow path, a breeze descended into the creek bottom, gently stirred the leaves and dropped its cool fall air. Off to the east, the moon was just peeking into the valley, and yet the western sky was still aglow with the last rays of the sun. As I admired the evening, I noticed one of my favorite cows grazing beneath a persimmon tree. I took a slight detour to check on her. I quietly greeted her by saying, "Hi, Silage Cow, what are you up to?"

She lifted her head as if to reply, "Hi, William, I'm eating some delicious persimmons."

I reached up for a branch. The cows had already picked the lowest branches bare of fruit, but by pulling down on the stripped branches, I was able to reach an upper limb loaded with freshly ripened persimmons. I plucked a couple and held out the fruit to Silage Cow. She knew me well and anticipated that I would give her a treat. She approached and sniffed. A bit of cow drool dripped on my hand as she rolled the persimmons into her mouth with her rough tongue. I listened as her molars crunched the seeds. She was an older cow; a matriarch of the pasture. I reached up to the branch again and shook it until several more persimmons fell to the ground. Each one making a quiet "plop" sound as it landed. Silage dropped her head and zeroed in on the fallen fruit. I plucked three more from the higher limb. I ate one and offered the other two for her to eat. As she took the persimmons from my hand, I rubbed the rough fur of her neck. She stretched out her neck as if to say, "Yes, please. Pet and scratch some more."

I talked with Silage, "You are a smart ol' girl, eating persimmons here while the rest of the herd has moved on. There's nobody here to steal from you."

I scratched behind Silage's ears and pulled out a bur that was tightly tangled in her curly gray fur. I sighed and said, "Well, I better get up to the house. Mom and Dad will wonder why I'm not back from deer hunting." As I walked away I glanced back to see Silage watching me. Then she dropped her nose to the ground and continued the search for persimmons.

It was Sunday evening. That meant school the next day. Since my home, in rural Jasper County, Illinois, was located in prime farming country, it was normal that a kid like me spent time caring for cattle. However, I spent much more time with the herd than I did with my peers; and it was only when I entered high school that I began to know more people than cows. Life has taken me away from the pastures and the cows of my youth, but my memories of caring for those cows will stick with me.

At college, I learned to be relatively normal. I went to classes, worked out at the gym, and enjoyed some good times with my classmates. Whenever I became less inhibited and let loose, I had a habit for telling cow stories. Those closest to me found them hilarious. On a good night, I would tell funny stories; other times I would tell sadder stories. In 2012, I went to a New Year's party, and as the night progressed, I began to tell cow stories. Then something odd happened; I realized that I was forgetting important details. The stories about my beloved cows were beginning to slip away. This was simply unacceptable. That night, I decided that I needed to record these stories. Over the next months, I feverishly wrote down the cow stories. As I wrote, it became apparent that these stories weren't just for me; they were too entertaining and insightful. Such an honest account of life on a cattle farm is missing in the literary world. These stories needed to be shared. For those who have raised cattle and for those who have never stepped foot on a farm; this book is centered on cattle, but it provides so much more. Welcome to *Cows I Have Known*.

Chapter 1: Operations

Cattle farming can be divided into two categories: beef and dairy production. On a farm that raises beef cattle, the primary objective is to produce a two-year-old calf, referred to as a "fat-calf" or "calf-fed" which is sent to market. On a dairy farm, the primary objective is milk production. The two systems are as different as night and day. Beef operations raise Angus, Hereford, Simmental, Charolais, Gelbvieh, and Limousin breeds. Most dairy operations have Holstein cattle. My knowledge of Holstein cattle is limited; however, I have found them to be tamer and less excitable than the beef breeds. At Gillespie Farms, the beef cattle were a complete mixture of aforementioned breeds and some others, too.

A beef farm consists of two parts: 1) pasture lands with brood cows and 2) a feedlot. In a brood cow pasture, one will find an adult bull and many cows. Each cow's job is to give birth to a calf and raise it to weaning age at seven or eight months. After giving birth, a cow normally comes into heat within two months—most are rebred in fifty to sixty days—so the annual schedule for a cow looks like this:

- ✓ graze and eat to your heart's content
- ✓ get bred by the bull
- ✓ have a calf nine months later
- ✓ raise the calf
- ✓ get bred by the bull while raising your calf
- ✓ get your calf weaned seven to eight months after giving birth
- ✓ graze and eat to your heart's content

The whole system is dependent upon the cow delivering a healthy calf. A brood cow that doesn't suffer serious illness or experience a catastrophe will live between fifteen to twenty years. Considering that length of time, it's easy to see how a farmer would become quite accustomed to each cow's subtle individuality.

Over many years, cows lose their teeth, and this causes their health to deteriorate. Once a cow can no longer keep up her health and raise a calf, she is culled. Culling means removing the cow from the herd and hauling her off to the sale barn. At the sale barn, meat lockers normally purchase the cull cows. Most of the meat from cull cows is ground into hamburger. This may seem sad, but culling a cow is better than letting her waste away and die slowly on the farm. The revenue generated from sales of cull cows is significant, which is helpful for the farm family.

When calves are weaned, they are corralled and separated from their mothers. Normally, they are hauled away from the brood pasture to a special pen in a feedlot. At this stage, they are referred to as "feeder calves." In the feeder calf pen they are fed a corn-rich diet, which promotes growth. The amount of feed is carefully regulated and increased incrementally. The calves eventually learn to regulate how much ground feed to eat, or "self-feed." Once the feeder calves learn to self-feed, they are considered "fat-calves" and are transferred to a new lot with a gravity-flow feeder of ground corn, plenty of hay, and water. At approximately two years of age, the fat-calves are loaded onto a cattle trailer and taken to the sale barn, where they are auctioned to various meatpacking plants.

Gillespie Farms

From the early 1980s to 2004, beef cattle production at Gillespie Farms consisted of two herds of brood cows, a herd of young heifers, and a feedlot. In 2004, the operation reduced in size to one herd of brood cows and the feedlot.

The cattle pasture started where the yard of the farm house ended. The aptly named "home pasture" was about eighty acres in size with five small ponds, a creek, and several tree-covered hillsides. At full capacity the home pasture contained forty-four cows, their young calves, and one bull. The other brood cow pasture was located five miles away from the house, near the small village of Bogota. It was a seventy-three-acre pasture with two ponds, a creek, and tree-lined bluffs. At full capacity, it contained thirty-five cows. The feedlot was located near the Bogota pasture. It was situated on flat land with some access to trees. At the feedlot, water was supplied by an automated system that ran off a well. Gillespie Farms had one other pasture, nicknamed the "slack pasture." The slack pasture was eight-and-a-half acres in size and it served as an area for young heifers to grow into adulthood before joining the ranks of the adult brood-cows in the pastures.

Of course, a cattle farm would not be complete without daily chores. The most common chore on any cattle farm is checking the cows. Those new to cattle may wonder, *What exactly are you checking?* The first priority is to ensure that all the cattle are within the pasture. Normally, this is accomplished by counting the cows. Second, it's important that all of the cows and calves appear healthy. Common physical symptoms of poor health include droopy ears, discolored manure, watery eyes, nasal discharge, sunken eyes, labored breathing, swollen hooves and weight loss. However, when a farmer checks the cattle, it's typically a change in behavior that gets noticed first. Then he can approach the odd cow to check for signs of illness. Examples of abnormal behavior may include laying down when all the other cows are grazing, kicking a back leg repeatedly, limping, not chewing cud while resting, and bawling. Another priority is checking that the food and water supply is adequate. The farmer is also vigilant for any potential problems that can be prevented, like a damaged fence. Mending fences before the cows start getting out is always a good idea.

Checking cattle is a daily chore that varies little from season to season. Sometimes checking the cows would get skipped for a day during the heaviest workload of harvest or planting, but we always made up for that by checking the cows twice daily when snow was on the ground.

Grinding feed and unloading it into the feeders at the feedlot was a chore done on a weekly basis all year. During the early spring, the fences would be checked prior to turning the cows out on their summer pasture. Often, April 17th or 18th was when the cows were released into the summer pasture. In the mid-summer, we would mow the pastures to limit the growth of weedy broadleaves and keep them from producing seed. As late summer progressed into fall, we fed large bales of hay to the cows because typically the weather turned drier and the pastures would be grazed short.

Chapter 2: Misconceptions

At night, cows sleep with their knees locked. As a country pastime, teenagers drive around, find a pasture, sneak up on a sleeping cow and tip her over … It's called cow tipping. **(Total misconception)**

There is no such thing as cow tipping. If someone claims he has gone cow tipping, press him for details. Ask him, "Did you actually sneak up on a sleeping cow and push her over? Or did you drive around drinking beer?" If there is any hesitation in his response, the latter is true. He did not tip a cow. More importantly, this scenario couldn't possibly work:

A.) Cows sleep with their front legs folded beneath them and their back end lying down.

B.) Cows have keen night vision, a superior sense of smell, and good hearing. There is no way that a car filled with idiots could drive up to a pasture and even get close to a cow. The headlights of the car, the smell of human—perfume, cologne, beer breath, deodorants, smoke, body odor—and the sound of the engine and radio would alert even the most impaired cow. A herd containing many sets of eyes, noses, and ears would detect strange people wandering around their pasture long before the humans would detect the cows.

Consider this; some rural teenagers use the myth of cow tipping to make complete fools out of gullible friends or family who don't live around cows. They con the victim into thinking that cow tipping is a real thing and a rite of passage.

Then they drive around the country drinking beer until they find a pasture. They tell their gullible friend to get out and find a cow. The nervous victim acts with false bravado, complies out of peer pressure and wanders about the pasture in the dark, looking for a cow. The pranksters poke fun at him and sometimes even drive off, leaving the victim in the pasture. It's a cruel prank. Furthermore, cattle farmers hate people trespassing in the pastures because especially at night the cows can become frightened and break out of their fences.

Cows are dumb. (Misconception)

I take offense to this statement. Cows are exactly as smart as they need to be. Their ability to identify individual humans and establish a social hierarchy is a testament to their intelligence. Cows are direct. When something is bothering them, they address it immediately. If they feel threatened, they follow their instincts. If they are hungry, they graze. They don't second guess their decisions. That being said, a herd of cattle can act in ways that are difficult to understand. A cow can act very wild, which is extremely frustrating to those dealing with her. But in the wild cow's defense, her actions are wise—usually when we are trying to corral a wild cow, the reason is to send her off to the processing plant because she is a pain to deal with!

Farmers don't name their cows because the cows are all going to the market. (Misconception)

False. Farmers name their cows, just not all of them. A cow earns her name. Those that get named tend to be the tamer cows or those that do something eventful. Some cows can become pet-like and actually enjoy attention and affection. For example, my mom currently cares for eighteen cows. She probably checks them twice daily and has nearly every cow named. Many are so tame that they'll approach just about anyone and seek attention or some grain to eat. Even folks with large cattle operations tend to have a few cows that they either really like or dislike. These cows get named. Considering how long cows can live, it's a good idea to be on a first-name basis with those that you'll see every day.

Farmers don't name many calves since most will be weaned, fed out, and sold. Another reason is based in superstition. When a calf is born, naming it immediately is a bad idea. It seems that naming a newborn calf greatly increases its chance of mortality. Those few calves that do get named usually earn their names from some physical trait, like the color of their fur. When naming a calf, the best policy is to wait about a week and make sure the calf gets started well.

A cow lying on her back will die. (Factual)

It is actually true that for cattle, goats, and sheep, lying on their back will result in death. Sometimes farmers will refer to this condition as a cow being "high-centered," but the technical term is "dorsal recumbency."[1] It can occur when a cow or calf or bull somehow gets knocked on its dorsal side, past the point of righting itself. This is a rare occurrence that may result from a cow that is sleeping on her side being butted onto her back by another cow. Dorsal recumbency can also result when a cow accidentally rolls onto her back during a difficult labor. Once on her back, she is trapped. The weight of the cow's rumen limits the diaphragm and blocks the esophagus. This causes the cow to have trouble breathing and gas pressure builds up inside the rumen. Normally the gas produced by digestion is vented by belching every one or two minutes. The heavy rumen expands with gas, further impairing respiration and circulation. The animal loses consciousness and will likely die within thirty minutes. If the farmer is lucky enough to discover a cow on her back that has not yet succumbed, the condition can be righted by rolling the cow over onto her side. It can be quite difficult and dangerous for a person to right a full-grown cow due to the danger of being kicked by flailing hooves. Many farmers have accomplished this task with the help of a loader tractor.

Cows are all the same. **(Misconception)**

People generally accept that dogs and cats have personality and exhibit traits that make their pets different from others. The same is true for cows. If you doubt that

---

[1] King, Carol. "Dorsal Recumbency: Getting Stuck Upside-Down." Pygmy Goat World Magazine, 1994. http://kinne.net/dorsrec.htm

statement, then you haven't spent enough time around cattle that are comfortable and grazing. Cattle that are wild or tightly confined seem to act the same; however, cows grazing in a pasture with plentiful grass, water, and shade will exhibit their personality if you observe them closely.

The individuality of cows becomes exemplified in the herd hierarchy. In the herd, it is important to remember that all cows are female, and all are mothers or expectant mothers. Typically, only one adult bull is present in the herd, and he does not lead the cows. No, rather he spends his time with them but is a bit distant in his interactions. Of course if a cow is in heat the bull will be actively pursuing her, but it's common to find the bull on the edge of the herd. On a hot day the bull will often be lounging in the pond or barn with the cows out grazing nearby. The bull is definitely part of the herd, but he is not included in the hierarchy of cows. The leader of the cows is always a middle-aged cow that is aggressive, healthy, and large. Below the leader is a second tier of aggressive cows that have earned a higher status, either through experience or brute force.

For example, the Bogota herd's second tier contained Corn-Eating Machine. This seemed unlikely since Corn-Eating Machine was an older cow that was small but very wide. However, Corn-Eating Machine maintained strong alliances and had knowledge and trust on her side. It was not uncommon to see Corn-Eating Machine watching over the young calves while their mothers grazed. She had earned her status. A new cow in the pasture might try to beat her out by force, but Corn-Eating Machine's high status peers would never allow it.

The bottom tier is composed of young cows, very old cows, and those that are timid. The timid cows may be perfectly healthy and strong but choose not to fight for a place in the hierarchy.

The easiest way to observe the hierarchy is at the corn trough. The leader and second-tier cows arrive at the trough first. When a lower-status cow happens to be at the trough, she is quickly butted out of the way. The lower-status cows squeeze into the trough wherever they can or go to the second trough. Some cows just don't bother with the rat race. At the Bogota pasture, we named a cow "Timid Cow" because she would approach the feeder, maybe get a few mouthfuls of corn and then back away when threatened by another cow. She had plenty of size and experience, but she just preferred not to fight.

The individual personalities of cows actually work to create a personality for the whole herd. For instance, at Gillespie Farms, the Bogota herd was preppy when compared to the home herd. In the Bogota herd, it was very common to see the higher-status cows head-butting others to assert their dominance. This aggressive nature also carried over to their dealings with us. You didn't want to be too comfortable around the Bogota herd. The home herd was tamer and less strict in terms of a hierarchy. At times we were unsure which cow actually was the boss in the home herd.

Farmers don't care if their cows are standing around in mud.
(Misconception)

The sight of cows standing in mud is definitely a concern for farmers, but it can be difficult to avoid. The narrow hooves of cattle act like shovels and tear up the soil. During the growing season when grass is actively sending down roots, the pastures can tolerate moderate grazing without damage. However, once the growing season has ended, the soil structure of a pasture is at the mercy of rainstorms. Saturated soils become weak and are easily disturbed by cattle hooves. In Illinois, the winters tend to freeze the soil and protect it for periods of time, but once the frozen soil thaws, it is very weak, and any cattle traffic will form mud. In the worst scenario, heavy rains occur in the late fall, then more precipitation falls in winter, along with multiple freezing and thawing events. To mitigate the problem of winter pasture degradation, many producers limit their cattle to a winter lot. The logic is sound: cattle are destined to destroy an area of grass around their hay feeders, so limiting the impacted area preserves the larger pasture. In areas with high hoof traffic, like winter lots and feedlots, the formation of mud cannot be prevented unless the ground is hardened. Hardening requires the use of gravel or concrete, which is expensive and permanent. Often, old hay bales are set out to improve bedding areas in winter lots. In the end, all farmers are concerned about the well-being of their animals. However, as the quip goes, *farmers are a lot like people; there are all different kinds.* Some show more concern, and some show less.

18

Cows have four stomachs. **(Misconception)**

While the digestive system of a cow does have four distinct compartments, it is misleading to identify the compartments as stomachs. The reticulum, rumen, omasum, and abomasum each function differently. When cattle graze, they pull plants into their mouth with a massive, rough tongue. In the front part of their mouths, they only have teeth on their bottom jaw. Rather than cutting, cattle press their tongue and bottom front teeth against the tough dental pad on the top of their mouths to pinch plants and pull the vegetation loose. Once a cow fills her mouth with plant material and swallows, that mouthful is referred to as "cud" or "bolus." The bolus travels down the esophagus to the reticulorumen, which is composed of the rumen and reticulum. The rumen is much like a forty or fifty gallon vat teeming with microbes that ferment the boluses. The reticulum is a portion of the rumen that is divided off for indigestible materials to settle. Woody stems, roots, rocks, metal nails, and wire pieces can accumulate in the reticulum for long-term microbial activity. Particles that are not degraded stay in the reticulum for the entire life of the cow. Sharp metal can penetrate the wall of the reticulum causing hardware disease.[2] Whenever the cattle take a break from grazing they have another job to do. A cow will allow a bolus

---

[2] Hardware disease can sometimes be treated by forcing a strong, cylindrical magnet down the cow's throat into the rumen. The magnet settles into the reticulorumen where it attracts the sharp metal fragment. If the metal is a nail or wire, the piece lines up against the magnet and is less likely to pierce the wall. Antibiotics are also administered to address the associated infection.

from the rumen to travel back up the esophagus to her mouth, where she'll further grind up the plant material with her twenty-four molars; twelve on top and twelve on bottom.[3] This activity is commonly referred to as "chewing their cud." The cow will re-swallow the finely-ground bolus, sending it back to the rumen, and continue the process.

The microbial activity of the reticulorumen produces significant amounts of gas that is vented by belching. Since cows belch every few minutes, they tend to keep it quiet. If one listens closely to a cow, the belching sounds like a gentle gurgling. The reticulorumen is followed by the omasum. The omasum serves as filter by allowing only the smaller particles to pass and as a buffer to help recycle the water and saliva present in the rumen. Larger particles are turned back by the omasum for more break down before they can pass. Particles that pass the omasum go to the abomasum, or a cow's "true stomach." It functions much like a human's stomach, with enzymes and acid being secreted to digest proteins. The abomasum is followed by the lower digestive tract that is similar to that of a human.[4]

---

[3] Hall, J.B., and Susan Silver. "Nutrition and Feeding of the Cow-Calf Herd: Digestive System of the Cow," Virginia Polytechnic Institute and State University College of Agriculture and Life Sciences Virginia Cooperative Extension, 2009: http://pubs.ext.vt.edu/400/400-010/400-010_pdf.pdf

[4] Umphrey, J.E., and C.R. Staples. "General Anatomy of the Ruminant Digestive System." Dairy Production Guide Fact Sheet DS31, Florida Cooperative Extension Service, 1992. http://mysrf.org/pdf/pdf_dairy/cow_handbook/dc15.pdf

Chapter 3: Felini

The greatest cow I have ever known came to the Gillespie Farm in a disaster. Her mother was a standard-looking Hereford that started giving birth in the wee morning hours one muddy and damp March Saturday. The cow lay down and pushed. As the cow strained the calf's feet and lots of blood came out. The calf fell out on the cold, muddy ground—along with her mother's prolapsed uterus. Dad quickly called the veterinarian. He arrived about a half-hour later. The cow was in such bad shape that we didn't attempt to drive her to the barn. Dad simply roped her to a nearby corner post, and the vet worked hard to put the uterus back where it belonged. The attempt was futile. The doc's hand went through the wall, and the cow bled to death right there in the pasture. With sadness and frustration my brother and I did exactly as we were told. Dad quietly said, "Take the calf to the barn. Rub it down with straw, and we'll feed it a bottle after I write a check for the vet."

The young calf had red fur on her sides and back. Her face and front legs were all white. While my brother Bob and I dried her fur with straw, she attempted to stand. First she would try to push her body off the ground with her back legs. She wobbled and attempted to extend her front legs. On the first few tries, she collapsed backward when she lost her balance. After a few more tries and some help from Bob, she stood up. Her legs still wobbled and she maintained a comical wide stance, but she was standing. Since the mother cow was dead, we had to provide milk for the calf, and the first feeding is always the most important. Newborn mammals need a mother's first milk called "colostrum." It contains antibodies and proteins necessary for the calf to survive. Fortunately, a powdered form of colostrum for calves is available at the local feed store. Dad kept some on hand for emergencies just like this. Mom whisked the colostrum powder into a pitcher of warm water and poured it into a bottle. When Dad finished his business with the veterinarian, he brought a bottle out to the barn. With little coaxing, the new calf nursed. Despite being born in terrible circumstances, she was off to a strong start.

After a few days of feedings, there was no hesitation when we entered the barn with a bottle; the young calf would stand up and let out a bawl the instant we opened the barn door. She would run over and frantically start looking for the bottle. Once the calf found the nipple and started nursing, she would wag her tail in joy. Mom and Dad took my little sister, Sarah, out to the barn to see the calf. Sarah had recently watched the classic Disney movie "Bambi" while at the babysitter's. She was part of the first generation to watch the movie in the home since it was released on VHS in 1989. Sarah named the young calf Faline after the beautiful doe that Bambi falls in love with in the movie. The rest of the family had never seen the movie, but the name stuck, although we always spelled her name Felini.

This photo of Felini with Sarah was taken just before Felini was moved to the slack pasture. At the slack pasture, Felini matured before being bred and becoming a cow.

Playing with our new pet calf became the favorite activity for me, Bob, and Sarah. Bob and I would arrive home from school in the evening, jump off the bus, and go running into the house. We changed into our play clothes and ran out to the barn to see Felini. One evening, I ran out to the barn and discovered that Felini was not alone. In the stall with her was a strange-looking black and white splotched calf. I was puzzled because we did not have black and white splotched cattle on our farm. This calf was from a dairy cow. Unbeknownst to me, Dad had traded a load of hay bales for a Holstein calf from a nearby dairy farm. The way he saw it, we were already bottle feeding one calf, and he had two boys old enough to care for calves, so why not get another calf to raise? Dad also knew it would be a fun surprise.

Bob named the bull Holstein calf Blacky, and as March ended and spring arrived, the two calves were doing great. Bob and I fed them before and after school. After school, we would commonly run around the corral with the two little calves. Bob would play with Blacky by lowering his head and gently butting him. Blacky would shake his head and put on the act like he was fighting with all his might. It was a show of playful affection. Then we would run circles. Sometimes we would chase the calves, and then they would chase us. During the summer, Felini and Blacky were released from their little pen to graze with the rest of the cattle herd. Every morning and evening the calves left the herd to wait by the barn for their bottles. The calves would let out a bawl to say, *"We're hungry, hurry up with my bottle."* Bob and I would mix warm water with powdered milk replacer and walk out to the barn. Whenever the calves spotted us, they paced back and forth at the gate. Bob and I would call out, "Felini, Blacky, Baaaaaaaa!" The calves would call "Baaaaaaaa" back at us as we approached. Once inside the pasture, Bob and I tipped the bottles down, and the calves would latch onto the nipples. The excited calves would wag their tails while they nursed.

Normally Blacky would finish his bottle first. Bob would run with the empty bottle, and Blacky would chase him, kicking up his heels as he ran. When Felini finished her bottle, I would also start playing. Often, Sarah would be out with us. She was too young to hold a bottle, but instead she held "horsy sticks." Sarah would gallop around the pasture with a stick in each hand and vividly imagine herself as a horse. The calves played right along with our antics.

As always happens, Felini and Blacky grew up, and in the fall they were weaned. Shortly after school started for Sarah, Bob, and me, the calves were taken to a special pen in the feedlot. Since Felini was a heifer, we had the option of keeping her on the farm to become a cow. After a month at the feeder calf lot, she and eight other heifers of the same age were transferred to the slack pasture. The west and north sides of the slack pasture bordered woods. This sheltered the pasture from the worst of the winter winds, and it also provided a special perk during the summer. A few large trees overhung the fence in the northwest corner and provided shade. The tree lines channeled the breezes through the corner. During the hottest part of the summer, the northwest corner of the slack pasture was always a refreshing spot. This pasture allowed the heifers to grow to maturity before being bred. We always kept a tame old cow in with the heifers to serve as a calming influence. The whole system was set up like a cow-in-training school. Our lingo reflected this; a group of heifers at the slack pasture was called a class, and when they moved to the brood cow pastures, we called it graduation. We rarely had problems at the slack pasture, and most of the problems we did have were related to the transport of heifers out of the pasture. It seemed that they didn't want to leave!

Felini's class was the best batch of heifers to graduate from the slack pasture. When the heifers were mature enough, we bought a young black Limousin bull and turned him loose to breed. Soon enough, we had eight pregnant heifers, one pregnant old cow, and a lazy young bull that had accomplished his task. Nine months later, the heifers started calving. We checked on the herd daily, and when Felini's udder started to enlarge with milk and her vulva started to dilate, we knew that she would soon calve. We were anxious for her to give birth and nearly camped at the slack pasture to make sure that she was all right. Much to our relief, she delivered a healthy bull calf.

Felini at the slack pasture, just moments after giving birth to her first calf. A joyous day on the Gillespie Farm!

Not long afterwards, Felini and her calf were moved to the home pasture, where she would be integrated into the herd. At that time there were forty-two cows in the home pasture. Felini and several of her comrades from the slack pasture became the newest cows in the herd. Unfortunately for them, they were on the very bottom of the pecking order. The low status didn't seem to bother Felini.

Her friendly disposition made checking the cows more enjoyable because we always took time to pet Felini. If we checked the cattle when they were asleep in the woods, Felini would be lying with her classmates from the slack pasture, and her calf would be nearby. I would scratch behind her ears and under her chin—areas that are hard for a cow to groom. Another cow would approach and shyly sniff my shirt. I'd turn around and let her sniff my hand. She would back away before I could pet her face. Over time, the other cows observed our interactions with Felini and decided that maybe the humans weren't so bad after all. Felini had a calming influence on the whole herd.

Chapter 4: Vacationing

My mother taught school for twenty-seven years. While she found teaching to be rewarding, it was also draining. She taught with more enthusiasm than her colleagues, but teaching at that level requires energy. Each year Mom would start teaching in the late summer with high energy levels, which declined throughout the school year until mid-May, when the schools closed for summer vacation. This was her time to forget about teaching school and recover. Dad understood this and tried to make some time for a small family trip right after the school year ended. This was normally a busy time for farming, and often the day trip had to be postponed.

In 1992, Dad was temporarily caught up on fieldwork when the school year ended. That particular year, Mom had endured a horrendous batch of soon-to-be-felons that were her students. She was more than tired—she had also lost faith in her profession. Mom and Dad planned a small family trip to Forbes State Park. Located about an hour's drive away, the park had a lake with a beach and an ice cream stand. The day after school ended, Dad planned to do the morning chores and then head out for the day. We would swim, picnic, and have some ice cream.

That morning, Dad got up early and checked on the Bogota herd and the feedlot. All the cows and calves there were doing just fine. He checked the home herd, but the count came up one cow short. Dad rode around the pasture on his three-wheeler until he found the missing cow. It was a large Hereford cow with a bloody discharge and calf's feet clearly sticking out of her vulva. It was the first calf for her, and things were not going well.

Back at the house, Mom noticed that Dad had been gone longer than expected. She kept us kids busy gathering up our beach toys and loading the car with our picnic supplies. Mom watched from the window as Dad rode the three-wheeler into the driveway instead of putting it in the barn. She knew something was wrong. Bob, Sarah, and I sat down on the porch and petted kittens while Dad called the veterinarian. "Hi Robert. This is Jim Gillespie. Hey, I've got a cow down here that seems to be having trouble calving. Oh I see. So you think it will be about two hours before you can make it down here? Okay, we'll see you then." Dad hung up the phone with a disappointed look on his face. Obviously, waiting for two hours to get help pulling the calf was bad news for the calf and the heifer.

It was ten in the morning; in two hours it would be noon. Two more hours dealing with the vet and pulling the calf would make it two. Add an hour's drive to the park, and it would be three—much too late for a relaxing day at the beach.

Mom had Bob and I change out of our swim trunks and put on our work clothes. She addressed us, "Dad is going to keep track of the cow down in the pasture. William, I want you to go with Dad. Bobby, you need to direct Dr. Robert back into the pasture when he arrives; stay close by and watch for him." I climbed in the work truck with Dad, and we drove down into the pasture.

The young cow had picked a beautiful spot to calve. The creek ran away from the bluff line, and the result was a narrow bottomland meadow with trees along its eastern side. Sunlight filtered through the canopy and dappled the short grass with light. A cool mist left over from the morning's dew hung in the air. The cow lay down and strained to deliver the calf, but only the feet emerged. The hooves of the unborn calf had begun to dry, indicating that she had been straining for several hours. Dad and I sat on the tailgate of the truck waiting for the vet to arrive. Eventually, he relieved me from waiting and suggested that I play in the creek.

I walked to the nearby riffle and looked for unique rocks, snakes, frogs, minnows, feathers, tracks, and anything else of interest. Soon I returned to the truck because it didn't feel right that I was playing while Dad sat waiting in a morose mood for the vet to show up.

Technically, Robert knew his stuff, and he probably was an excellent small animal veterinarian, but as Dad and I sat waiting, we both wished that Ken was coming down to help instead. What Robert lacked was a certain ease in dealing with large animals. He was awkward around the cattle, and that did not go unnoticed by his patients. Cows just did not respond well to Robert's presence. Regardless of our preferences, we needed help. Robert was the veterinarian on call, so things would just have to work out. When Robert arrived, he and Dad roped the cow to a nearby tree. The young Hereford fought the rope initially but then resigned to the situation. Using the jack, Robert was able to pull the calf. As we suspected, it had died during the prolonged labor. Robert examined the cow to check for the possibility of a twin. He concluded that there was just the one calf, and we released the cow from the rope. She wobbled a bit and lowed to her dead calf. After licking it a few times, she gave up and slowly walked back to the herd.

While Robert washed up his equipment, Dad wrote out a check for his visit. Dad was hoping that he could still salvage the day and make the trip happen, but it was not to be. This was disappointing to him—he had worked hard to make time for the trip. However, cows don't calve on a schedule, and the best we could do was hope for better luck next time. Late that afternoon Dad took all of us fishing down at the farm pond. It was fun, but it certainly wasn't the trip that he wanted for Mom.

A few years later, the same young Hereford cow who had caused the cancellation earned her name. Bob and I had grown up considerably in those years, and we were now helping out with the annual cattle vaccination. This was always an eventful day. The home herd consisted of forty-four cows, one bull, and all the young calves, and each one would have their turn in the cattle chute. The day started by corralling the entire herd in a pen behind the west barn. We separated out a group of seven or eight and herded them into the main barn stall. From there, we pushed two or three into the smaller confining stall. The stall was purposely tight because it was the last stop before pushing the cows into the squeeze chute. The cattle would get nervous while going through the process, which caused many of the cows to defecate before we pushed them into the chute. It didn't take long before fresh manure covered our clothes. The job was dirty and hazardous, so we approached it with humor.

Bob and I pushed a 250-pound bull calf into the head gate, and Dad quickly shut the gate around the calf's neck, capturing it. Mom asked, "Is this one a bull?" Bob responded, "He sure is." Mom handed the clamps to Bob. The large stainless steel clamps were used to castrate calves. The two-handled instrument worked by pinching between the calf's body and scrotum. The thick hide would withstand the pressure without tearing, but the vas deferens tube and the spermatic blood vessels would break. The calf was then a steer. Being young males ourselves, Bob and I had a good deal of empathy for the bull calves. We tried not to think about what we were doing, but it was necessary task. We could not have a bull in the feedlot impregnating heifers meant for market. To overcome our anxiety, we sang our own version of the Pointer Sisters classic, "I'm So Excited":
I'm so excited, and I just don't like it.
I'm about to lose my nuts, and I just don't like it!

I lifted the calf's tail high over its back to keep him still while Bob crouched down and clamped right where the scrotum attached to the calf's underside. It let out a high-pitched bawl. Meanwhile, Dad implanted the calf's ear with Ralgro[5] and attached ear tags. Ken, the veterinarian, injected

---

[5] Ralgro is the brand-name for a booster implant containing the active ingredient zeranol. It is implanted in calves meant for the feedlot. The product raises the level of growth hormone and insulin, promoting muscle growth.

the calf with Ivomec[6] and vaccinated the calf for a number of diseases. Mom refilled the syringes and wrote down notes about each calf. She stepped over near the back of the chute, and Bob handed the clamping instrument back to her. Dad opened the head gate and turned the steer loose into the pasture; it walked away swishing its tail and lifting a leg in obvious discomfort.

Bob and I turned back inside the barn and drove the large Hereford cow into the confining stall. I recognized her immediately—"Bob, this is the one that had trouble calving a few years ago on that day we were supposed to go down to Forbes," I said. Bob waved his hand over her back and commented, "Look how flat her back is! You could build a city on that." We laughed at the ridiculous image of a city built on a cow's back. Mom heard Bob's joke and said, "That would be a good name for her! City-On-Her-Back"

Just then, Mom pulled open the rear door of the squeeze chute. Bob and I pushed and yelled until City-On-Her-Back relented and walked into the chute. When Ken checked her pregnancy status, he felt a large calf in her uterus and commented, "There's a good-sized calf in this cow. She should calve before too long." After vaccinating, City-On-Her-Back was released from the chute, and about a week later she calved. In the years that followed, she had many more calves and established a reputation as a good mother. She also

---

[6] Ivomec is antiparasitic agent developed by Merck. It contains the active ingredient ivermectin which is effective against round worms, eye worms, lung worms, cattle grubs, sucking lice, and mites.

developed a pleasant demeanor around us humans. Her large size helped her rise through the ranks of the cow's social hierarchy even though she wasn't very aggressive.

Chapter 5: Bumblebees

1988 was a dry year on the farm. By mid-summer, the pastures were parched, and the grass that normally grew all season was grazed shorter than Astroturf. In the backyard, cracks formed in the soil, and the fearsome velvet ants made their appearance early.[7] The drought affected everything. Day after day, the sun would shine bright and high temperatures would bake the landscape. On some afternoons the western sky would bank up with clouds. We'd watch the clouds hoping that a thunderstorm would develop and bring rain to the farm. Large cumulonimbus clouds would form, and distant rumbling could be heard. We thought of the parched fields and how badly the rain was needed. It seemed imminent. We'd keep looking at the line of storms marching toward the farm from the west, but right before we expected the sky to let loose a deluge, the storm would split around our farm. Other farmers just a few miles to the north and south would receive a nice rain shower while our land barely received a drop. This happened so often that Mom became superstitious. She would say, "Every time I watch the clouds, they split and go around the farm. I'm not watching them anymore."

---

[7] The velvet ant (*Dasymutilla occidentalis*) is a unique species of wasp with wingless females that are bright red and black in coloration. They erratically travel along open ground and deliver an extremely painful sting to victims that step on one with bare feet. Male velvet ants have wings and lack a stinger. At Gillespie Farms this wasp tends to appear during the driest part of the late summer. (Borror & White, A Field Guide to the Insects, 1970, ISBN: 0-395-07436-3)

The singing of the cicadas only reminded us of how dry it was. The pastures provided little for the cows to eat, so we were forced to start feeding hay early. Normally, the cows are fed hay from mid-September through April, but in 1988, we started in July.

The dry weather also meant the hay fields produced fewer bales; our stockpile of hay bales, needed to feed the cows during the winter, would be short. Thankfully, we had a few bales left over from the previous year. Dad decided he would feed them to the cows before putting out any of the new hay cut that year. Every few days, Dad would take the open Case 1070 tractor and move out an old bale for the cows, which seemed to have disdain for the older bales of hay. They quickly made head-butting the bales a sport. It worked like this: Using the bale fork attached to the tractor's three-point hitch, Dad would set the bale on the hay pile. He pulled the tractor away, shifted it into neutral, scampered down from the tractor, ran to the empty bale feeder, and flipped it over the bale. Then he cut and pulled the twine off the bale. The cows saw the seconds between the bale being set down and Dad flipping the feeder over the bale as their golden opportunity. They ran in and butted the bale, tearing it up and making a royal mess. Sometimes the cows crowded in so quickly that Dad couldn't get the ring on the bale. This was despicable cow behavior and very wasteful of scarce hay.

One day at lunchtime, Dad mentioned that the next bale to be moved out contained a nest of bumblebees. Now, bumblebees have been a particular nemesis of mine since my first encounter with them as a toddler. I don't remember the scenario, but I've been told that Bob and I were playing in the chicken yard when I was about two years old. We accidentally stirred up a nest of bumblebees hiding out in an old pump, and they stung me relentlessly and caused me to swell up like the Stay Puft marshmallow man. My fear of bumblebees was equal to Dad's excitement over finding the nest. His enthusiasm stemmed from experiences he had as a teenager on his grandpa's farm. Back then, the young Jim Gillespie would find bumblebee nests and visit them later with his trusty old tennis racket. He would gently stir the nest to agitate a few bees. Three or four would fly out to defend the nest and instantly be served out of existence with quick swings from Jim's tennis racket. He would stir the nest again and step back for more fun. This was pure sport for him, and the threat of getting stung only added to the excitement.

At the lunch table, Dad hid his eagerness over finding the bumblebee nest, but he hinted that we should watch him move out the bale of hay. Naturally, I was worried for his safety, but he had a plan that we didn't know about.

The cows finished off the previous bale and were milling around the pasture looking for something to eat. It was time for Dad to move out the suspect bale. He started the old tractor and drove out to the hay stockpile. As he revved up the engine, the radiator fan kicked up dust. He backed the bale fork up to the hay bale, and, lucky for him, the vertical beam of the bale fork sealed off the entrance and exit of the bumblebee hive. He drove the bale out, set it down, and quickly drove away. Bumblebees began streaming out. Instead of stopping the tractor and putting the feeder ring on the bale, Dad left the bale unguarded. The cows started head-butting the bale into oblivion. With bravado, the lead cow charged into the bale, and the bumblebees attacked her viciously. She let out a panicked, short "BLAAHHH," and ran from the bale. She turned to look back in disbelief and was promptly stung by at least five more bumblebees. She let out another panicked "BLAAHHH," and ran straight into the pond for refuge. Splash! The second-tier cows head-butted the bale right after the lead cow, and the bumblebees kept streaming out of the bale. Each cow would attack the bale, get stung about five times, let out a "BLAAHHH", and run straight into the pond. Splash! It served those cows right for wasting so much hay in a dry year. Mom, Bob, and I watched and laughed at the antics from a safe distance. For a time we all forgot about the dry weather.

Chapter 6: Cow Language 101

Since cattle were first domesticated, humans and the cows have understood each other. Of course, cows do not interpret spoken word, but they can be trained to respond to commands. Nearly every farmer has a sound that he or she makes to tell the cows, "come here." It is a good thing to have cattle trained to a call because if the cows ever escape from the pasture, being able to call them back saves the farmer a lot of trouble. Unfortunately, no universal call has been adopted. On the Gillespie Farm, we use two sounds: honking the truck horn and yelling "Sooook, Sooook, Sooook, Sooook, Wooooooooooooo! Sooook Cows!" I've heard farmers yell "Woooo" only, ring a bell, and say "Heeeeyyyyyy Cooowwwws!" Cows accustomed to one call may not respond at all to one of the other calls. Our neighbor Terry had some health trouble last year, and we helped out by stopping at his farm and doing his chores. Whenever I fed his calves, I called, "Sooook, Sooook, Sooook, Sooook, Wooooooooooooo! Sooook Calves!" and the calves simply looked at me like I was from another planet. Apparently, Terry used a different call.

Of course, humans that care for cattle also become trained. They learn cow language. For those readers without a herd nearby to observe, I will provide a brief synopsis of cow language. It's common knowledge that cows go "MOO," but that is an oversimplification. The proper spelling of a cow's primary vocalization would be more like "MMHHHRREH." Cows with young calves vocalize softly to them with this call. It can mean, "Come here." "Here I am."

or "This is my calf." When a similar vocalization is made with more volume and for a longer duration it can mean, "Seriously, calf, get over here!" "I'm hungry! Feed me some corn!" or "Where on earth is my calf?"

A cow's moo can be referred to as "lowing," "bellowing," or "bawling". Lowing and bellowing have a more general connotation, whereas bawling tends to indicate that the cow or calf is calling to express a problem. Cows bawl when they are isolated, hungry, thirsty, can't find their calf, excited, or in discomfort. Cows also make a snort that sounds like a "huffffffff." They make this sound by constricting their nostrils and exhaling. It typically expresses a cow's feeling of annoyance. While cows also blow their nose to dislodge mucous, their snort is more prolonged. Cows are generally not aggressive; however, they may become aggressive when one handles their newborn calves. Cows can make a low-pitch guttural grunting sound when they are being extremely defensive. It is an obviously threatening sound.

Bulls have vocalizations that tend to be of a higher pitch and sound nothing like moo. A bull typically threatens other bulls by "bellering," performing a broad-side threat, pawing the ground, and head-butting inanimate objects. "Bellering" is slang for bellowing. When a bull displays, his bellowing is repetitive and longer than the calls made by cows. In the broad-sided threat posture, the bull arches his back, tenses his muscles, and tips his head downward. To look even more menacing, he will use his front hooves to dig in the ground and throw dirt in the air. If he really wants to show off, he will rub his body along static objects such as barns, fences, or trees. He may also head-butt those objects. It's normal for a bull to perform like this for his cows and any other bulls around.

An example of a cow performing a broad-sided threat; notice the aggressive tilt of the head and the flexing of neck muscles.

An example of a cow in normal grazing posture; she is feeling calm.

Cows also use the broad-sided threat posture. For example, a cow of high social status will display to discourage cows of a lower status from approaching the feed trough. Cattle universally threaten by shaking their heads at their subject of frustration; however, they do not signify emotion with their ears like horses, cats, and dogs. Generally, alert ears indicate that a cow is curious, while droopy ears can signify poor health. How a cow holds its ears can also be a trait of that particular breed. Brahma cattle have naturally droopy ears.

Not all cows exhibit body language to the same degree. Unless you are familiar with an individual cow's temperament and expressiveness, it is always best to give her plenty of respect. Cattle are mostly docile, but they are responsible for two-thirds of injuries caused by farm animals.[8] The most severe injuries and fatalities occur from cattle head-butting a victim against a static object or the ground.

I also have a healthy respect for the destructive power in the back legs of cattle. Cows, calves, heifers, bulls, and steers all kick in the same manner. If you are picturing a mule raising its hindquarters and kicking straight back, wipe that thought out of your head! Cows do it differently. They raise one leg to the side and kick out and back. It's a

---

[8] Cordoba, Connie. "Understanding Dairy Cattle Behavior to Avoid Animal-Related Accidents on the Farm." University of Wisconsin-Madison Department of Dairy Science and the Babcock Institute Farm Safety Facts Sheet, 2005: http://babcock.wisc.edu/sites/default/files/documents/en_behavior.pdf

lightning-quick kick, and it can be very damaging. A swift kick to one's knee can seriously injure the joint. To mitigate the danger, cowhands stay out of the zone that's one to four feet away from the hind legs of skittish cattle. When loading cattle into a chute or trailer, it is impossible to stay away. The solution is to place oneself squarely against a cow's backside. Without the distance for a hoof to gather speed, a kick lacks momentum and is much less damaging. This adage is true for cows kicking their hooves or people throwing their fists: avoid if possible, but if avoidance is not possible, get squarely against the subject and they cannot hurt you nearly as badly.

Every farmer and cowhand gets kicked eventually. It hurts. Hopefully, the kick hits muscle and not the kneecap or groin. After I'm kicked, I tend to get nervous and try to stay back. This is exactly the wrong thing to do when working with cattle. The worst thing to do is be three feet away when a cow decides to kick. The most painful injury that a cow ever inflected upon me was from a kick straight to the thumb. I was loading a huge Charolais cow into the trailer, and she was not cooperating. She finally started to move, and I didn't keep up with her. I was running behind her through the chute when she sent her left hoof crashing straight onto my thumb, jamming the bejesus out of it. I couldn't grip anything with that hand for several days—not until the swelling went down. I have been lucky; that was a rather mild injury.

Cows also seem to understand some human body language. They can spot a pushover. While I would never support being cruel to animals, there comes a time when being able to stand your ground against an aggressive cow becomes important. All cowhands know that a cow's skull is thick and boney, so hitting a cow with your fist or hand is just a good way to break your hand. You need a club or boots. A hardwood club about three feet long is a very effective deterrent when used properly, which means swung very hard and accurate enough to hit the cow's head. A good pair of boots comes in handy when no club is available. Kicking a charging cow Chuck Norris-style right on the nose almost always stops her. Just be prepared to repeat or quickly retreat if the cow decides to charge again.

Chapter 7: Corn; A Love Affair

It is believed that cattle were domesticated in the Middle East about 10,500 years ago,[9] and corn or maize cultivation started in Central America about 9,000 years ago.[10] For 8,500 years, humans grew cattle and corn, but wide oceans separated them. Then, in 1492, Columbus discovered the New World, and thus began the Columbian Exchange. Cows were soon introduced to the Americas, and corn was introduced to Europe. I like to imagine the first meeting of cows and corn: A famished Spanish cow with sweeping horns and fur of red and brown is led down a ramp from a wooden sailing ship. She steps off the ramp onto the sandy tropical beach, thankful to be off that damn boat. She is led by the sailor past piles of exotic goods ready to be loaded onto the ship for the return trip to Europe. A barrel gets knocked over in front of the cow, and small multicolored ears of corn spill on the ground. With the rope lead in one hand, the sailor stops to help pick up the ears of corn with his free hand. The cow drops her head and takes a big sniff, then opens her mouth and picks up an ear. The cow crunches the ear of corn with her molars. The taste of crushed corn hits the cow's tongue, and the angels start singing!

---

[9] Mctavish, E. J., J. E. Decker, R. D. Schnabel, J. F. Taylor, and D. M. Hillis. "New World Cattle Show Ancestry from Multiple Independent Domestication Events." *Proceedings of the National Academy of Sciences*, April 9, 2013: E1398-1406.
http://www.ncbi.nlm.nih.gov/pubmed/23530234
[10] Carroll, Sean B. "Tracking the Ancestry of Corn Back 9,000 Years." *New York Times,* May 24, 2010:
http://www.nytimes.com/2010/05/25/science/25creature.html?_r=0

Cattle absolutely love the taste of corn. If a cow could do a cartwheel, she would do it for ground corn. Farmers often feed a small amount of ground corn to the brood cows as a supplement to their diet of grass and hay. Feeding the cows corn in the trough can become a ritual that trains the cattle to come at a call and enables the farmer to check the cattle easily. On the Gillespie Farm, cows are trained to come to the sound of a truck horn in a very simple manner—honk the horn and put feed in the trough. The herd comes running for corn. Once all the cows are around the trough, it is easy to count them and circle around the group to look for any that will calve soon. A little ground corn can also help bait a wary cow into the corral and calm down a cow in duress.

Most of the corn grown in the Midwest is formally known as yellow dent corn or *Zea mays* var. *indentata*.[11] The name refers to the dent that forms in the crown of the kernel once the corn dries. Dent corn was developed by a northern Illinois farmer named James L. Reid and his father, Robert Reid in the mid-1800s.[12]

> "In 1846 when my father Robert Reid moved from Ohio to Delevan Prairie he brought with other goods his seed corn. This corn was known in Brown County

---

[11] McMahon, Margaret J., Anton M.Kofranek, and Vincent E. Rubatzky. *Hartmann's Plant Science*. Upper Saddle River, NJ: Prentice Hall, 2002.

[12] Curran, William R. "Indian Corn. Genesis of Reid's Yellow Dent," *Journal of the Illinois State Historical Society* XI, January 1919: 576-585. https://archive.org/stream/jstor-40194511/40194511#page/n11/mode/2up

Ohio as the Gordon Hopkins corn. It was not a yellow corn but reddish or flesh colored which gave to the shelled corn the appearance of being highly mixed. It was quite late in the spring of 1846 when my father arrived in Delevan. Uncle Daniel Reid who had settled here some years previous had the ground prepared for corn and the field was at once planted. The crop was good but imperfectly ripened. The best of it was selected for next year's seed but being immature the stand of corn for the crop of 1847 was very poor and had to be replanted. This was done by putting in the missing hills with a hoe and using for that purpose a small corn that was grown in the neighborhood at the time known as the Little Yellow corn. I am unable to give anything of the history of this variety; but what I call Reid's Yellow Dent has been bred from the result of that cross, by selection, to what it is today -- an almost pure yellow corn of medium size and medium early in maturing." (James L. Reid, as quoted by A.D. Shamel)[13]

Reid developed yellow dent corn by crossing corn varieties on his farm in Tazewell County. Dent corn is high in starch content and very useful as animal feed. Currently, forty-seven percent of corn grown in the United States is used in animal feed, while twenty-four percent is processed into ethanol, four percent is used to make sweeteners, nineteen

---

[13] Shamel, A.D. "The Art of Seed Selection and Breeding." *The Yearbook of Agriculture 1907*. Washington D.C.: US Dept. of Agriculture Government Printing Office, 1908. P221-236.

percent is exported, and six percent is used in an amazing variety of other products[14].

The majority of corn grown on Gillespie Farms is yellow dent corn, and every year we devote a few acres to plant a seed corn test plot. This enables us to test out several varieties of hybrid seed corn and see which ones we like for yield and habit. An extra perk of the seed corn test plot is the minority corn that's grown. The end rows of the plot along the road are planted to sweet corn. It matures before the yellow dent varieties, and it's removed near the end of the season to display the various hybrids in the test plot.

We eagerly anticipate the sweet corn ripening. On a normal year, this happens around the first or second week of August. At first you have to hunt for the ripest ears. After four or five days of hunting, the rest seem to ripen all at once, and we have a surplus. This is our chance to stock up on sweet corn for the entire year. However, you can't simply pick ears of sweet corn, bag them, and put them in the freezer; the corn must be picked, shucked, cut off the cob, cooked, cooled, bagged, and frozen. Anyone who has participated in this process knows that it is labor intensive, but homegrown sweet corn in February is well worth all the trouble.

---

[14] Illinois, University of. "Ethanol, Food and Fuel Issues." University of Illinois College of Agricultural, Consumer and Environmental Sciences, March 2009:
http://web.extension.illinois.edu/ethanol/foodvfuel.cfm

There's also another benefit: the cows make this activity fun because they, too, love sweet corn. We start by picking the sweet corn early in the morning before the day heats up. Usually, we pick four or five feed sacks full of corn. To shuck the corn we drive the work truck out into the pasture and park under a shade tree. The cows immediately notice the abnormal activity and become curious. After yelling, "Sooook, Soooook, Sooook, Sooook, Whoooooooooooo! Sooook Cows!" a few times, the herd starts running to the truck. Soon the truck is surrounded by bovines. We stand up in the bed of the truck and throw the shucks and silks over the sides. Hungry cows surround the truck like sharks, and a feeding frenzy ensues. The cows stretch their necks and reach with their tongues to take shucks from our hands. We place each shucked ear in a cooler beyond the cows' reach. The event is such a hoot.

Cows and humans share the affection for sweet corn with a formidable foe—the raccoon. Raccoons absolutely love to devour sweet corn. Any gardener knows that growing sweet corn requires some type of deterrent to prevent the complete destruction of his or her patch. We mitigate the deleterious effects of the raccoons four ways. First, we plant a patch big enough so that destroying it entirely would require a substantial effort on the part of the raccoons. Second, we always plant the patch on a field end away from the preferred habitat of raccoons: barns, brush piles, and fence rows. Third, we attempt to thin the population of raccoons during the winter trapping season. Lastly, we encircle the sweet corn patch with an electric fence positioned about four inches above the ground.

Unfortunately for us, it seems that raccoons still manage to ravage a large portion of the sweet corn patch. They attack by first breaking down the cornstalk and then gnawing through the shucks to the delicious kernels. Raccoons are finicky about the ears they eat. When the ear they have is not to their liking, they must knock over the next stalk and take a few bites to test the new ear's flavor. It is as if they are thinking, *Ah, we're in sweet corn heaven. I'll take a bite here and there, smash this and that.*

The raccoon damage is frustrating for us humans, but it has a silver lining for the cows on the Gillespie Farm. Damaged stalks and ears are gathered and fed to the cows. While every cow prefers a perfectly untouched ear of sweet corn, she doesn't turn up her nose to an ear that's been chewed on by a raccoon. This is especially true when every other cow in the herd is trying to get the stalk that just landed in front of her!

The process of salvaging sweet corn for the cows goes like this:

1. Using a machete, chop off the stalks at the ground and load them into the bed of the work truck.
2. Smile as the pile of stalks in the truck bed grows and you can envision happy cows.
3. Drive out to the pasture honking and calling. Watch as the cows perk up and start running toward you.

4. With a driver keeping the truck just creeping along, throw the sweet corn stalks out of the truck bed for the cows.
5. Count the cows and laugh as they dash from stalk to stalk eating the ears.

Those who say there is nothing to do in the country would change their minds if they had a sweet corn patch and a herd of cows.

The author feeding sweet corn shucks to Good-Gray-Cow.

Chapter 8: The Rise and Fall of Corn-Eating Machine

A bit of mystery surrounded Corn-Eating Machine: It was family legend that she was raised on a bottle by my Grandpa Omer and that her mixed-breed heritage included Jersey. This legend never seemed plausible because Jersey is a breed of dairy cattle, and many years had passed since my Grandpa Omer had cared for the cattle. However, in my earliest memories of the cows, Corn-Eating Machine was already an old cow, so it is possible that my Grandpa Omer did raise her. Regardless of her upbringing, she had amazing longevity. She loved corn and was tame, typical of a calf raised on the bottle, but she also had a mean side. Maybe early on Corn-Eating Machine's behavior was just a playful nature, but as she got older, she became devious. We all knew to watch out for her. She was shorter than most cows and very wide. In fact, she was wider than she stood tall. Her face was white while the rest of her body was black. She had a few gray hairs around her face and eyes that seemed to say, "I've seen it all." Through sheer social skill and age, she maintained a high status in the hierarchy of the Bogota herd. Often, she acted as the herd babysitter—four or five young calves remained in her care while their mothers grazed. Most of the time her behavior was commendable, and she didn't cause trouble. We would let our guard down around her; then when we least expected it, she would head-butt the bejesus out of us.

On one particular occasion, she nailed me while I sorted calves to be weaned. The Bogota pasture, which she called home, was set up with a cattle trough in a holding pen at the southeast corner. At one end of the pen was a tight corral. On this occasion we called the cows and poured ground corn into the trough. While the mothers were preoccupied eating corn, we quickly drove their calves into the corral at the end of the pen. Since we only wean calves that are older than seven months, we had to sort out the younger ones. They would stay in the pasture with their mothers while the older calves were hauled away. Dad and Grandpa were standing in the corral discussing which calves to sort out, and I was blocking the opening of the corral. My back was turned to the cows at the trough because I was focused on the calves. Corn-Eating Machine finished eating and then stalked up behind me. Without any warning—wham!—a stiff head butt lifted me off the ground. I landed on my feet, shaking with shock. I whirled around to see Corn-Eating Machine standing there with a smug expression on her face.

While such actions were not cute, Corn-Eating Machine's behavior was not dangerous and so was forgivable. That is, until one day, early in the summer before my twelfth birthday. It was the tail end of the planting season, and Dad was busy in the fields. At lunch he told Mom, Bob, Sarah, and I to check on the tall Horned Cow in the Bogota Pasture. The cow had given birth to a calf the day before. He was an adorable little bull with black fur everywhere except for a little white spot on the top of his head. Dad was worried that the new calf had not nursed. If that was the case, we needed to get colostrum in the calf as soon as possible.

After lunch, we drove the work truck back to the pasture, opened the gate gap, set it aside, and drove into the pasture holding pen. We honked the horn and dumped two buckets of ground corn into the trough. Our intention was to bring up all the cows, including the Horned Cow. If we could capture her in the corral, then we could bring her calf up and watch for him to nurse. If he didn't nurse, then we would have to run the Horned Cow into the head gate and work with the calf. However, we weren't surprised when the Horned Cow stayed about fifty yards away from the feed trough and the pen. While the other cows ate, she nervously eyed us. Bob and I quietly tried to get behind the Horned Cow and drive her into the pen. She saw right through our tactic and took off running north. We were beginning to get frustrated with this uncooperative cow. About 200 yards away the cow stopped. We waited a few minutes for the Horned Cow to settle down.

Mom decided that the best thing to do was drive the work truck into the pasture, and just look if the cow's nipples had been nursed. If the nipples were clean and the udder was marked with calf slobber, then we would conclude that the calf had nursed. If the nipples were swollen and dirty, then we needed to take action to get some colostrum in the calf. Mom drove the work truck back into the pasture in a hurry. As we approached her with the truck, Horned Cow immediately started walking away. Mom parked the truck and we all piled out. Mom helped Sarah climb in the back of the truck where she could watch us, yet she would still be safe. At six years old, Sarah was accustomed to fending for herself while we tended to farm chores. Mom walked with Bob and me over to the cow. As we approached, the cow walked about 150 yards away from us. We followed her until finally she stopped and let us look at her. We couldn't honestly tell if the calf had nursed or not. We were discussing our options, when Bob noticed that a few stragglers at the feed trough were calmly walking out of the pasture through the open gate gap. We had left the gate open as a matter of convenience; we were going to drive right back through after checking the horned cow. Bob ran to the truck. In a hurry to catch the escaping cows, Bob picked up Sarah from the bed of the truck and set her on the grass. He needed to drive back to the gate quickly, and since the pasture was bumpy, Sarah couldn't safely ride in the bed of the truck.

Bob drove off, and Sarah stood there alone in the pasture, about 150 yards away from us. Mom and I watched helplessly as Sarah turned her head to see Corn-Eating Machine only twenty yards away. An intense sinking feeling came over me as Corn-Eating Machine turned toward Sarah and started to charge. Mom screamed, "NNNNNOOOOO!" as we sprinted toward Sarah to intervene. Corn-Eating Machine got to her first.

The cow hit Sarah hard, knocking her to the ground several feet away from where she stood. Mom and I arrived just moments too late. Mom rushed to Sarah, and I ran straight for Corn-Eating Machine. The cow bolted off in the opposite direction and then stopped to face-off with me. I rocked back on my feet and prepared to fight with kicks. Instead of charging me, Corn-Eating Machine let out a huff and sauntered off. Behind me, tears streamed down Sarah's face. Mom was consoling her and checking for injuries. Sarah was shaken and bruised, but otherwise okay. That cow didn't know it, but she had just messed up big time. Head-butting me was one thing, but attacking my little sister was completely unforgivable. My hands trembled with a combination of fear and rage. Corn-Eating Machine didn't know it, but she had just messed-up BIG-TIME.

Not long after mauling Sarah, Corn-Eating Machine gave birth to a set of twin calves. Her new calves needed some extra milk to stay healthy. To make bottle-feeding them more convenient, we transferred the trio from the Bogota pasture to the home pasture and kept them in the barn lot. At the home pasture, she was on my turf, with the cows that I looked after every day. Without her cronies at the Bogota pasture she would soon be put in her place. I kept sturdy sticks near every entrance to the barn and enforced a strict rule: If Corn-Eating Machine threatened or even looked at me funny, I'd whack her. If I didn't have a club, I would kick her nose for such offenses. Brutal, yes, but she attacked my six-year-old sister without provocation. My violence against Corn-Eating Machine was motivated by revenge and fear. I knew what she was capable of and in retrospect; she brought out the darkest side of me. The cows of the home herd were even more brutal than me. Corn-Eating Machine had enjoyed a high social status at the Bogota pasture; now she was at the bottom. The very bottom of the pecking order in a forty-five-cow herd is a rough place to be. She got butted away from the corn trough; she got butted away from the hay ring; she got butted just because she was new. The home herd cows didn't know it, but she deserved every butting.

Corn-Eating Machine was never accepted into the home herd. Perhaps her pride kept her from making alliances at the bottom and working her way up. Regardless, whenever I would go check the cows in the south woods, Corn-Eating Machine would never be with the herd. She would either be on the edge of the herd or 100 yards away. If she had a young calf at the time, it would be right with her. However, once her calves got a bit older, they would join the other calves of the herd, and Corn-Eating Machine would be alone. Over the years, she continued to raise healthy calves and her behavior improved. While I never trusted her, I eventually developed a fondness for the old cow. When she was finally culled from the herd, I almost missed her. I'll always wonder just how old she was when she left the farm and if there was any truth to the legend.

This photo of the author was taken the summer prior to Corn Eating Machine's attack. No wonder Corn Eating Machine ran when this little rascal came sprinting at her! The bantam rooster the author is holding was named "Governor."

Chapter 9: Fibbing Face

Grasshoppers jumped ahead of the truck as Bob and I drove back the dusty dirt road to the pasture. He stopped at the gate and I jumped out of the passenger side to open the gap. It was just a short section of fence that was stretched tight between two corner posts. A loop of number nine wire held the top of a short post and kept the gap tight. I had to pull the section of fence extra tight with my right arm and slip off the loop with my left hand. It was always a bit of a challenge and the short post was worn to a polish from the years of daily handling. I opened the gap and laid it back so Bob could drive through.

As I hopped back into the cab I looked at Bob, "Whew, it's getting hot out again."

Bob nodded, "I think the old girls will all be down at the creek."

I smiled, "They'll be easy to count."

We bounced along in the truck as Bob followed the well-worn path down to the bottom. He parked near a little bend in the creek where the cows liked to sleep. There the herd was lazing away happily. I started by counting the cows that were cooling off by wading in the creek. Bob started by counting the cows that were laying in the shade.

I met up with Bob by a downed tree and swatted a deerfly that landed on my head, "Ugh, I must have counted wrong; I only got twenty-six."

Bob sighed, "Dang-it, that's what I got! Let's count'em again."

This time I circled around and counted the cows in the shade first and finished by counting the cows in the creek. We met by the same downed tree.

I shook my head, "Twenty-six."

Bob rolled his eyes, "Twenty-six; we're still one cow short." He thought for a moment and continued, "Let's drive around and see if we can't find her."

I nodded, "Sounds good to me!"

Missing one cow is usually indicative of a situation that needs attention. She is A) off calving somewhere, B) very ill, C) outside the fence, or D) dead. While Bob drove, I sat in the passenger seat and searched the pasture like a hawk. From time to time I would have him stop while I glassed a brush line with the binoculars.

I shook my head, "I don't know where she's at. I mean, we went back to the spring, we drove around the Armor Hills, we passed by the old hay feeders, and we can see most of the north hills!"

Bob shrugged, "Maybe we ought to go count'em again?"

I set down the binoculars on the seat between us, "Yeah, maybe she's joined up with the herd by now."

We returned to the bottom and recounted the lazy cows. Once again we only found twenty-six.

Bob sighed, "Dang-it, we're still missing one. How about this; let's check that all the named cows are here."

We walked together and found Floppiness, Bullah, Timid Cow, Horned Cow, and the White-Tailed Cow. All the named ones were present. I said, "Well, Bob, I guess we need to walk the bluffs and the ravines."

He nodded in agreement, and we split up to search for the cow on foot. I covered the hidden areas to the west while he searched the areas to the east. Within half an hour, we were both back at the truck.

"I didn't find anything!" I admitted as I wiped the sweat from forehead.

A slight crazed look came over Bob's face as he pulled off his sweat-stained cap, "Me neither. I don't know where the hell she's at."

It was nearing noon, and the overhead sun had raised the temperature to ninety although with the humidity, it felt more like one hundred. A pesky deer fly buzzed around my head, "Bob, the only place we haven't checked is around the pond."

The pond itself wasn't a hiding place, but the thicket of autumn olive and small ash trees growing around the pond could easily hide a cow. The cows grazed in the brush, but even with their trampling, it still wasn't easy to traverse. Often, visibility was limited to five yards in the tangle of branches, thorns, and leaves. As the younger brother, I got the duty of snaking my way through the center of the jungle, while Bob looked in from along the edge. On the north side of the pond, I finally encountered our missing cow.

I recognized this cow as recent addition to the Bogota herd. Her fur was a distinctive beige color with a few splotches of white on her face. She was standing happily in a narrow opening amongst the shade of twenty-foot-tall ash trees. Behind her was a newborn calf with sleek cow-licked black fur. I stepped a bit closer for a better look at the calf. I was still about fifteen yards away when the cow calmly began to walk towards me. She seemed perfectly serene and happy until she was about two feet away. Then, without any kind of warning, she dropped her head and switched to KILL-THE-HUMAN mode. My happiness over finding the cow gave way to terror right in the nick of time. I quickly side-stepped behind a small tree and scrambled around the trunk as the cow charged after me on her rampage. I saw an opening in the brush and jumped for it. I burst out from the thicket into the open pasture at a full sprint, running like a deranged, murderous cow was after me—which was exactly the case. Bob saw me running and yelled, "WHAT'S GOING ON?"

With a full dose of adrenaline, I yelled, "SHE WAS GONNA KILL ME!!" Bob caught up with me near the truck. Thankfully the cow didn't bother to pursue me out of the thicket, but I wasn't going to waste any time looking over my shoulder!

63

"What happened?" he asked.

I tried to catch my breath. "Bob, she tried to get me! I found her and it was like she was just fibbing that she was going to walk by me in the thicket. She never shook her head, pawed the ground, or showed it in her face!" I tried to calm down a bit, "She has got a nice little calf in there." I was totally shocked by how quickly she had turned into an aggressive mother bear. Bob quick with the names, put "fibbing" and "face" together. From there on that cow was known as "Fibbing Face."

Timid Cow

After Fibbing Face pulled that stunt, she lost points with me, but soon, Fibbing Face's overall demeanor and the way she treated other cows caused all of us to share a disdain for her. In the Bogota pasture, we had a cow that would often hang back from the feed trough. She was mostly black in coloration with some white that trailed from the splotches on her face down along her neck. While she wasn't an anxious cow, she was a bit shy and timid when the other cows were aggressive. Over many years of noticing her behavior, we began to call her "Timid Cow." She was an excellent mother and had been with the Bogota herd for many years. About two years after Fibbing Face was introduced to the herd, Fibbing Face decided that Timid Cow was one cow that she could beat out of the social hierarchy. Usually, the establishment of rank just involved the occasional head-butting at the feed trough, but one early summer day we witnessed the true Fibbing Face come out.

On this early summer day Bob and I filled two buckets with ground corn from the bulk feed storage at the feedlot. We set the buckets in the bed of the work truck. The tailgate sounded its normal "KA-CHUNK" as I slammed it shut. I hopped in the cab with Bob as he turned the key. The truck started and Rhett Akins "That Ain't My Truck" came on the radio. We drove back the dirt road to check the Bogota herd. Bob honked the truck horn as we approached. The morning air was a comfortable temperature, and the cows were scattered about, grazing in the meadow near the trough. Our honking drew their attention. The cows bawled at us and excitedly made their way to the trough, walking and galloping. We hurried to dump the feed in the trough before all the cows arrived. I climbed up and stood tall in the trough with an empty bucket in my hand. I counted the cows as they lined up.

"Bob, I think we're one cow short."

While I recounted, Bob walked around the outside of the trough and counted the cows' behinds. He replied, "Yeah, I only got twenty-six. I'll get the truck."

I climbed down from the trough and opened the gate gap so he could drive through. I closed the gate gap behind the truck and hopped in the cab. As Bob let out the clutch he said, "It's odd that we're missing one because the whole herd was grazing just north of the trough."

I nodded and then shrugged, "I'm not sure which one is gone. Floppiness, The Horned Cow, Bullah, and Fibbing Face were all at the trough."

The morning air was not yet hot, but we suspected that some cow was already enjoying the shade down by the creek. She was probably cool and comfortable, and decided that the rat race for corn wasn't worth her trouble. Naturally, the first spot that Bob and I would check was along the creek, but as we drove away from the trough, we couldn't help but notice that some of the cows were acting a bit strange.

I looked in the mirror, "What's wrong with Fibbing Face?"

She had left the trough and was following behind the truck at a trot, as if she held some vested interest in where we went. Fibbing Face ran with her head held high in indignation of everyone.

Bob glanced back, "Weird cow."

As the truck crested the hill we spotted our missing cow. It was Timid Cow. She was grazing in the shade of the big ash tree. She looked up at the truck then focused on Fibbing Face running behind. Timid Cow began to retreat. Fibbing Face saw Timid Cow running away, and she passed the truck in pursuit. Fibbing Face kicked up dust as she sprinted toward Timid Cow. Bob stopped the truck, and we watched helplessly as Fibbing Face dropped her head and viciously butted Timid Cow.

"What the hell?" Bob muttered.

Timid Cow was clearly trying to flee, but Fibbing Face continued to pummel her. This didn't make sense because normally a cow fight would end when the loser ran off. The assault continued as the two cows struggled and dropped out of sight into the creek channel.

I looked at Bob, "We gotta do something!"

Bob shook his head, "There's nothing we can do. You know, we've got a shotgun behind the seat, but we can't shoot Fibbing Face."

"Ugh, I wish we could!"

We hesitantly stepped out from the cab of the parked truck. As we started toward the creek, Fibbing Face reappeared. For a moment we feared for our safety and froze in our tracks, but she paid no attention to us. Fibbing Face trotted off to join the other cows. Bob and I looked at each other and seemed to share the same dreaded thought; Did Fibbing Face just kill Timid Cow? We immediately walked over to the creek and looked down the channel to see if Timid Cow was still alive. We spotted her hiding in the shady pool of water. Timid Cow seemed okay. There were no visible injuries, but the poor cow had just taken the beating of her life. Fibbing Face had seemed to pick out Timid Cow just because she chose not to fight. Fibbing Face's behavior was not cow-like; it was much more human-like. From that day forward, I harbored a great hatred for that cow. The thing I always enjoyed about the farm was escaping from human

"Fibbing Faces" present at my school. A cow had just taken that away from me.

The day of reckoning for Fibbing Face would come. In a few years, she lost the physical strength of her youth. She developed sore hooves and limped around. She started losing weight, and a decision was made to cull her off the farm. I was glad for the day we pushed her ass in the trailer.

Chapter 10: Fawn in the Grass

It wasn't just the cattle that made visiting the pastures memorable. Anytime one goes outdoors, the opportunity to see a bit of nature presents itself. These opportunities become enhanced when one spends time with a cattle herd. While I would not consider cows as part of a natural ecosystem, cows are attuned to the natural world. It's not uncommon to see cows curiously looking outside their pasture. If I would take the time to pay attention to the cows' behavior, their gaze would reveal deer, coyotes, foxes, and other wildlife that would have gone undetected. One particular trip to check the Bogota herd remains vivid in my mind. The herd was grazing on a portion of the pasture that we nicknamed the "Armor Hills." This area was located far from the feed trough. Since the cows were so far from the trough, Dad decided to skip calling them. They wouldn't all come to the feeder from back there. Instead, he drove the work truck back into the pasture to count them. A deep ditch prevented us from driving all the way back to the Armor Hills, so Dad parked the truck and we continued on foot. The cows were actively grazing. As we walked through the herd, the only sound from the cows was, "Munch, Munch, Munch, Munch, Munch." We had nearly circled the whole herd when Dad stopped and stood motionless. His action caught my attention. He pointed to a spot in the grass one step away from where he stood. I looked over and saw something nestled in the tall grass. It was about the size of a cow pie and held perfectly still. The young fawn was curled up with its little black nose almost tucked in by his back legs. Its fur was a surprisingly bright shade of red, with little white dots scattered about. I thought to myself, *That mother doe was smart to hide her fawn amongst the cattle here. There are twenty-six other mothers that would discourage any coyotes from eating her fawn.* As we walked away from the herd, I noticed Floppiness and Horned Cow looking over the fence into the hayfield. On the far side of the hayfield, along the woods, the mother doe was watching us.

For Whom the Cows Bawled

Of course, there were other interactions with deer. July 1995 was drier than usual, but on one particular day, high-level clouds were blowing in from the west and the humidity was beginning to rise. This type of weather pattern was odd for mid-summer when most clouds and rain showers result from convection. The corn growing in the fields was right at the tasseling stage, and we were hopeful that the clouds would produce a nice rain shower. While the sky began to darken, the sounds of cicadas intensified. The cows happened to be peacefully grazing near the west barn when a distressing sound echoed from the southern bottoms; "BLLLAAAAAAAAHHH! BLLLAAAAAAAAAAAHHHH!" The cows tensed up and turned to face the sound. Their large ears pinpointed the source. "BLLLAAAAAAAAHHH! BLLLAAAAAAAAAAAAHHHH!" Without hesitation, Red Rip, City-on-Her-Back, Killer, and three other lead cows started running toward the sound. Their sense of urgency told us that something terrible was happening. Bob looked at me and said, "Let's get down there!" At a dead run, we followed the cows down into the pasture bottoms. The cows led us straight to the source. They lined up along the fence, stood tall and menacing, and nervously looked toward the sound inside the neighbor's tall corn. The sound was more muffled now. "Bllllaaaaahhh." Thinking the sound could be coming from one of our newborn calves, Bob and I crossed the fence and walked toward the source. About forty yards into the tall corn, we spotted corn stalks moving. Bob and I advanced. Just ahead, the corn gave way to an opening of flattened stalks. A large black dog glanced at us and then disappeared into the corn. To the right, a larger German shepherd dashed off noisily, knocking over corn stalks as he ran. In the middle of the disturbed clearing was a half-grown fawn, mortally wounded from the dogs' mauling. Bite marks were scattered all over its body. The only place not bitten was the neck. Apparently, the dogs were too stupid to bite the neck and end the fawn's suffering. As the broken legs of the fawn twitched, Bob and I heard Dad approach in the work truck. We walked back the boundary and met Dad as he turned off the engine, "What was that?"

Bob replied, "Two big wild dogs just killed a fawn. You got a gun?"

"Yeah, your Remington." Dad looked past us to where the sound had originated, "I thought it might be a fawn."

Bob continued, "Well I don't think the shotgun's of any use now. The dogs took off, but if we see them around here again, they need to die."

I added, "I hope they don't go after our calves."

Bob recommended a shoot-on-sight policy, and I completely agreed. Dogs capable of taking down a half-grown fawn could easily kill a newborn calf, and we definitely did not need any feral dogs running around killing wildlife.

Bob and I climbed into the back of the truck. As we rode back to the house, the smell of rain filled the air. Just as Dad parked the truck, big drops of rain started falling from the sky. Our anger at the dogs subsided to feelings of relief for the crops that needed rain. Lucky for the dogs, we never saw them again.

Chapter 11: Leptospirosis

It was the summer that I turned thirteen and not many years after Felini's class had graduated from the slack pasture. We had a new class of seven heifers that showed some real potential. These heifers were all the daughters of our Red Limousin bull in the home herd. Most of their mothers were Herefords. The heifers exhibited the muscled build and red coloration of their Limousin father. They had the pleasant demeanor of their Hereford mothers. Since the heifers' father was the bull in the home herd, all the young slack pasture heifers would be going to the Bogota herd. Otherwise the heifers' calves would be inbred. In late summer, we acquired a young handsome Black Angus bull and turned him loose in the slack pasture to breed the fifteen-month-old heifers. We also kept an old cow in with the young herd to act as a calming influence. They spent the following winter in the slack pasture where we put out bales of timothy and clover hay for them to eat. When the weather turned frigid, we kept open a drinking hole in the pond by chopping through the ice with an ax. Nearly daily we checked on the heifers by feeding them a bucket of corn at the trough. By early spring, the heifers were starting to widen out, and their first calves were born in May. In June, we caught up on fieldwork and had more time to devote to the cattle. One morning we decided that the time was right to move the new cows and calves from the slack pasture to the Bogota herd. We fed the slack herd a bucket of feed at the trough, then corralled them in, sorted out the bull and the calming old cow that would stay behind, and loaded the new cows and calves into the trailer. After a short ride, the young cows and calves were turned out of the trailer at the Bogota pasture. With fresh grass and plenty of water in the pond and creek, the young mothers would raise their calves just fine, or so we thought.

Not long after we moved the new cows and calves, the oldest calf born at the slack pasture went missing. A thorough search turned up a dead calf without any indication of what could have killed him. Since all of the other cows and calves seemed healthy, we had to accept that the calf was lost and move on. It's not uncommon for a cow to lose her first calf, but this one had seemed fine. That was troubling.

About a week later, another calf went missing. This, too, was a calf that belonged to a new cow from the slack pasture, and when we found the dead calf, again there were no clues to help us figure out a cause of death. With the death of the second calf, we decided to check on the Bogota herd more often. We always checked them in the morning by feeding them corn at the trough, but now we would also walk through the herd in the evening or at the least just drive by them to quickly look for problems.

A few days later Dad and I drove back to the pasture and checked the Bogota herd in the evening. We made sure to check the younger calves. Immediately, we noticed a sick calf that belonged to a slack pasture cow. This particular little calf had dark red fur and was running around playing the previous day. Now it was hunched over, barely able to walk or hold its head up. We placed it in the truck bed, and I restrained it while Dad drove us to the corral. We called the veterinarian. Ken was the vet on call and said he would be at our farm in about an hour. Dad and I went back to the corral at the Bogota pasture and waited.

Suspecting that more could be amiss, Dad and I thoroughly checked all of the calves in the herd. Sure enough, one of the other calves born at the slack pasture was just beginning to get ill. We drove it into the corral, too. The vet arrived just before eight, right when it was beginning to get dark. Dad opened the gate to the pasture and quietly told Ken that we had found another sick calf. When Ken approached the corral, flies buzzed around my head as I lifted the first calf to its feet. The calf's condition had deteriorated—it had gone from being a beautiful healthy calf to a noodle. In the moments I took attempting to get the calf standing, it died. Ken knowingly shook his head and said, "Let's take a look at the other calf." I set down the dead calf while Dad roused the live one. Its condition was also getting worse. I walked over and helped hold the calf steady while Ken checked his temperature. "Yep, running a fever." He listened to its lungs. "Sounds clear." Ken started asking some questions about the calves. Dad told him that these calves were all from new heifers moved over from our slack pasture. As Dad spoke, I noticed a warm sensation on my foot. The sick bull calf was urinating on my boot. In the dim glow of the flashlight, I saw that the urine was red with blood. I spoke up, "Hey Ken, this calf's got blood in his urine." Ken looked down, drew a deep breath and said, "Hmmm, Let's do an autopsy on the calf that just died. Let me get a few things from my truck,

I think I might know what's going on here." Ken returned with some surgical knives, Ziploc bags, and a Styrofoam cooler.

"Jim, you've heard of leptospirosis right?" Ken asked.

Dad tipped back his sweat-stained ball cap, "It can cause cows to abort late-term, right?"

"Exactly. But it can also kill calves if the conditions are right. You guys moved these calves and their mothers into this pasture from another lot. Are you watering them out of a well over there?"

Dad answered, "No, we've got a small pond that we dug out a few years ago. They drink out of that pond and any other puddles or ditches they feel like drinking out of."

Ken squeezed his temples, "Hmmmm, that doesn't exactly go along with my hypothesis, but I still think that it's lepto. I'm thinking that for some reason those heifers weren't exposed to lepto over in that pasture. They had their calves over there and everything was fine. I'm guessing that lepto is present in this pasture, like nearly everywhere around here, and the new cows don't have a problem with it because of their age and weight. Then as these new calves started getting bigger, they drank water in the pond and creek instead of just nursing the cow. As soon as they started drinking water, they got sick. Now, this is just affecting those calves born to the new heifers, because the calves born to cows already in this pasture get enough resistance from their mothers. Those cows already carry some antibodies from having lepto."

Quietly, Dad replied, "Well I wouldn't know why the slack pasture would be lepto-free, but that sure makes sense. What can we do?"

Ken said, "Well let's treat this sick calf with some strong antibiotics right now. Then let's collect the kidney from the dead calf and send it to the Animal Disease Lab in Centralia for testing."

We got right to work. Ken grabbed a hypodermic needle and a bottle of antibiotics from his truck. He held the bottle at a distance so his aging eyes could double-check the label. Then he quickly inverted the bottle and inserted the syringe. Ken shot several CC's of air into the bottle and withdrew the equivalent CC's of medicine. He pinched the calf's neck skin on one side and shot in half the dosage, then pinched the calf's neck skin on the other side and shot in the rest of it. Then we turned our attention to the deceased calf. I flipped it onto its back while Dad focused his flashlight for Ken to see. Ken cut open the chest cavity down to the pelvis. He examined the calf's organs and removed the kidneys. He placed them in a Ziploc bag and set the bag in the Styrofoam cooler with ice. Ken spoke, "Jim, the quicker this cooler gets to the lab, the better. I can send it FedEx tomorrow morning, or if you got time, you can take it down there." Dad responded to the question by nodding his head and said, "Yeah, I'll just drive it down tomorrow morning. Does the lab open at eight?" Ken nodded.

Before Ken left for the night, we made plans to vaccinate the remaining calves that were moved from the slack pasture. He would put together the vaccines and needles needed, and we could pick up the box from his office the next day. Hopefully the other calves would not become exposed before we treated them. Out of seven healthy calves born to the heifers, three had died from lepto, one was ill but had been treated with antibiotics, and three appeared to be healthy. That night as we drove home from the pasture, Dad and I both assumed the treated calf was a goner too.

The next morning, Dad was up extra early checking the cattle; though I doubt he slept much that night anyway. He asked me if I wanted to go with him to deliver the cooler to the Animal Disease Lab in Centralia. You bet I did. I wanted to know what had happened, and I did not want to lose any more calves to lepto. In my time working on the farm, we had lost plenty of calves, but usually it was during the winter or early spring, and it was often a more gradual death. A typical scenario might be as follows: a weak calf might get sick with pneumonia; we'd treat it with antibiotics; it would get scours; we'd give it albon; it would get pneumonia again and couldn't recover. A calf dying from lepto was a new event altogether; a calf is healthy one day and dead the next. From a producer's standpoint, I felt helpless. We were lucky to discover the third afflicted calf before it died. If we had skipped checking them that evening, it is likely that both calves would have been dead, and we would have still been clueless to the cause.

The drive to Centralia took about an hour and a half. Dad was quiet as usual on the drive down. My twelve-year-old mind wandered, and I began imagining the lab. I pictured a large, shiny building full of sharply dressed experts in lab coats and goggles. They'd be busy looking through microscopes, centrifuging bottles, mixing chemicals, using Bunsen burners, agitating samples, taking notes, and solving problems. I imagined Dad and me walking into the building through some glass double doors where we would be greeted by a sharp-dressed receptionist. She would jot down a few notes and take the cooler from us. Dad and I would leave, and we'd receive a letter in a few weeks officially confirming that the beautiful calf with red fur died from leptospirosis. I snapped back into reality when Dad pulled the truck in front of a windowless dumpy brick building and said, "I think we're here."

We walked inside the building through a windowless single door. Inside the lab, everything was still. If work was being done, it wasn't happening at a fast pace. A disheveled middle-aged man wearing a lab coat was leaning against a messy counter. He acknowledged our presence by motioning us over to a lab counter where we set down the small cooler. He asked what we needed. Dad politely told him that we've collected the kidneys from a calf that we suspect died from leptospirosis.

The lab tech snapped back, "Well you don't really know what killed your calf, or you wouldn't be here." He turned his back to us and continued in a condescending tone, "Lots of diseases can kill cattle this time of year. It's real important that you keep the flies under control in the pasture. You do use fly control, right?"

Dad and I were completely taken aback. We were being treated like five-year-old-schoolboys. Dad shot back, "Flies didn't cause this calf to die."

The lab tech slowly turned to face us and replied, "No, no, you don't understand. The flies carry diseases that kill calves."

Dad sighed audibly and replied, "Okay." He wrote down our address, and we walked out of the building, furious. Back in the truck Dad muttered, "That son of bitch! What the hell! Willy, it's not a lack of fly control that killed those calves! Does he SERIOUSLY think that we're TOO STUPID to know that flies carry diseases?!"

I replied, "He treated us like we were five-year-olds. I'm a kid, and I'm insulted!"

We fumed for a few minutes. Then Dad clutched the truck and shifted it into reverse. He calmly turned to me, "Will, when we get home, we'll look after the calves that are left and maybe we won't have any more trouble for a while." It seemed like a long drive home, but we were back before noon.

While Dad and I were gone, Mom picked up the box of vaccines and supplies from the vet's office. She and Bob had already treated the calves. We arrived home not long after they had finished vaccinating the three calves and returned to the house. The ill calf had gotten up and nursed its mother cow, so maybe there was some hope for its survival.

A few weeks later, we received a letter from the Centralia Animal Disease Lab. According to their analysis, the calf had died from "oak poisoning." It almost seemed like a joke. First of all, I had never heard of any local producers in this area losing calves from oak poisoning. Second, it was mid-summer, and none of the oak trees in the pasture would drop acorns until the fall. Third, no oak trees had fallen in the pasture, and even if an oak tree did fall, all of the cows would gobble up the leaves before their calves could consume enough to cause any adverse conditions. Here was the perfect situation to incorporate the term "oak poisoning" into our lingo to mean any conclusion that is completely irrational, but in this case it was just too frustrating and sad to ever talk about. I seriously wonder if the kidneys were even tested for leptospirosis, or if the lab simply ran a test for kidney failure. This could have been the case since kidney failure occurs with both leptospirosis and oak poisoning mortality.

Chapter 12: A Herd of Difference

The home herd and the Bogota herd were geographically separated by about five miles. Occasionally a cow would get transferred between the herds, but as a rule, the two groups never mixed. Unsurprisingly, the demeanor of the two herds was quite different. Between the ages of eleven and fifteen, I was attuned to the body language of the cows. At the time I felt that none of my cow language knowledge translated understanding the language of my adolescent peers. The other middle school kids seemed to talk constantly. They repeated the same stories numerous times and their verbal banter often had a threatening tone. Perhaps my familiarity with animals and their language is why I preferred being with the cows instead of my peers.

In retrospect, the differences between the home herd and the Bogota herd of cattle can be explained. I considered the home herd as "my" herd. The pasture was located just outside of the yard; no driving was necessary to check them. All I had to do was walk out the garden gate and go see the cows. During the winter season, we kept the cows nearby in the winter lot. Most of them would be huddled around the hay feeders. Checking them was entertainment for me. Hardly a day passed when I didn't go see the cows. I had favorite cows that I always made a point to see: Felini, Good Gray Cow, Swimmer Cow, South America, Julia Gulia, and an older gray cow that would later be named Silage Cow.

In the summer, my pets could be found in the south woods between the hours of ten am and two pm. At least most of the cows would be in the woods. Swimmer Cow was an attractive Hereford with the typical red fur on her body and white fur on her legs and face. She had a tendency to mosey away from the herd while they were sleeping in the woods. She preferred to spend the hottest hours of the day in the pond. She loved the water and would venture out to relax in the deepest part of the pond. There, she would stand nearly submerged, like a hippo, with just her head and back above the surface. The white fur of her legs was permanently stained by the dark muck on the bottom of the pond. After two pm the cows would start moving out of the woods and begin grazing nearby. Around four pm the herd would either be grazing their way up the west side of the pasture toward the winter lot, or grazing up the east side of the pasture near Elmer's Branch. At dusk they would be near the north extent of the pasture. During the night they would graze southward and in the morning they could be found in the creek bottoms. By nine am they would be headed towards the woods for their mid-day siesta. I knew their habits and grazing pattern like the back of my hand.

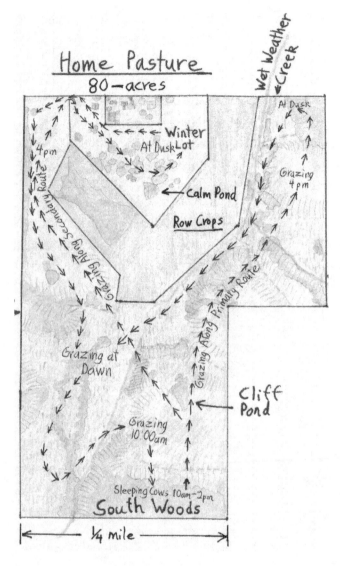

Home Pasture
80-acres

Wet Weather Creek

At Dusk

Grazing 4pm

4pm

Grazing Along Secondary Route

Winter At Dusk Lot

Calm Pond

Row Crops

Grazing Along Primary Route

Cliff Pond

Grazing at Dawn

Grazing 10:00am

Sleeping Cows 10am-2pm

South Woods

|← ¼ mile →|

The summer grazing pattern of the home herd; they were the most fun to check when sleeping in the woods midday.

The forty-five cows of the home herd had a social hierarchy, but it wasn't clear cut. I could identify a certain group as being the top-tier cows and another group that was the bottom-tier. The rest of the cows were somewhere in between and fought very little. Part of the reason for this was the herd size. The larger group enabled most of the cows to avoid conflict. Since the herd was large enough, the status of those cows was ambiguous. For example, Swimmer Cow fit into that group somewhere between the bottom and top; she almost never fought.

The Bogota herd was smaller, and the mid-level group for the average cows was nonexistent. I joked with Mom and Dad that "my" cows were simply better behaved than the Bogota herd. There was a kernel of truth to my joke. I didn't have any favorite cows in the Bogota herd. We had plenty of them named, but most of the named cows were notable because of nefarious behavior. Fibbing Face, Corn-Eating Machine, and the wild Horned Cow fell into that category. A few cows were named because of physical attributes—the White-Tailed Cow and Floppiness being the most recognizable. Dad normally checked the Bogota herd, and he was always in a hurry when checking them. He simply took two buckets of ground corn to the feed trough at the southeast corner of the pasture and honked the truck horn. The cows were very accustomed to this routine and would come running. Those of the Bogota herd were clearly more antagonistic than "my" cows. The twenty-seven cows would rush up to the feeder and aggressively butt each other for the best spots at the trough. Floppiness reigned supreme using pure, brute force. She was cream-colored, with big ears that flopped up and down as she ran. Part Charolais, Floppiness was nearly twice the size of the smaller cows. Her enormity gave her a distinct advantage. I didn't like her behavior or that of the other high-status cows at Bogota.

The social hierarchy of the Bogota herd was a model for what I saw at school. Three or four girls would ruthlessly suppress the others so that these three or four would receive all the attention. When I was standing in the feeder of the Bogota pasture, I could see the same thing happening. The only difference was the top tier cows didn't hatch elaborate schemes against the lower status cows. I could see the cows of lower social status standing away from the feeder in silence, while cows of higher social status hogged all the corn. I was fluent in reading cow Language. I knew that when a cow tipped her head down and tensed her neck muscles, she was putting on the act of looking tough. It was like an adolescent girl flipping her hair and looking down her nose to say, *"I'm the prettiest."* The intended effect was the same: put down the lesser girl without overt action. When a higher tier cow butted away the lower tier cow, it was like the popular girl starting a rumor about her foe. The cows used brute force; girls used shame and embarrassment. The feeding trough at the Bogota pasture was an ugly place. It was unfortunate that the actions of a few cows caused a trickle-down effect, and thus made the whole herd seem ruthless.

On a day-to-day basis, the situation could seem hopeless for the lower tier cows; however, the status quo was fluid and unpredictable. Sometimes, a few cows of the top tier would get culled. This was much like the turmoil in school when a preppy girl moved away. The only difference being the culled cows were going to McDonalds. Often, the top-tier cow developed sore hooves. This condition would slow down the aggressive cow and render her unable to assert her dominance. It was analogous to the top-tier girl developing acne.

In the Bogota herd, a cow of lower social status could bide her time and slowly work her way up the social ladder. However, a cow of high social status was not more valuable to us humans. As a "higher power" over the cows, we decided whether a brood cow should be kept or culled. The criterion was based on the cow's ability to raise a healthy calf. All other factors were secondary. Looking back it's ironic to think of all the struggles for rank, when status doesn't mean squat.

Chapter 13: Earl's Barn

Normally, the cows on Gillespie Farms were fed round bales of hay. These giant bales of hay weigh somewhere between 1,000 to 1,600 pounds and are very tightly wound. The fact that these bales are so dense enables us to store them outside for a long period of time, like a year. Water is both shed and absorbed into the first layers, but it doesn't soak through the entire bale. It works like a thatched roof. Small square bales are much different. They tend to weigh forty to seventy pounds and are compressed in such a manner that once the strings are cut, you can remove flakes of hay from the ends of the bale. The small square bales must be kept dry and covered storage space is always in short supply on a farm. However, in 1994, my dad purchased some land that he had been farming for a neighbor named Earl. Most of the land was row crops, but some was also pasture with a pole barn on it. Being a typical Midwestern pole barn, it had sliding doors on the east and west ends, a solid wall to the north, and an open lean-to on the south. Once the paperwork was finished and we officially owned the land, we started sprucing up the place. We repaired the old barn, rebuilt the fences, and got the pasture ready for the day that we could open a gate between the original Bogota pasture and the adjacent new section we called Earl's hills.

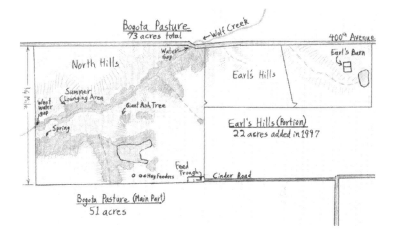

Earl's Hills added 22 acres on the east side of the Bogota pasture. The new barn was very interesting to the cows.

It was a fun day when we opened the gate between the two pastures. At first, the cows were skeptical. Then they grazed and walked forward a bit. Once they had clearly made it into Earl's pasture, a few cows looked back to see if we were protesting their escape through the gateway. With a bit of spunk, the cows kicked up their heels and celebrated their new pasture.

Contained within the Earl's hills was the barn. For many of the cows in the Bogota herd, this was a strange new thing because there was no barn in the main portion of the Bogota pasture. Our largest cow, Floppiness, decided that she liked spending time in the barn, and she could often be found lounging there when the other cows were out grazing. The new land and barn was a great addition to the farm. The extra acres of pasture meant that we could expand the Bogota herd from twenty-seven to thirty-five cows.

That summer we made a point of square baling many wagonloads of our best clover and timothy hay to store in the barn. This stock pile of square bales would serve as emergency feed that could be used for ill cattle or to feed the herd if the other food sources ran out. The shelter provided by the barn also meant we had a dry place for cows to calve in the snowy winter. We used the drive-through portion of the barn to store our heaviest tractor and disk. By mid-summer, we had the barn well stocked with square bales of hay. We even had the tractor and disk put away. Everything was in order.

Storms came rolling in that Friday. With the work wrapped up, it was time for my parents to enjoy a long-overdue night out. Their friends Gary and Linda met up with them, and they headed off to Effingham for a steak dinner. It was an uneventful evening for Bob, Sarah, and me. We ate the meatloaf Mom had prepared for our supper, did the dishes, and then watched "Nash Bridges" on TV. We particularly loved the character Joe Dominguez, played by Cheech Marin. He always seemed to be getting into funny predicaments that spiraled out of his control until the character, Nash Bridges, played by Don Johnson, showed up and saved the day.

The show ended and it was nearing bedtime when our parents returned to the house with Gary and Linda. They had just sat down in the living room when the phone rang. Dad answered it. His eyes got wide as he blurted, "Oh, no!" He hung up the phone and yelled, "Hey, Patty, we've got a problem. Earl's barn is on fire. Call Kelly at the volunteer fire

90

department for me!" Mom dashed over to the phone table and found Kelly's number in the Rolodex. I ran out to the truck with Dad and Gary in disbelief. As we pulled out of the driveway, an orange glow lit up the clouded northern sky. We knew that it was too late to save anything.

It was a four-mile drive to the pasture. By the time we arrived, the barn was engulfed in flames that licked high into the night sky. The intense heat warped the corrugated metal sheathing. Sheets that fell off the exterior revealed a tractor and disk that were already destroyed. Kelly Geier showed up with the fire truck within a few minutes. He set up the truck and approached my dad, "I'm sorry Jim, but it looks like we're too late to extinguish the fire. We'll pull down some timbers and try to determine where the fire originated from, but it's probably best to let it burn out." He was stating the obvious, but it was still a heavy blow. We had worked so hard to fill the barn with our best hay. On top of that, we had parked the tractor and disk in the barn to shelter it. Now it was burning along with all the hay. Dad nodded in agreement to Kelly's plan.

Dad spent the rest of the night parked near the barn. He was afraid that late-night partiers would see the flaming barn and drive back to investigate. Dad turned on the headlights of his truck to turn them away.

In the morning, we closed off the cows from that area of the pasture. There was no need to chance a cow or calf getting hurt while snooping around the burning barn. It continued to burn all through the next day until it finally went out on Sunday. On Monday, the insurance adjuster drove out to see the barn. He took one look at the charred remains and checked the box for "total loss." It was now time for cleanup.

After spending Sunday sitting around the porch in a somber mood, it was nice to be moving forward. A local scrap hauler came over, and we worked together to load the burnt sheets of corrugated metal onto his trailer. The metal sheets were flimsy and broke apart easily. Every time they bent, little flecks of oxidized metal popped off. We had to be careful to keep that grit out of our eyes. The few pieces of unburned timber were piled up and reignited. What had been a Case 2290 tractor was now difficult to recognize. All the tires were gone. The windows in the cab were hardened puddles of glass on the heat-warped metal floorboards. Any metal that wasn't steel melted. All the steel warped. Square beams holding the disk together appeared round. The intensity of heat was hard to fathom. The tractor and disk had value only as scrap metal; they were winched onto a flatbed semi and hauled away to be recycled like soda cans. Nothing could be salvaged. Chunks of burned concrete and any residual charcoal were buried with a bulldozer about a week later.

The source of the fire was never determined. It was a stormy night, so it's possible that lightning struck the barn and started the fire. It could have been arson. Regardless of the cause, the barn, 1,000 square bales, and a tractor and disk were destroyed. Insurance helped to replace the tractor and disk. We ended up with a Case IH 2294 and a used Krause disk. The peace of mind that a cattle farmer has when knowing he is prepared for emergencies with shelter and feed, was lost.

This photo was taking the day after the fire. Little remained of the barn or the 1,000 square bales of hay stored inside. The Case 2290 tractor and the disk were reduced to scrap metal. Notice the smoke rising from the smoldering hay in the background.

Chapter 14: Red Rip and the Ducks

Our farm was special because in addition to cows, cats, and chickens, we also had ducks—pet ducks, to be exact. They earned their keep by providing comic relief. Whenever the weather was rainy and the ground was muddy, the ducks were happiest. Most of the time we had big white Pekin ducks, but occasionally we would have a mallard or some Rouen ducks. They loved the pond in the cattle lot. It was shallow, muddy, and perfect for dabbling. At night, the ducks stayed in the duck house, a small building that protected them from being eaten by marauding raccoons. The duck house was located in the backyard. On a daily basis the ducks would leave the backyard and go down to the pond in the pasture. For the most part, the cows paid no attention to the ducks. The ducks dabbled in the pond, foraged around the pasture for cow pies to muddle, and visited the chicken house for cracked corn. One day the ducks discovered a secret. Out in the pasture was a metal creep feeder. This feeder was simply a self-feeder that is set up so only small calves can enter it. The term "creep" describes the slow progression of feed down into the trough. It works by gravity. We kept the creep feeder filled with a mixture of ground corn, oats, and pellets, which we referred to as "calf crunch." Supplementing a calf's diet with creep feed can be a big help to those calves that aren't quite getting enough milk from their mother. A creep feeder's trough is set about a foot off the ground, which is the perfect height for calves, but a stretch for ducks. The height proved to be an obstacle for the ducks and resulted in one of the funniest things I've ever seen. Somehow the ducks figured out that the creep feeder was full of tasty feed, but in order to get any grain they had to stand as tall as they possibly could and shovel their bills full of calf crunch. I did not realize that this was going on until one day I was checking the cattle and walked behind the creep feeder. I noticed six duck bellies lined up under the creep feeder and heard them shoveling their greedy bills full of corn. Those mischievous ducks!

Bellies of the pet ducks raiding the creep feeder meant for the young calves. Also notice the light snow. Yuck!

In the home herd we had a young, bulky cow with all red fur that we called Red Rip. She was an aggressive cow by nature, and whenever she had a calf, she turned especially gruff and defensive. Around the same time that the ducks discovered the creep feeder, she was raising a young bull calf that was full of spunk. He ran about the winter lot playing constantly, and he found the ducks to be very entertaining. They developed a bit of a game. The calf loved chasing the ducks, and the ducks loved going to the creep feeder, but in order to get to the creep feeder and the pond, the ducks had to cross the pasture. Red Rip's calf would be there, waiting to kick up his hooves and chase the ducks. The ducks could usually make it from their duck house through the yard, out into the pasture, and down to the pond without being harassed. However, when they got the urge to go eat some creep feed, they'd be caught. Red Rip's calf would either be in the creep feeder already, or he would quickly run over and give chase. The race was on! The terrified ducks would run and flap their hapless wings to reach the safety of their pond.

Red Rip's calf also seemed to enjoy playing with us humans. When we walked near him, he would kick up his heels and run toward us like he was going to charge. Then, at the last moment, he would veer off to a spot where he could stop and shake his head at us. Sometimes he would even let us pet him. However, Red Rip did not approve of us petting her calf, and whenever she saw us touch him, she would let out a low "muah" and walk our way. She would also shake her head to act intimidating.

Red Rip's calf grew quickly, and he was weaned and transferred to the feeder calf lot in late winter. By early the next spring, Red Rip was growing wide with the pregnancy of her next calf. All around the farm little hints of spring lifted our spirits. It was early April and the woodcock males started their courtship calls. We could hear them at dusk, spiraling high into the sky. In the woodlands, spring beauties and bloodroot flowers were just beginning to bloom. Mom and Dad knew the time was right to look for morels, so they took

Bob, Sarah, and me on a short walk to look for the prized mushrooms. We had high hopes of finding the very first tasty morels that popped up through the leaves. We spent about an hour straining our eyes and found a few of the precious fungi. Seeing the first hints of spring and finding morels put us all in a good mood. As Bob and I rode back to the house in the bed of the work truck, the chorus of spring peepers surpassed the sound of the engine. We couldn't help but smile. Suddenly Dad gunned the engine and passed right by the normal parking spot for the work truck. Instead he swung left in a hurry and drove back to the gate of the winter pasture. He stopped the truck with a jerk and bailed out. He let out a quick yell, "C'mon, kids! Help me."

Dad had spotted Red Rip out on the nearest hay pile with four hooves up in the air; she was "high-centered," a common term for dorsal recumbency. Red Rip was a big cow, and the large calf inside her only made things more difficult. We only had minutes to save the cow's life. Dad opened the gate and ran out into the pasture with the rest of us following behind. We splashed through the mud to reach her. Dad got there first and threw his shoulder against Red Rip's broad flank. Bob and I raced through the mud and piled in beside him. She began to move. "ONE, TWO, THREE!" We all heaved and Red Rip rotated back over on her side. She swung her head and was able to tuck her front legs beneath her body. The poor cow looked rough. The dark red fur around her face was matted with mud. Her back was wet with manure. She groaned as the stinky trapped gases began to gurgle up from her rumen. We pushed Red Rip to stand, but it took some time for her to comply. When she finally rose to her feet, she turned toward us. The look on her grizzled face seemed to say, "Ugh. That was horrible."

Red Rip on a cold winters day. As usual, she's giving me a tough look and demanding respect. Always a defensive mother, her personality was passed along to her calves. In Chapter 22 she earns my respect as an ally.

Chapter 15: Izzy (Where is He?)

South America was a sharp-looking black cow with a white patch on her face that looked very much like the continent of South America. She graduated with Felini's class of heifers and was part of the home herd. During South America's time, the home herd had forty-four cows and one bull. It was summer break from high school, my favorite time of year. Instead of watching the minutes slowly tick by on the clock at school, I was doing the thousands of little jobs that needed done to keep the farm running in tip-top shape. One of my favorite jobs was checking the cows. It required just a bit of strategy. The cows grazed during the late afternoon and night. Shortly after dawn, they would usually be grazing in the creek bottom, and by ten in the morning, they could be found relaxing and sleeping in the woods. For those who have never seen it, a herd of cows relaxing in the woods is a very pleasant sight. The cows are so content and peaceful. All the mothers are chewing their cud with their calves lying nearby. Often, the little calves get so sleepy that they lie flat out on their sides. It's the prime time to check the cows; they're easy to count and one can walk close by to check over each one. It was also the perfect time for petting the tame cows, like Felini.

South America was named for the white patch at the top of her face. In this photo she is approaching for some sweet corn shucks.

One particular morning, my count came up one cow short. I was about to begin my search for the missing cow when South America came waltzing into the woods with an innocent expression on her face that said, *nothing is going on here*. But a quick look at her udder and the bloody mucous on her back end told me that she had just calved—probably within the last twelve hours. I immediately asked her, "Where is he, South America?" Of course, she just stared at me. She didn't have to say anything; her dark brown cow eyes said, *None of your business.* But it was my business. Judging by her udder, the calf had likely nursed. However, a cattle man can never rest easy until he sees the new calf nursing.

I tried to drive her away from the woods, back in the direction she came from in hopes that she would lead me to her calf. Sometimes this tactic works. No dice—not this time. I decided that I would return to the house and tell Mom and Dad what I had found and head back to the woods to follow South America when the herd started grazing again.

Back at the house, Mom was picking green beans in the garden. As I walked by the rows of okra and started down the path between the green beans, Mom stood up and wiped her dusty hands on her shorts. "Well, what did you find?"

I replied, "I think that South America calved."

Mom smiled, "Oh good, is he all black?"

I nervously chuckled, "Well, I didn't see her calf, but it sure looks like she calved. She's got a big udder and some dried-up bloody membrane around her tail. I tried to drive her back to her calf, but she just walked in circles."

Mom nodded, "How about we go back down this afternoon and look for him then?"

I shrugged, "That's kind of what I was thinking. Maybe she'll go to her calf when the cows start grazing about three."

Mom handed me a bucket of green beans and tomatoes. "Take these up to the house. I'll help you look for the calf this afternoon; but first, let's go fix some lunch."

After lunch I had to help Dad move some hay bales, and we didn't make it back down to the pasture until almost five o'clock. Our plan didn't work. When Mom and I approached the cows, they were grazing in the bottom and they looked at us like, *what are you doing back here?* South America followed the herd and nonchalantly munched away. She was determined to keep her new calf hidden. I walked some of the brushy areas to look for the new calf. No luck.

That evening we gave up on the search, but by the next morning, I was determined to find the calf. Dad went with me to check the cows. When we saw South America, he teased her: "Where is he? Where is he? Huh? Where is Izzy?" Against our better judgment, the unfound new calf had a name, Izzy. Now, if we could just find him. I had always been good at finding calves, and this young cow was beginning to make a fool out of me. I left South America in the woods and searched the brush along the old dead creek channel. I searched the trees of the eastern hill and then the trees near the cliff. I was returning to the herd when I decided to check the backside of the dam on the cliff pond. The area was covered in honeysuckle, and the location was rather secluded. Bingo! There was Izzy perfectly hidden in a jumble of vines. He was covered in horseflies! I stepped over to Izzy and squatted down next to him. I reached out to brush away the awful biting insects.

Then in the blink of an eye, Izzy bolted and took off like a rocket. In mere seconds he crested the hill and was gone, leaving me dumbfounded. I muttered, "Shit!" and quickly went after him. As I scrambled to the top of the hill, I looked across the open pasture and the little calf was nowhere in sight. He had flat-out disappeared. This was most troubling because there simply wasn't a single hiding place in the short grass between the pond dam and the fence. Beyond the fence was the neighbor's soybean field—lush, tall soybeans that would easily swallow a little black calf. I thought to myself, *What have I done? Now South America won't even be able to find her own damn calf.* A few seconds ticked by as I considered the situation, *The area is wide open except for the soybean field. That calf had to run into the bean field. Maybe, just maybe, I could walk along the fence and find some kind of sign where Izzy crossed into the soybeans.*

I ran over to the fence and starting searching for signs such as bent over grass, upturned bean leaves, or broken over weeds. I also watched if any fur was caught on the barbed-wire fence. I moved along the boundary slowly. With unimaginable luck, I found some fine black hairs stuck in the bottom barb of the fence. Izzy had run under the fence there. I stood tall and noticed the faintest trail of disturbed leaves going out into the soybean field. I thought, *Things might turn out good yet.* I crossed the fence and followed the trail for

103

about twenty feet. Then I spotted the little black calf nestled deep down in the shade of the tall soybeans. I pounced on him immediately, before the calf had a chance to run. Izzy kicked and squirmed like a child throwing a tantrum as I picked him up. I muttered, "Izzy, I'm taking you to your mom, and I'm going to see you nurse, dammit!"

It was a long, hot walk with the eighty-pound calf from the soybean field back to the cows in the woods. Izzy kept up his kicking fit for about half the trip. Dad and South America were there to meet us. I set down Izzy, and he ran again until South America let out a small "mmmmuh" and went after him. Dad and I backed off about forty yards and found a good log to sit on. I cooled down for a few minutes, and we watched as Izzy circled around South America and then started nursing. What a relief!

Chapter 16: Little Red Cow

Growing up on the farm, I quickly became accustomed to some amazingly disgusting sights. It used to be a game on the school bus to name the grossest thing that you'd ever seen. I never lost this game. Heck, I even played that game in college and soundly defeated the suburban kids who thought roadkill kittens would win.

The poor Little Red Cow tested my ability to withstand disgusting sights. It was early summer and the tall fescue grass was growing faster than the cows could graze it down. I was checking the home herd about two hours before they would head to the woods and sleep. It was a cloudy morning, and the cows were grazing in the meadow just south of the woods. I counted the forty-five cows and was about to leave when I walked by the Little Red Cow and decided to pet her. She was pretty tame and didn't mind me brushing off the horseflies. As I scratched behind her ears, I noticed an awful rotting flesh smell. *Hmmm, not good,* I thought. I walked around her and noticed that her udder didn't look right. I parted the grass to see that a portion of her udder was rotten flesh, serving as a maggot hotel. I nearly gagged. The Little Red Cow must have gotten mastitis in one of her nipples. The infection destroyed a quarter of her udder, and the skin was simply rotting away. I looked at her calf nearby. He seemed perfectly healthy. I shook my head in disbelief, *How could the Little Red Cow have kept her calf healthy while suffering with such a severe abscess in her udder? My goodness, she is one tough cookie!*

I was faced with the decision of what to do. Apparently, the Little Red Cow was over the worst part of the disease, but an exposed gangrenous wound is no picnic. I returned to the house, and this became our lunchtime discussion. Dad mentioned that we had some screw-worm[15] balm in the barn. Screw-worm balm is a disinfectant for open wounds in animals. It comes in a spray can, much like spray paint. Also like spray paint, it contains some pigment so that one can see where the disinfectant has covered an area of the animal. This screw-worm balm happened to be blue. The plan was for me to get the can, go down to the pasture, and spray the infected part of the Little Red Cow's udder with screw-worm balm. *No problem!*

After lunch I cruised back down to the woods on the three-wheeler. Since the day was cloudy, the cows cut their siesta short and were already out grazing. I came across the Little Red Cow in about the same area that I found her in the morning. She looked a bit tired, as if the disease had taken more of a toll on her than I initially realized. I said, "Easy girl, this should help." I popped the cap off the can and prepared to spray some graffiti on her udder. *-TSSSS-* With lightning-quick speed, she kicked the can right out of my hand. "Whoa!" After a few minutes of searching for the can in the

---

[15] The screw-worm is the larval form of the fly Cochliomyia hominivorax or the New World screw-worm fly. It is believed to be eradicated from the United States, but is still present in tropical regions of Central and South America. The maggots are parasitic and feed on living tissue of warm-blooded animals. Spray for controlling screw-worms in wounds is effective against maggots of other fly species.

tall grass, I found it and thought, *You dummy, that spray was probably cold to her.* I put the can under my arm to warm it up a bit. Now I had her full attention. She moved away and looked at me like, *What the hell was that!?"* I said, "Sorry Little Red. Be good now; no more kicking." I walked up to her and tried to spray the dead portion of her udder again. This time she allowed a few more seconds of spraying before the can went flying. I was getting mad at her for kicking, but I was still pleased that she only kicked the can and had not kicked me. I thought, *Okay, I'll try this one more time.* When Little Red finally settled down enough I sprayed the dead portion of her udder again. I must have nailed it really well. The portion was obviously blue, but the whole damn quarter was moving and convulsing as the hoards of maggots started to exit in mass. I gagged.

The next day, I sprayed her udder again. This time the Little Red Cow only kicked once, and the maggot population was way down. After a few weeks, the dead flesh fell away. We all suspected that she would have trouble raising her next calf with just three-quarters of an udder, but we didn't cull her that year because we all liked the Little Red Cow.

February

The next year, she was due to calve in late February, and the cold winter weather was testing the limits of our endurance. I would check the home herd every morning by taking a walk amongst the cows in the winter lot. It was a small area, and normally the cows would be concentrated around the hay feeders. I climbed up onto the bales and counted the cows. If they were all present, I continued by checking over the herd for illness and looking for any cows that were beginning to calve. The previous evening I noticed that the Little Red Cow looked as though she could calve. Her udder was swelling with milk, and her vulva was enlarged, a condition farmers call "springing." I was excited that one of my favorite cows was soon to calve, so I made a point to find her first thing the next morning.

The sun was just under the horizon of the eastern sky when I stepped outside onto the porch. That morning's low temperature was about twenty degrees. The rubber of my gum boots was hard and stiff as I pulled on the frozen footwear. Just for fun, I kicked a post on the way out to the pasture and confirmed that my boots were like bricks. I climbed up on the first bale feeder and looked for the Little Red Cow. She wasn't there. I immediately started searching for her by walking east over the crest of the hill. She wasn't in any of the normal hiding places. I turned and looked south toward the calm pond. My eyes were drawn to a cow lying upside-down outside of the pasture in the bottom. It took a moment for the image to register, and then I realized it was my Little Red Cow. I took off running across the frozen ground pock-marked with cow tracks. As I neared her, I noticed a small newborn calf lying beside her. His front feet were tucked underneath his body, and he shivered as I approached. I scrambled across the barbed-wire fence and ran out to the Little Red Cow. Her eyes and legs moved! I had arrived in time; she was still alive. I threw my shoulder against her flank and shoved. It was just enough force to roll her onto her side. She swung her head to get stabilized. The

Little Red Cow had nearly succumbed to dorsal recumbency. She took labored breaths, and then began to belch. While she was recovering, I checked on her calf. He was small, coal black, and appeared to be healthy. I started rubbing his sides to warm him up. I looked around at the damaged fence and slide marks on the ground. In my mind, the scenario began to piece together: *The Little Red Cow decided to give birth to her calf where the fence ran along the base of the hill. It was a secluded spot that was sheltered from the wind. Cows often lay flat on their side during labor, and when she did this, she accidently rolled onto her back. In her effort to become upright again she slid down, broke through a portion of the fence, and ended up in a shallow ditch at the bottom of the hill. Fortunately, the ditch was dry. Her calf must have been born during this ordeal. Apparently, the calf inherited his mother's spunk. It had managed to stand, walk out of the ditch and lie down on the edge by his dying mother's head.* I had gotten lucky to find them when I did.

I picked up the newborn calf and carried him through the damaged fence to a grassy spot on the top of the hill. I kept rubbing his sides to warm him up. Soon, the Little Red Cow rose to her feet. She wobbled a bit and then followed my path up the hill to be with her calf. I checked the rest of the cows and returned to the house to tell my story at breakfast. I was so proud that I had saved the Little Red Cow.

She stayed healthy for several more years. Despite losing a quarter of her udder, the Little Red cow was still able to provide enough milk for her new calves. To this day, I regard her as one of the nicest cows for only kicking the spray

109

can out of my hand and not kicking one of my knees when she had the chance.

Chapter 17: Grinding Feed

When I was young, grinding feed was my least favorite job on the farm. It happened every Saturday morning. The process started innocuous enough; ride with Dad down to Wakefield Mill to pick up protein supplement. Just a few miles away, the mill was much more than our stop for cattle feed supplement; it was our primary supplier of everything farm-related. The business consisted of a feed mill, a hardware store, a grain elevator, and a local meeting place. It was invaluable convenience for us. All of our farm equipment, barns, and fences required constant maintenance and repair. Every conceivable item required to keep a farm running could be found in the hardware store. The store building set close to the road with a weathered brick exterior. Inside, the walls were lined with shelves that contained everything from garden seed to barn door hinges to colostrum mix for newborn calves. The floor was wooden, with travel paths from dirty boots worn deeply into the grain. The store was laid out with a center aisle devoted to office desks hemmed in by high countertops. The business was run by the Geiers—Kelly, Margaret, and Richard. Kelly kept his desk behind the counter of snacks. Snickers, Paydays, Peanuts, M&Ms, and little sacks of potato chips filled the display case. To the left of his desk was a DTN[16] screen that

---

[16] DTN stands for data transmission network. The business began in 1984 as an FM broadcast that would provide subscribers with current weather and commodity market information. Later the business updated to computer terminals at the subscriber's location that were updated by a signal sent to the subscriber's satellite dish. DTN has now switched to mostly internet delivery of data. The

displayed up-to-date market prices and weather radar maps. A column supporting the ceiling ran next to his desk and provided a place for Kelly to keep pictures of his family. Behind Kelly was Margaret's desk, with a computer, printer, low file cabinets, and an occasional sewing project. Farther down the aisle, Richard kept a desk, with a computer dedicated to playing solitaire. The north wall was filled with shelves of paint, motor oil, and cleaners. Between the center aisle and the shelves was a bench for farmers to loaf on. Nearby a soda machine stood and provided twelve-ounce cans of Pepsi, 7UP, Root Beer, and Mountain Dew for fifty cents each.

Dad and I would park at the feed mill and cross the road to the store. Once inside, I would scan the loafing bench to see which neighboring farmers were present. Normally their conversation focused on other farmers that were not present. Sometimes an awkward silence fell when we walked in. Dad would step up to the counter; "Four bags of supplement and two sacks of peanuts." Kelly was always friendly and would hand us the peanuts from the snack counter. Then we would follow Kelly out to the feed mill building. He would dolly a stack of fifty-pound bags of supplement to the edge of the loading dock and then heave four bags into the bed of our truck.

From there we would drive up to the feedlot. It was only about 4 miles north of the Wakefield Mill, but Dad always took his sweet time and rarely broke the forty-five

---

company is based in Omaha, Nebraska.

mile-per-hour mark. He would pull the truck under the pin oak trees. We kept the feed grinder hooked up to the Allis Chalmers D-17 in the barn. It usually started strong. First, I would have to disengage the grinder's fly-wheel. Next Dad would start the power-take-off shaft that ran the grinder. He would help me unload the bags of supplement into the mixing hopper. Then he would drive the tractor and grinder around the barn to the bin where he would back it under the auger, and I would re-engage the fly-wheel. As indicated, it was a tedious process with about twenty more steps. When Dad would finally back the feed grinder into the barn and the job was finished, the saga of feed grinding continued. I would get back in the work truck and instead of riding home, Dad would drive around for at least another half-hour while my stomach growled and he looked for ducks to hunt. In actuality, grinding feed could be done in less than forty-five minutes, but if it was duck season, Dad always made the job last twice as long.

When Bob and I got older, we started doing the job on our own. The task became substantially less painful. We streamlined the process and did it as quickly as possible. Still, it was never a particularly pleasant job. It was always loud and dusty, and the feedlot was often muddy. When it wasn't muddy, it was hot outside and the biting flies would target us.

Technical Difficulties
I always thought that the feed grinder was a dangerous piece of equipment because it had so many moving parts. The machine absolutely roared when running corn from the bin into the hammer mill. One day the grinder

113

was acting odd. When Bob and I started running corn into the hammer mill, the grinder surged like it would get a glut of grain and then the flow would choke off. This was strange, but we couldn't find an obvious source of the problem. We kept the grinder going; that is, until the grinder made a loud "K-chunk!" sound and the slip clutch started squalling. I immediately shut off the unloading auger from the bin. Bob quickly shut down the tractor. We were both worried that we had seriously broken something. We walked around the grinder looking puzzled. None of the mechanical parts seemed broken or out of place. After a few minutes of investigation, we opened up the hammer mill assembly and discovered the problem: the grisly remains of a pulverized raccoon. Apparently, the raccoon had crawled inside the hammer mill earlier. Once inside, he was unable to escape. He stayed out of our view while we added supplement into the back port of the grinder and drove out to the bin. When we started unloading grain from the bin, the coon was holding on inside the machine in such a manner that it would temporarily block the flow of grain. On the outside of the machine, we were completely oblivious to what was happening. At some point, the raccoon lost its grip and slid down into the spinning hammers. What a horrible way to go! Since the feed grinder was only designed to grind grain and not raccoons, the machine plugged immediately. We cleaned the blood, fur, and gore out of the hammer mill, then closed up the mill again. Bob turned on the tractor and started the grinder, and I started the unloading auger on the bin. Everything worked like a charm. We finished the job and moved on.

Chapter 18: Killer Cow Extraction

With prom approaching at Newton Community High School, the school administrators put together a little demonstration to show how paramedics extract victims from a car crash. Of course this was an attempt to remind the students to avoid drinking and driving. The demonstration was scheduled for Friday morning. I was looking forward to not sitting in class and besides, the thought of a spoiled prep crunching-up their shiny new car after doing something stupid was mildly amusing to me. At the time I was fifteen and I didn't really consider the full magnitude of a classmate ending up in a serious wreck.

However, fate decided that I would not be attending the demonstration. Events in the pasture made that morning quite memorable for me. We knew that Killer Cow was about to calve. The all-black cow had been in the home herd for some time. She had earned a reputation and a name for being terribly aggressive whenever she had a calf. The previous year's calf wouldn't nurse on his own, so Dad had to work with Killer Cow in the barn to make it happen. She proved to be dangerous and nearly unmanageable. However, when her calf was about a month old, she calmed down considerably and acted like a normal cow.

That particular Friday morning, she was nowhere near the herd. My dad found her in a small creek, mired up to her belly in mud, with the front hooves of her unborn calf sticking out. Dad returned to the house and called the veterinarian while I jumped into my overalls and coat. I met Dad out by the barn as he started up the loader tractor. We grabbed a lasso and a chain, and then headed down to where Killer Cow was stuck. I opened the gate gap, and Dad drove into the pasture. I stayed behind at the gate to direct the vet when he arrived. In short order Ken the veterinarian drove up. I hopped in the truck with him and as I slammed the door, I told him about the situation. "She's down in the creek, stuck up to her belly in mud. There's two feet sticking out and they look like front feet, so I don't think the calf is breached."

As the truck started rolling forward Ken asked, "Can we get her out of the creek? It will be a mess to pull the calf in that deep mud."

I nodded, "Well yeah; Dad's got the tractor back there, so I suppose that we could pull her out first. Although…. it's probably better that we don't."

Ken gave me a confused look, "Why's that?"

I hesitated, and sighed, "Because her name is Killer, and she is the meanest cow on the farm."

Ken let out a little snicker that translated to; *What have I gotten myself into?*

While I had been waiting on the vet, Dad had driven the loader tractor down to the creek. He had parked on the solid bank above the creek and got the lasso out. Ken and I arrived just as he was roping the cow to the tractor. Killer was living up to her moniker by thrashing her head at Dad. Ken and Dad attempted to tie the rope into a halter, but Killer fought them viciously. Seeing that their efforts were in vain,

116

they just kept her tied with a chokehold. The rope was wrapped around the frame of the loader tractor, and I kept tension on it so that the wraps wouldn't pull loose. Should Killer choke down, I could give her some slack. If she continued to behave badly, I would keep that rope tighter than hell.

Dad and Ken climbed down into the muddy creek behind Killer Cow. Her legs were stuck in the deep mud and that muck tried to suck the boots off Dad and Ken. They quickly set up the pulling jack and were able to pull out a healthy calf. He was larger than normal, which is what caused all the trouble for Killer. Her pelvic muscles convulsed in waves. I cringed just imagining the amount of pain she must have been experiencing. The vet gave her a shot of antibiotics to help fight off infections that can develop after such a difficult birth. Then Dad and I had to get her out of the creek. We all knew that this part could be bad. Killer thrashed at us so aggressively that we could not tie the rope into a halter, so with fear at what might happen next, Dad put the tractor in the lowest reverse gear and proceeded to pull her out of the creek by her head. I backed away a bit and watched Killer's neck stretch. I prepared myself to witness her head pop off, miraculously it stayed attached, and she slid up on the creek bank. Dad motioned for me to back away as he approached the cow and flipped open the latch that released the rope around her neck. Killer viscously shook her head at him and managed to stand up on wobbly legs. She was still ready to attack, but her legs could do no more than a creep forward. Dad hopped back up on the tractor, and we left Killer and her new calf right there in the valley. As we drove away I looked back. Killer started licking her calf.

Once back at the house, I changed out of my muddy bibs and coat. Dad drove me to school in time to catch the very end of the paramedic's vehicle extraction demonstration. That morning I had already been part of a different, but very real, extraction.

Whenever she had a young calf Killer Cow was an ultra-defensive mother. Here she is mid-winter, resting on a pile of old hay.

Chapter 19: Silage Cow

I really wish that I had memories of Silage Cow as a calf, but I must have been too young. My first recollections of her are of a middle-aged cow on the smallish side with gray fur that was rough, like a rug. Her face was expressive, with deep brown eyes, a gray nose and rounded ears that reminded me of a teddy bear. Silage Cow became friendlier as she grew older. She had a gentle nature and was a top-notch mother. I can only recall Silage being aggressive on one occasion, and during that event she was on my side.

Silage Cow earned her name during the winter of 1995. The preceding summer was drier than usual, and by fall our stockpile of hay was woefully short of lasting the winter. Dad decided that cutting some of our worst drought-stricken corn for silage would be a good way to keep the cows fed. We hired a nearby dairy farmer with silage equipment to do the work. The corn field was chopped and piled up at the Bogota barn lot.

Silage feed is analogous to sauerkraut, except silage is made from chopped corn plants instead of cabbage. The vegetative corn plant, or "stover," is cut with a machine, which is pulled behind a tractor, called a silage chopper. The chopper takes the standing corn, chops it off at the ground, and runs the stalk through something that works like a wood chipper. The chopped corn is thrown out of the machine into a specialized silage wagon. The wagon has an unloader device that is necessary because silage doesn't flow like grain—it has to be moved. The silage is either blown into a tall silo or a large bag, or it's emptied onto a compressed pile.

On Gillespie Farms, we lacked a silo; so Dad decided to make a silage pile on a hardened slab of lime at the Bogota barn lot. The sides of the pile would be flanked with large round bales of hay that served as retaining walls. Wagonload after wagonload was hauled from the field and dumped on the pile. To ferment properly, the pile needed to be compacted, which was accomplished by driving over the big hump with the Case 2290 tractor. I can distinctly remember our old farmhand Ray Swisher working on this task. He drove back and forth over the pile as the wagonloads came in from the field. Once the field was cut, the pile was covered with thick, black plastic. Dad piled crushed lime along the edges of the plastic to weight it down and seal it. Old tires were thrown on top of the plastic to prevent it from blowing away. While the pile would not win any awards for farm aesthetics, it was functional.

Inside the silage pile, aerobic bacteria consumed the ambient oxygen and carbohydrates in the plant material producing carbon dioxide, water, and heat. The oxygen in the pile was consumed within one or two days; then the anaerobic enterobacteria in the pile produced more acetic and lactic acid.[17] These acids caused the pH of the silage to drop from neutral to five. When the pH fell below five, the anaerobic homo-fermentative bacteria became dominant and

---

[17] Amaral-Phillips, D. "Important Steps During the Silage Fermentation Process." *University of Kentucky Dairy Animal and Food Sciences Extension*, 2000: http://afsdairy.ca.uky.edu/extension/nutrition/milkingcows/forages /silagefermentationprocess

produced more lactic acid. The silage pile became more acidic. When the pH neared four, the microbial action slowed, and the silage was preserved. As the outside temperatures cooled in the fall, the interior temperature of the silage pile stayed about eighty degrees.

When Dad pulled the plastic back and exposed the silage face during the winter a strong sweet and sour aroma wafted up along with steam. The smell was comparable to sauerkraut. To this day I associate the smell with happy cows.

As the winter set in, we began feeding the silage to the cows. This was a multi-step process.

1. Drive up to the barn by the Bogota feedlot in the work truck. The radio was always set to my Dad's favorite radio station, 95.7 WCRC. It played country music, which could be good or torturous, depending on the DJ.
2. Convince the loader tractor and the old green truck to start. The old truck was barely functional, and its condition earned it the nickname, "The Green Bomb."
3. Using the loader tractor, fill the bed of The Green Bomb with silage from the pile.
4. Drive back to the trough of the Bogota pasture.
5. Shovel out a third of the steaming silage from The Green Bomb into the trough.
6. Check the cows of the Bogota herd.
7. Drive The Green Bomb to the home pasture.
8. Shovel the rest of the silage out of the truck into the feeder.

9. Count the home herd and check for problems. Pet Felini, Good Gray, and Silage Cow.
10. Return The Green Bomb to the Bogota barn lot.
11. Arrive at home with my stomach growling.

I would take my boots off on the porch and step inside the warm house. Sometimes my arrival would be met by the wonderful smell of freshly baked chocolate chip cookies.

On weekdays, I was in class at the Newton Community High School, and I didn't have time to help, but when the weekend rolled around, I went on every trip to feed silage. Our close interactions with the cows while shoveling silage into the feeders caused them to grow very tame. At the time, Silage Cow was not yet named, but she had a habit of quickly running up to the feeder and claiming the spot along the driver's side of the truck bed. This was a prime spot at the trough because plenty of silage was shoveled out in front of her. She was already a tame cow, and once she was in position and feeding, she was impossible to move. After we emptied the truck bed of silage into the feeder and needed to get back in the cab, we literally had to climb over her back. She was that intent on eating silage. Her name started as a description—"That one cow that loves silage so much." Then it was simply shortened to "Silage Cow."

Many cows acquire their names through bad behavior. Unfortunately, many good cows never get named because they give birth to healthy calves and need little attention. Silage Cow's moniker was based on her love of silage feed, but it was her tame and gentle nature that earned her a name. Silage Cow's demeanor simply brought a smile to my face whenever I saw her. I remember one very cold evening in January when I went out to check the cows. I was sick with a fever, but I couldn't stand being cooped up in the house any longer, so I went out and walked among the cows. A biting cold wind blew flurries across the landscape. The snowflakes danced along the frozen mud and gathered in hoof prints. Silage Cow was resting on the hill above the calm pond with a dozen other cows. I sat down next to her and leaned back against her shoulder. I took in a heavy breath with my mouth bypassing my congested sinuses. She turned her head to me and gave me a sniff. I replied in a sick, nasally tone, "Yeah, I'm not doing so good." She held her head against me and continued to chew her cud while I rested there for a few minutes before moving on.

Silage's personality seemed to reflect a deep understanding of her human caretakers and her role as a mother. In all of her years on the farm, she only once had trouble calving. It was early spring, and the cows were antsy to be released from their winter lot into the rest of the pasture. We spotted Silage Cow off by herself and knew immediately that she was calving. I donned my chore coat and went out to check her. When I approached, she looked at me with big, brown, sorry eyes. There was only one foot coming out of her birth canal, which meant the calf couldn't be delivered unless we repositioned it. I dashed back to the house and recruited the help of Bob and Mom. We grabbed a bucket of warm water, sisal twine, and a lasso. Silage wasn't near any trees or posts that we could rope her to, so we simply approached her gently. I set the coiled lasso on the ground and touched Silage's face. She stood perfectly still as Bob dipped his hand in the warm water then slide his hand into the birth canal. He strained to reach the calf's other leg. Finally he quietly said, "There it is; bent way back."

Bob struggled to grasp the slimy leg. He waited out a contraction and then redoubled his efforts. Silage looked back at Bob and Mom through the corner of her eye but stayed still. I whispered to console Silage, "Easy girl, just a minute, easy now."

Mom motioned for me to come help pull. Bob had repositioned the calf just enough to get both front legs up in the birth canal. Silage contracted as we tied loops of twine on both of the front feet. We pulled back and down. Another inch of the calf's front legs appeared. Silage pushed again, this time we gained three more inches. I could hear Silage breathing heavy as she shifted her weight and pushed again. I could see the calf's head in the birth canal. We were gaining. I heard Mom consoling Silage, "Almost there girl, you've almost got him." Silage contracted while Bob and I pulled in unison. The calf's shoulders were exposed and we knew that we were close. I heard Mom say, "Come on Silage, just one more push." With that Bob and I were able to pull the calf out onto the ground. Mom cleared the mucous away from his nose, while Bob and I hoisted up the calf to drain any fluid from his lungs. The calf moved his head and his chest pumped. Silage turned around to claim her new calf. I backed away and picked up the coiled lasso that we didn't need. From a distance Mom, Bob, and I watched as Silage licked her newborn calf. We stood in awe, because every other cow on our farm would have moved away or struggled against us. Not Silage, she was one of a kind, and she worked with us to deliver that large bull calf with coal-black fur.

As it happens with all cows, many years of grazing wore out Silage's teeth, and she became thin and frail. We kept her on the farm as long as we could, but eventually the day finally came when she was culled. I remember herding Silage into the barn. She stood quietly in the barn while Dad backed up the trailer. Mom and I petted her back, and Silage turned her head to us. Her brown eyes were still bright. I opened the trailer and she loaded up willingly. It was as if she had just said, "Goodbye." I didn't ride along on that trip to sale barn. I will always miss Silage Cow.

An elderly Silage Cow munching on sweet corn shucks that she had just pulled from Laura's hand. (You'll learn more about Laura in Chapter 35.)

Chapter 20: Kids in Charge

It was a rare situation when Bob, Sarah, and I took care of the farm by ourselves, but every once in a while it did happen. As a rule, Mom and Dad didn't travel. With two herds of brood cows, the feedlot, and a small herd of heifers, the cattle were a huge responsibility. There was a gloomy joke in my family that whenever Dad was away, a cow or calf would die. Once he went on a pheasant-hunting trip for a few days. During that time, Mom and Bob struggled to help a calving heifer at the slack pasture. Their best efforts were to no avail and the calf died. When Dad arrived home, his first words to Mom were, "Well, what died?" An epic fight ensued—Mom felt insulted by Dad's comment, because she and Bob had worked so hard to save the calf. The entire event only added credence to the superstition, even though we knew it was irrational. Still, it always seemed that the cows had the most trouble in the times when we were least prepared. So when Dad decided to join Mom for a school teacher's conference in Chicago, we all understood the dire implications.

The plan was that while Mom would gain the professional development hours required to keep her teacher's certificate, Dad would tag along and enjoy a behind-the-scenes tour at the Adler Planetarium and the Shedd Aquarium. With the parents gone, Bob, Sarah, and I would be taking care of the cattle. We would undoubtedly face some major problems.

Mom and Dad left on a Friday evening in March. During the night, two inches of wet snow fell on the cold, muddy ground. Since we expected the worst, we went to check the cattle together on Saturday morning. We walked around the home herd's winter lot and found damp cows huddled around the hay feeders. The cold, clammy air stung our faces. The cows looked absolutely miserable, but okay. We moved out a junk bale of hay for bedding. Bob used the loader tractor to set it near the hay feeders. A few cows ventured over to head-butt it. They acted rowdy, like they were getting away with something, but in reality they were just spreading out the old hay for their calves to rest on. Then we moved on to our next chores. Sarah and I climbed in the work truck with Bob, and we headed up to check the Bogota herd. During the drive, I couldn't help but notice how the gray, overcast sky kept the daylight at bay. Despite the conditions, we were in good spirits because we shared a sense of pride that we could take care of things. Apparently Mom and Dad thought so, too. With George Jones singing "He Stopped Loving Her Today" on the radio, we drove the dirty work truck to the Bogota pasture. At the gate, Bob honked the horn, alerting the cows that it was time for corn. We dumped three buckets into their trough as they approached. Seeing this, they picked up their pace. I stepped up and stood on the end of their feed trough. I started counting, and I heard Sarah comment, "I see a white one back there still." I directed my attention away from the trough and looked toward the hay feeders 200 yards away. A white cow was lying down looking away from us. I replied, "Sure enough. Let's walk back and check on her."

We found the white cow in very rough shape. Her wobbly legs could barely support her weight, and the muscles around her pelvis spasmed. Next to her was a coal black calf that looked much larger than a newborn. She had given birth to a real whopper. He was wet and shivering but appeared alert and healthy. Bob, Sarah, and I discussed our options. We decided that the best plan was to get the cattle trailer, load up the pair, and take them to the barn, where they could recuperate in a dry place. There, we could feed the cow ground corn and flakes of clover hay without all the other cows rushing in to steal her feed. She could recover better with some individual attention.

We drove the work truck from the pasture to the pole barn at the feedlot. Bob backed up the truck, and I hooked it up to the cattle trailer. He pulled out of the barn, and I climbed back into the truck. The cloudy sky darkened to a more depressing shade of gray, and snow began to fall. As we drove back to the pasture with the trailer, a Dwight Yoakam song droned on the radio until Bob turned it off in disgust. I opened the gate, and we drove back to the hay pile.

Under normal circumstances, a cow is unwilling to enter a cattle trailer. One must first corral the cow and drive her through a chute into the trailer. On this particular day, we had an inkling that things might work out better. As we approached with the trailer, the old cow perked up, but stayed lying down. She was in rough shape. I got out of the truck and directed Bob as he backed up the trailer's tail end to about ten feet away from the cow. I opened the back gate of the trailer, which let out a metallic creak as it swung away. I walked over to the calf and tried to pick him up. Usually a newborn calf weighs between sixty and ninety pounds[18] and that weight can be carried. This calf was different. He must have been double the normal birth-weight. After straining and grunting, I decided that picking him up wasn't necessary and simply dragging him into the trailer would work just fine. Meanwhile, Bob and Sarah coaxed the old cow onto her feet. Without the slightest hint of threatening or hesitation, she followed me and her calf right into the trailer. I had never seen a more cooperative cow. She looked at me with tired eyes that seemed to say, "I'm so glad you came. Please take us anywhere warmer and drier."

We unloaded the pair at the feedlot barn. Bob climbed up to the hayloft and threw down a square bale of clover hay. I got her some grain to eat while Sarah fetched a bucket of water. The old Charolais was squared away. Still wobbly, she powered through standing and munched on the ground feed. We roused the calf so that he was standing. Then Bob, Sarah, and I quietly left the stall. We stood outside of the barn for a few minutes and then peeked in through the door to see the massive newborn nursing.

Later that evening, Mom and Dad called to see how things were going. Things were good. We had saved the day for a cow and her calf, plus we had made a pot of chili for supper. Right when Mom called, we were nice and warm

---

[18] Herring, William O. "Calving Difficulty in Beef Cattle: BIF Fact Sheet," *University of Missouri Agriculture Extension*, 1996: http://extension.missouri.edu/p/G2035

inside the farmhouse, enjoying the chocolate chip cookies she had baked for us earlier. In our world, we were celebrating a small victory.

Chapter 21: White-Tailed Stupidity

Animal breeders get excited whenever a new offspring is born with unique coloration or markings. These features distinguish breeds. Consider the Hereford: all cattle of this breed are dark red with a white face. Another example is the Belted Galloway, which is easily identified by a white band, or "belt," around the midsection. On Gillespie Farms, we, too, became enamored of a lineage of unusually marked cows. This all started with a Charolais-Hereford mix. Her fur was tannish-orange in color, with the exception of her tail, which was pure white. This trait must have been dominant, because each of her calves was born with the same white tail. It didn't matter if we had a Hereford, Limousin, or Angus bull, her offspring always had a white tail. When this trait first appeared, Dad decided that we should keep this cow's heifer calves and send them to the slack pasture after weaning so they could become cows. Over the years, White-Tailed Cow had several heifer calves. We were delighted whenever a white-tailed heifer was in one of the slack pasture classes. Little did we know of the big mistake we had made. At first it seemed rather benign. White-Tailed Cow's first calf became White-Tailed the Second, and she developed very large nipples with the birth of her second calf.

Stick out your thumb. The ideal cow has four nipples that are each about the size of your thumb. Go to a soda machine and buy a can of Mountain Dew. The second white-tailed cow developed can-sized nipples.

A newborn calf instinctually looks for nipples between a cow's back legs; however, when those nipples are the size of soda cans, it's impossible for the calf to nurse them. Whenever White-Tailed the Second gave birth, we had to intervene to help the calf nurse. First we herded the cow and the calf into the corral. Then we hauled the headgate out of the barn out to the corral. We set up the headgate and forced the cow down the chute and into the headgate. Dad milked her oversized nipples into a pitcher. We poured that milk into a bottle and fed it to the calf. After milking, the cow's nipples would shrink down a bit, and we attempted to get the calf nursing on the cow. Usually this process had to be repeated. It was exhausting, and it seemed that White-Tailed the Second always calved right before we planned something fun. It wasn't long before I developed a disdain for White-Tailed the Second.

Within the next few years White-Tailed the Third and Fourth also developed oversized nipples. While their calves had cute markings, we had to work with each one to get it nursing. It was pure lunacy to promote this line of genetics. It took some convincing, but finally my Dad admitted that the white-tailed cows were an absolute pain to deal with and agreed not to save any more white-tailed heifers. I found his response to be well-reasoned, but not drastic enough. I wanted the farm to be rid of the white-tailed lineage as soon as possible. However, Dad wouldn't go along with my plan. Instead, we had to continue working with the white-tailed cows for many years. As all cows do, they aged and were culled one by one until we only had two left. One was yellow with a white tail and the other was black with a white tail. Both were part of the Bogota herd.

It was the summer after I graduated from high school. Dad had recently started working for the Illinois Department of Natural Resources managing a state park, and I worked hard to help out around the farm. We badly needed to haul off cull cows from the Bogota pasture to the sale barn, but this job required two or three people to conduct, and with Dad away at work, culling cows just kept getting put off. By midsummer, I decided that I might be able to take care of the task by myself. I had been checking the cows, and I had them well trained to come up to the feeder. I skillfully herded the cull cows into the corral and called Dad to tell him that I had caught the cows and was going to haul them to the sale barn. It was a quick call, "Hi, Dad. I just wanted to let you know that I caught the three cull cows at Bogota, and I'm going to haul them off ... Yep, I got the two old black ones with sore feet and the white-tailed cow." I then called up a friend from school, "Hey, you want to go for a little road trip? Just come on down to the house, I've got to load some cattle in the trailer, then we can go to Salem, get some lunch, and drive back." He lived in town and I hadn't seen him much since school had let out for the summer. I figured we could catch up and he probably wanted to get out of Newton for a while.

I loaded the cows and arrived back at home just as he showed up. He parked his car and said, "Will; I'm glad you called. My mom was driving me nuts."

I laughed and mocked, "Ronnie! Take out the trash!"

He shook his head and rolled his eyes. I patted the side of the trailer and said, "We'll be gone for a while. With these old girls in here, I can't go very fast."

Ronnie laughed and climbed in the passenger side of the truck. We joked and told stories as the truck and trailer jostled all the way down to Salem. Having him along kept me alert. I constantly checked the trailer in my mirrors.

I was a bit nervous when I pulled into the sale barn because Dad had always driven the cattle trailer and took care of the business. The building was broad with a corrugated steel roof. The front quarter of the building had exterior walls and housed some offices. Right behind the offices was the show ring, the area where the cattle are herded through during the auction. Bidders sit in the benches above the sale ring, and at the Salem sale barn, the seating rose up over the offices. It's much like a theater, except the stage is at ground level, covered with wood chips, and gated off. Behind the show ring was an expansive area full of holding pens for livestock. This part of the building had no exterior walls, and instead contained lots of strong holding pens composed of weathered wood. Above the holding pens was a long catwalk that allowed potential buyers to get a good look at the cattle before auction time. It was a fascinating structure. I approached the offloading chute and swung out wide with the truck and trailer so that I could back up straight. As I started in reverse, I thought to myself, *Some complete idiots haul cattle down here, so just relax, this will go fine.* I hid my anxiety and backed up the trailer perfectly. The cows were reluctant to leave the trailer but with a little bit of yelling and prodding, they stepped down onto the wood chip-covered floor of the sale barn. From there, I herded them into a narrow raceway. One of the sale barn employees shut the gate behind the cattle. Relieved that the cows were unloaded and seemed fine, I walked over to the elevated booth adjacent to the raceway. At the booth, one of the workers leaned over and glued numbered tags to the back of each cow. As I stepped up into the booth, he greeted me, and handed over a clipboard. I wrote down my dad's name and address for the cattle check. He gave me an unloading receipt and then I walked back to the truck. As I opened the door, Ronnie said, "Is that it?"

I replied, "Just about. I've got some feed to give the cows. I'll park this rig over there and we'll carry it to their pen."

As I pulled the truck and trailer away, another rig was driving up to off-load cattle. Once out of the way, Ronnie pulled the square bale out of the truck bed, and I grabbed the bucket of ground corn. We carried the feed into the cow's holding pen and dumped it in the trough. Since cattle are sold per pound, we wanted them to be full.

As we left the sale barn, I was proud of myself for getting the job done. On the return trip, I drove a bit faster, but Ronnie and I weren't in any particular hurry. We stopped in the little town of Louisville, Illinois for lunch and arrived back at the farm around one o'clock. The next day, the cows were herded through the show ring and sold to the highest bidder. On Saturday, Dad received the cattle check in the mail. We were just coming in for lunch when he stopped by the mailbox and grabbed the mail. As we sat down at the kitchen table, he opened the cattle check, which listed three black cows. Dad looked at me funny and said, "Did you haul off the White-Tailed Cow?"

I replied, "I sure did. I took the black one with a white tail that doesn't have a calf right now."

He let out a loud sigh and said, "That's the wrong one. You were supposed to haul off the yellow white-tailed cow with a weaning-sized calf."

I shrugged and said, "One less white-tailed cow is a good thing, even if it was the wrong one."

Mom chimed in, "Jimmy, that yellow one's calf isn't weaning size yet."

Dad argued, "But the black cow was still young."

Mom was drying her hands by the sink, and I noticed her silently mouthing the words to me, "YOU DID THE RIGHT THING."

Dad sensed Mom's mocking and said, "What was that?"

She tossed the dishtowel over his head, and the whole family laughed.

Chapter 22: Calf-Killer

She was all black, like many of the cows on the Gillespie Farm. She also had a secret. She had killed her first calf. At the time, we had no idea. Her first newborn calf was found in a puddle. As best we could surmise, the calf fell out of the cow directly into the water and drowned. Unfortunately, our assumptions were wrong. After the death of her calf, we should have loaded her up into the cattle trailer and taken her to the sale barn where she would have ended up in Big Macs and Whoppers. Instead we gave the black cow a second chance and moved her from the Slack pasture to the home herd. Her second pregnancy went well. She was due to calve in early April. The weather was pleasant that Saturday, with plenty of sunshine and temperatures in the upper forties. The cows were in the winter lot near the house, and thankfully the ground had dried enough to solidify much of the mud. Mom and I heard an aggressive "BLLLLAAAAAGGGHHH!" coming from behind the little pond south of the house. This sound was completely out of place and could only mean a serious cow fight was in progress or some kind of trouble. Mom and I sprinted out through the garden gate and into the pasture to see what was happening. All the cows were in a flat-out run toward the calm pond. This was disturbing. I had never seen such panic in the cows before. It wasn't a stampede; it was a scramble. Mom and I ran along with all the cows. When we arrived at the little pond, we couldn't believe our eyes. Below the dam the black cow was aggressively head-butting her newborn calf! The calf was still wet, and every time it tried to stand up, she would butt it, knocking it down. It took a moment for Mom and I to understand what was even happening. Mom turned to me with a look of shock, "We've gotta get that calf!"

I replied, "I might be able to run in there and pick it up."

As the deranged cow kept knocking her newborn to the ground, Mom nodded, "Let's get the truck so you'll have a place to put the calf once you've picked him up." Just then, the black cow butted her calf into a shallow ditch. Now unable to head-butt the calf, she dropped down to her knees and struggled to get her head against the calf down in the ditch. While Mom and I were figuring out what to do, all of the cows had arrived in the hollow and lined up with us. The onlookers stood about twenty yards back from the insane black cow. The cows were letting out loud, angry bawls—they were furious! As Mom and I turned to get the work truck, something incredible happened. The gentlest cow on the farm, Felini, charged out of the ranks of spectators and butted the black cow in the flank. Chunks of dirt flew as the black cow whirled around and started fighting Felini. Felini was trying to save the calf. While Felini was not much of a fighter and lost ground to the crazed black cow, it didn't matter because in an instant the very aggressive Red Rip rushed in to provide back up. In the mere seconds that followed, Good Gray and Silage Cow dashed down into the thrashing fray. They were all trying to keep the cow from killing her own calf! This bought precious time for Mom and me to get the truck.

As we ran up to the house, we met Sarah on her way down. Mom yelled, "Come on, Sarah, we've got to get the truck back there." Sarah jumped in the truck with Mom while I opened the gate. We rushed back to the hollow. Sarah climbed into the bed of the truck. She positioned herself in preparation to take the wiggling calf from me when I brought him to the truck bed. Mom stayed in the driver's seat, and I ran over to pick up the calf. As I darted in, the black cow's attention turned away from battling with the other cows or killing her calf, to killing me. She charged me before I could even touch the calf. A full dose of adrenaline kicked in, and I started backpedaling. In the blink of an eye she closed the distance and got her head against my chest. Somehow my reverse sprint matched her charging velocity and I escaped unharmed. The cow returned her attention to the calf. Again, she dropped to her knees and struggled to head-butt the calf in the ditch. I was shaken. Mom yelled to me, "Will! Go get the loader tractor!" My heart pumped out of my chest as I sprinted to the barn and fired up the old loader tractor. I drove it as fast as I could without bouncing out of the seat. As I approached the cows, Mom climbed up on the fender with the lasso. I positioned the tractor so the loader bucket was just above the calf. He was protected now. Back at the truck, Sarah nervously watched as Mom and I climbed over the hood of the tractor and into the bucket. The black cow turned to us and tried to attack, but inside the elevated tractor bucket, Mom and I were safe. Somehow, we managed to get the rope around the black cow's head and tie off the other end of the rope to the chain hook. We scrambled back up the hood of the tractor, and I hit the hydraulic lever that lifted the bucket, thus tightening the rope around the cow's neck. She began fighting against the rope. When the black cow thrashed to the down-hill side of her calf, I saw my moment of opportunity. I slammed the tractor in reverse and pulled the cow and her pounding hooves away from the calf. Thankfully, in the game of cow-versus-6,000 pound tractor, cow always loses. As I reversed up the hill with the tractor and cow in tow, Sarah ran down to the ditch and helped Mom carry the calf to the truck. I watched as Sarah situated herself on the tailgate and held the calf while Mom drove away. The truck bounced over the bumpy ground and the calf squirmed but Sarah held him tightly and kept him safe.

I backed up to a flat spot on the top of the hill, shifted the tractor into neutral, and cut the engine. I heard Dad's truck pull in the driveway. He arrived home from work just as Mom and Sarah were taking the calf to the barn. Calf Killer continued to thrash for a while until she began to choke down. I lowered the loader bucket a little bit so she could regain her breath. Calf Killer stood motionless. The other cows slowly filtered out of the hollow and returned to the hay feeders. I sat in silence and noticed that my clothes were soaked with sweat. The back of my neck felt clammy. I wasn't sure what to do next. After few minutes of cooling, I looked to see Dad walking from the barn over to the hill where I was keeping the bovine felon tied to the loader tractor. He approached the tractor and rested his arm on the fender, "You alright?"

I shook my head in disgust then nodded, "Yeah…. We kinda had a mess here, Dad. Did Mom tell you what happened?"

He nodded and pointed to the tied-up cow, "You know, this cow lost her calf last year. It was over in the slack pasture and she had it in a little puddle. Now, I'm thinking she killed it."

Calf Killer seemed resigned to the situation of being tied up. I shrugged, "Now what do we do with her? I mean, I'd like to put a bullet in her brain." Of course I knew better.

Dad gave me an understanding look and spoke softly, "I guess we let her go?"

I stood up from the tractor seat, "Well, she's calmed down now."

Dad stepped toward the cow to release the latch on the lasso around her neck. I spoke up, "OH NO YOU DON'T!"

He stopped and I motioned, "I wouldn't trust this cow as far as I can throw her; you better back up just in case." I crawled over the hood of the tractor to the bucket and reached down. I flipped open the latch of the lasso. Calf Killer simply skulked away toward the hay rings without incident.

Back at the house, Mom had just stepped in from the barn. She called over to Kaufman's dairy farm and asked if we could buy some fresh colostrum for the new calf. Fresh colostrum from a Holstein cow is better than any colostrum mix, and this calf needed every advantage he could get. Dad drove over to the Kaufman's and picked up the milk. I don't think they ever charged him a dime. He returned just before dark. Mom prepared a bottle and when we took it to the new calf the poor thing nursed it like a champ.

Dad fed the calf a bottle the next morning, but then in the evening, we herded Calf Killer into the barn. She seemed to be in a somber mood when we roped her neck and tied her to a post. With persistence and patience, Dad was able to get the little calf to nurse on Calf Killer. We repeated this for the next two days. Finally we became confident that she would not try to kill her calf again, so on the third evening we turned both Calf Killer and her calf out of the barn. From that point forward she was able to raise her calf.

Not long after her calf was weaned, Calf Killer was loaded up into the cattle trailer with three old cull cows and taken to the sale barn in Salem. Dad and I unloaded the cows just before dark. Under the lights of the sale barn the casual observer would have seen four cows walking down the center aisle of the sale barn to their holding pen, but my eyes saw three cows and a killer. To this day, it amazes me that none of us were injured in the ordeal.

Chapter 23: Fences

Landscape

In 1800, the landscape of Illinois was much different than the grid of farm fields seen today. The south-central region that I call home was where the prairies and woodlands met. It was not a clear division, but rather a complex blend of wide-open tall grass prairie that yielded to deep woodlands in the drainage ways and wet areas. Indian grass and big bluestem dominated the prairies; oaks and hickories dominated the woodlands. Many areas were neither all grassland nor all woodland; they were savannahs with a mixture of both. At that time, the land area of what would become Illinois was part of the Indiana Territory. The 1800 census reported that only 5,641 people of European descent lived in all the Indiana Territory.[19] It is likely that fewer than half that number lived in the 57,918 square miles that would become Illinois.

The early settlers immigrated to the southern portions of the Indiana Territory along the major rivers. They brought cattle with them and built crude fences around their crop fields to keep out grazing cows. Since the first farms were surrounded by sparsely inhabited forests and prairies, the cattle were allowed to graze freely in the areas surrounding the farm. In 1814, the General Land Office in Shawneetown opened and began selling federally owned land. By 1840, twelve General Land Offices were open across the state.[20] The availability of cheap land increased

---

[19] http://www.in.gov/history/files/interritory.pdf

immigration. The influx of settlers transformed the wild Illinois landscape. Woodlands were cut for timber, prairies were plowed, wetlands were drained, and nearly all flat areas were converted to row crop fields.

In 1818, Illinois achieved statehood. The following year, the English Common Law for fences became statute. Those in state government believed that all the land area would become settled, and as the density of farms increased, the Fence Act would become necessary. The Fence Act of 1819 did not address the free ranging of cattle, rather it focused on what was considered a legal fence, the proportioning of fencing responsibilities between neighboring farms, and how fence disputes would be settled. By the 1870s, the density of farms brought an end to cattle being allowed to roam freely. In 1872, the Illinois Domestic Animals Running at Large Act was passed. This law prohibited farmers from allowing livestock to roam freely around the countryside. It also recognized livestock owners as the responsible party liable for damages caused by escaped animals. The cattle were then confined by fences.

In the late 1800s, all farms had livestock. Most farms had cattle, sheep, and fowl. Each animal provided the farmer with a needed commodity: beef and milk; mutton and wool; meat, eggs, and down. However, as the road system improved, farmers no longer needed to be completely self-

---

[20] "Records of the General Land Office, 1800-1908." *National Archives and Records Administration*, http://www.archives.gov/chicago/finding-aids/land.html

reliant. In the mid-1900s, central-Illinois farmers focused more on crop production. They sold off their livestock and converted the former pastures to fields. This trend has continued throughout the state, and currently only twenty-three percent of Illinois farms have beef cattle production.[21]

The landscape has also seen another shift. Farms in the nineteenth century relied on animal power and manual labor. In order to raise crops, farmers had to live very close to their fields. A farmer lived along a road with his land surrounding him. Over time, the original farmsteads on land sold by the General Land Office have been split, sold, and inherited multiple times. Today's farmers have parcels of land scattered over many miles from their base of operations.

Interestingly, the Illinois Fence Act of 1819 has not been amended to reflect the changes in agriculture. The law dictates that fencing responsibilities between adjoining landowners be equally divided. Thus, two neighboring landowners with a fence between their properties are each responsible for half the cost of building and maintaining a fence. This arrangement made sense in the 1800s when all farms had livestock, and a farmer's land was centrally located so that having a boundary line fence would be mutually beneficial to a farmer and his adjacent neighbor. Today, a cattle farmer benefits from a fence, while an adjacent landowner without cattle would receive no benefit from the same fence. The outdated law is unjust and cattle producers rarely attempt to recuperate a portion of the fencing costs

---

[21] http://www.agr.state.il.us/about/agfacts.html

from their adjacent landowners without cattle. However in 1995, a civil court case was brought by a cattle producer named Wallis. Wallis sought half the costs for fence construction from his adjacent landowner that did not own cattle. Ultimately, the court ruled against Wallis but failed to create a clear legal precedent in the matter.[22] Perhaps the court's message was that a cattle producer seeking half the fence costs from an unwilling neighbor is not likely to recuperate those costs in civil court.

Raymond's Nightmare

The Illinois Domestic Animals Running at Large Act identifies the cattle farmer as the culpable party for his cows' escapades, and hence, the source of a cattle farmer's greatest nightmare. A neighboring farmer faced this nightmare not long ago. The Kuhl's kept the tidiest farm around; their equipment was always clean, their fields were weed-free, and their cattle were sleek Black Angus. Raymond Kuhl kept a herd of twelve brood cows in the twenty-four acre pasture adjacent to his home. From his back deck he could overlook nearly all the pasture while enjoying his morning cup of coffee; a handy arrangement for checking the cows. The winter had just ended and the landscape was coming back to life; across Raymond's pasture the grass was greening and chorus of spring peeper frogs rang out. As night fell, the cool,

---

[22] Endres, Bryan A., and Lisa R. Schlessinger. "A Move Towards a More Fair Division: Envisioning a New Illinois Fence Act," *University of Illinois Department of Agricultural and Consumer Economics Agricultural Law and Taxation Briefs*, December 13, 2012: http://farmdoc.illinois.edu/legal/articles/ALTBs/ALTB_12-01/ALTB_12-01.pdf

humid air accumulated along the wet ground. During the night as Raymond slept, someone with nefarious intentions opened the gate to his cattle pasture. Apparently, the warm spring weather had brought out more than the just frogs. Regardless, his cows ended up walking southward down the two-lane blacktop, Bogota-Wakefield Road. The cows were nervous and stayed in a tight herd.

In the dark pre-dawn hours a thick layer of fog had formed. Before the sun came up, a crotchety old trucker named Floyd cranked up his diesel tandem axle dump-truck. The airbrakes let out a "Shhggronk" as they lifted and Floyd pulled out of his driveway. He headed south down the Bogota-Wakefield Road on a route that he had likely traveled thousands of times. One could joke that he was so familiar with this stretch of road that he could drive it blind-folded, which was essentially the case on this foggy morning. He was about four miles from his home when he passed by Raymond's house. In an instant, Floyd's truck plowed into eight black cows that he couldn't see. The collision obliterated the cow's bodies and forced several beneath the truck. Floyd slammed forward against his steering wheel and lost control. The massive truck veered off the road and over-turned.

The wreck totaled Floyd's truck and sent him to the hospital with a broken arm. His insurance had to replace the dump truck and pay the medical bills; so the insurance company filed a lawsuit against the cattle farmer, Raymond, for damages. Since the Illinois Domestic Animals Running at Large Act recognizes the livestock owner as the responsible party for the cows' containment and Raymond had made every effort to assure the containment, this quickly became a contentious case. Raymond hired a lawyer to argue that he provided *reasonable care in restraining such animals from so running at large.*"[23] The case went to trial. Arguments focused on the strength of the gate and the quality of Raymond's fencing. Worry kept Raymond and his family up at night. When the case was finally settled, it was decided that Raymond's fencing and gate were adequate. He was not held liable for damages caused by his escaped cows, but the ordeal marked the end of cattle on Kuhl's farm. Not long after, all the remaining cows were sold.

As difficult as this situation was, it could have been worse. Floyd could have died in the collision. He could have been driving a fuel tanker truck instead. Such a fuel truck could have ruptured and sent a stream of fuel running into the creek full of spring peepers. It could have ignited...It's probably best to stop listing the "could have" scenarios. The take-away message is this; having escaped cattle is a serious problem.

---

[23]http://www.ilga.gov/legislation/ilcs/ilcs3.asp?ActID=1714&ChapterID=41

Chapter 24: Watergaps

Raspberries

My family didn't talk much about the rain. It just needed to stop, but it kept falling; day after day. We had planted our corn a week before the "climatic shift" and the plants had emerged, but now after a week of heavy rain, the fields looked terrible. Instead of bearing green leaves, the corn plants were a sickly shade of yellow. We had planted soybeans in the days preceding the rain, but nearly all the seed rotted in the ground. Now the fields smelled like mushrooms and catfish, and every step across them sounded like "squoosh, squoosh, squoosh." Knats and mosquitos flourished in the standing water. The only thing more pervasive than the insects was the oppressive humidity. One could hide from insects in the house, but the humidity soaked through everything. It was June. We should have been wearing our leather work boots and baling hay, but instead we were stuck wearing our rubber boots and fantasizing about a dry spell to replant our fields. The old farmhouse smelled strong of mold and mildew. A slow leak in the roof caused the crack in the horsehair plaster to open up over my bed. Little pieces of grit fell onto me as I lay awake at night listening to the rain pour on our roof.

Morning came slowly, and the overcast sky kept me from waking fully. I hadn't even heard my brother leave at three o'clock to go milk cows at a nearby farm. It was still dim and early when I sat down at the kitchen table to eat breakfast. I always woke early. I couldn't help it; I lacked the ability to sleep in. My usual breakfast was milk-soaked

Cheerios, and this morning was no different. I heard Dad's footsteps coming down the stairs. He wandered to the refrigerator and pulled out a soda. I heard the can open. After a big gulp he asked, "I'm going to check the calves at the feedlot; you wanna go?"

While I wasn't completely alert, I knew that it would be best to avoid riding around with my depressed father as he cruised by the flooded fields at thirty-five miles per hour. I quickly came up with a reasonable excuse, "No, I think I'll stay here and get the stuff ready to fix watergaps."

With that he took another swig of diet coke, picked up his hat and left. As I finished my bowl of cereal, Mom stepped down the stairs.

I finished my glass of milk, "Good morning Mom; did it rain all night?"

She brushed back her hair, "Yeah. It rained pretty much all night again."

I set my cereal bowl in the sink, "Well, I guess Dad went up to the feedlot. I might check the watergaps... I wonder if the creek is still too high?"

Mom nodded, "Maybe you should wait till this afternoon." She set a mug on the table and continued, "How many raspberries did you pick yesterday?"

"I've probably got half a gallon in the fridge."

Mom smiled, "Well, sounds like I should make a pie."

I perked up, "Hmmm... If I wait till this afternoon to do the watergaps, this morning I could check the Cut-off Woods to see if there's any raspberries there."

Normally, appreciable raspberries patches aren't found in a woods, but the Cut-off Woods had recently suffered a tragedy. The sixteen-acre parcel had been covered with a towering stand of hardwood trees. The land had belonged to some distant family relatives who needed money. They had auctioned off the woods to a logging company for top dollar. Unfortunately, the company had a contract order of logs that needed to be filled over the winter. That winter's weather was unusually wet and warm. The soil stayed saturated and never froze. During the overcast winter days the whine of chainsaws was punctuated with the crash of felling trees. It spelled the end of the impressive oaks and hickories. The heavy log skidders and trucks rutted and compacted the soil. Once the logging was completed, my dad looked to the future and approached the logging company. He purchased the land and what was left of the once-glorious woods. I can clearly remember the first time we walked across the land as a family. We stood at the edge of the log loading area and looked over a landscape that was reminiscent of a WWI battlefield. The loading yard was nearly devoid of vegetation. Tree tops and stumps had been pushed into big piles along the sides. The massive piles had gaps where waist-deep ruts with standing water trailed out into the woods. Some of the smaller trees left behind whipped over once their supportive elders were removed. Stumps like table-tops dotted the landscaped and brushy tree-tops laid everywhere. It was nearly impossible to traverse.

The first years that my family owned the woods, we planted hundreds of trees in the scarred landscape. It was our early-spring ritual. This particular year while planting trees I had noticed the thick purple canes of raspberries. I took a mental note of their location, along a log skidder trail, and knew that in June I needed to return and check for raspberries to pick.

Now, just two months after planting trees and discovering the raspberry canes, our farm was in the middle of the nastiest wet spell we had ever endured. As I drove up to the woods, I thought to myself. *Going on a little adventure to look for raspberries will keep me occupied so I won't have to scout our sickly fields with Dad.* It was mid-morning and I really didn't expect to find much as I climbed out of our old Chevy Lumina. I slapped on some mosquito repellent, grabbed my repurposed gallon ice-cream bucket and foraged ahead in the humidity and thick brush. The weeds and briars were over my head and water dripped on me as I pushed my way through. Finally, I found the deeply rutted log-skidder trail that led back to the raspberry canes. I slapped a pesky mosquito and sighed; *This is going to be a miserable waste of time.* I pushed through ten more yards of thick weeds and briars then stumbled upon the Shangri-La of raspberry patches. Both sides of the rutted track were lined with a solid six-foot wall of purple berries the size of the tip of my thumb. I reached for the first sprig and plucked off three which I promptly ate. Delicious! I reached out for another sprig, with

153

just the right amount of coaxing several berries fell into my hand. I managed to fill my gallon bucket with raspberries in record time. I backtracked through the thick brush to the car and hurried home. I couldn't wait to show off my bounty!

When I arrived, it was a depressing scene. Dad sat moodily in his brown chair. He wore a disgusted look on his face. It had nothing to do with me and everything to do with the miserable condition of our crops. Mom was past the point of trying to cheer him up. She ignored him. The house was awash in a deafening silence. Instead of bounding through the door grinning ear to ear about the wonderful raspberry patch I had found, I quietly sat the gallon bucket of raspberries on the kitchen counter. From the cabinet below the sink, I pulled out a huge enamel steel bowl. I did some quick estimation. *Two gallons.* Then I grabbed another gallon bucket and headed right back out to my raspberry heaven. There was no way in hell I was going to stay around that miserable scene.

I followed in my previous trail of knocked over weeds and briars. It was much easier negotiating my way through the brambles this time. I slowed down and took some time to enjoy picking berries in such a beautiful patch. I was standing up to my waist in canes with my feet invisible beneath the thick foliage when a blur of red fur with white spots suddenly launched itself from between my feet. I was so startled! It felt like I jumped ten feet in the air. It was the fawn of a white-tailed deer that I had nearly stepped on. The fawn clumsily bounded away through the briars. I took a moment to catch my breath and reign in my thumping heart. Through

154

some miracle I had managed to keep from dumping my half-full bucket of raspberries. I smiled at my luck and thought to myself, *Ok you idiot, go empty your bucket before it ends up completely full and you spill it!* Once again I backtracked to the car. This time I dumped the gallon bucket into the big enamel bowl and headed straight back to the patch. As I walked through the weeds, I noticed that my hands were stained a deep dark purple from the berries. Purple hands from picking raspberries are a symbol of pride that one shouldn't wash off too quickly, much like race numbers painted on a tri-athlete.

I repeated the routine of picking the gallon bucket half full of raspberries and then returning to the car to dump the bucket into the enamel bowl. Before noon I had filled all my containers. This equated to four gallons of raspberries in one morning, a personal record.

Lunch at home was exactly what I expected. Nobody said much. Bob was tired from waking up at three to milk cows at a neighboring farm, Sarah was shy at the table, and Mom was frustrated with the whole scene. My dad wore the same disgusted and disappointed expression on his face that was beginning to look permanent. He spoke, "We're going to have to replant every one of our beanfields." He turned to me and continued, "Well, I guess that we'll go fix the water gaps this afternoon." I munched on my roasted deer sandwich and said little.

The part of a pasture fence that crosses a creek is referred to as the "water gap." This is normally a short

155

section of fence that is stretched from bank to bank and runs across the channel bottom. Wires are attached to steel T-posts driven into the streambed. It is a temporary fence by design. Whenever the creek floods, the water gap tends to first pile up with sticks, logs, brush, leaves, grass, and then wash out. If the water gap is built with too much integrity, all of the debris stays caught in the fence, and a massive logjam forms. Such a logjam can lead to more flooding or erosion of the creek channel around the logs. If the water gap is built too light, it's an invitation for marauding cows to escape. *A very bad situation.* Sometimes, even if the water gap is built just right, it still creates a logjam.

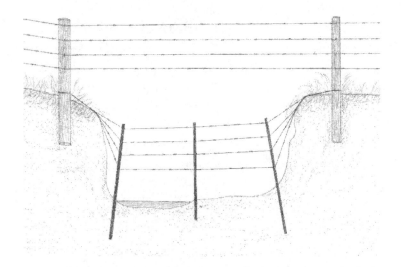

A cross-sectional sketch of a water gap; the water wasn't always so low!

On Gillespie Farms, we had four water gaps and after every large rain event we knew that the water gaps would have to be checked and likely repaired. We spent many mornings repairing water gaps. That afternoon Dad and I started by loading up the work truck with tying wire, a few steel posts, some barbed wire, a sledge hammer, fencing pliers, and the chainsaw. The sun was trying to break through the clouds as we climbed in the truck and drove up to the Bogota pasture where we could park the truck close to the water gap. That way we could see if the water level in the creek was low enough to actually repair the water gap. In the background, Natalie Maines of the Dixie Chicks sang, *Wide Open Spaces* as Dad stopped the truck on the bridge and looked down at the water gap, "Willy, it looks like we're going to get wet feet."

I replied, "Oh well; it's not the first time. How bad is it?"

Dad wiped his brow on his shirtsleeve, "Just a couple of logs. It's not torn out."

He pulled the truck up to the closest culvert. Dad grabbed the old chainsaw and pulled the cord four or five times before it puffed out smoke. By the tenth yank Dad was winded but the chainsaw had growled to life. As he chopped up the logs into manageable sections, I rolled them into the deepest part of the channel and let the running water carry them away. Once the logs were clear, I retrieved the sledge from the truck and we drove the posts back down into the sandy bottom of the creek. I tied the loosened barbed wires back to the posts. We were finished with the first water gap.

From there we started back to the farther west water gap. About half-way down the Wolf Creek at the Bogota pasture, the water flowed around a huge rock that was a source of endless marvel. The boulder was dark gray with light-colored chunks of stone throughout. It was an igneous conglomerate. Apparently, the Illinoisian Glacier had pushed it down from far north, but in the creek the rock looked like it came from outer space. Fixing water gaps was typically a tough and dirty job, but it entailed visiting the creeks. The flowing water, gravel bars, riffles, and rocks were always a source of inspiration to me. Seeing the fish, turtles, and snakes was my reward for fixing water gaps.

When Dad and I finally got home we had a different sort of reward; Mom had baked several raspberry pies. She smiled and teased me, "Willy, what am I supposed to do with all of these raspberries?" She still had three gallons of raspberries leftover in the refrigerator.

I grinned and shrugged, "I don't know, but I'm definitely going back out to the patch again tomorrow!"

Alcohol

The setting of the upstream water gap in the Bogota pasture provided more than natural wonders. The creek ran nearly parallel to the road 400 North for a distance before it veered slightly south and passed under the road and into our pasture. Since the road crossed the creek at such an oblique angle, the bridge was built thirty-five degrees to the rest of the road. Sober drivers followed the road signs, slowed down and turned to cross the bridge. However, the bridge proved to be a trap for those unwilling to meet the criterion of sobriety.

Apparently the trap had been set on a Saturday night when unbeknownst to us, a neighbor of the Bogota pasture threw a real wild party. Later we heard that things turned serious when one of the neighbor's inebriated friends left the party in his pickup truck and returned on foot. He had driven his truck off the bridge and into the creek. Somehow, the party crowd was able to extract the truck from the creek, but failed to notify us of any damaged fence. We were unaware of that night's events until the following afternoon.

Dad was driving around at forty miles per hour looking at the crops when he happened to notice some dried sand on the road. Thinking this was abnormal, he looked down as he drove across the bridge and noticed a problem. The water gap was missing, and broken debris from a vehicle was everywhere. Fortunately, the cows had not yet discovered the missing section of fence. Dad recruited our help to fix the water gap and pick up all the debris. While most of the mess consisted of broken glass and empty beer cans, we also happened to find two baseball gloves, a cassette tape of REO Speedwagon songs, and an assortment of tools. We counted ourselves lucky because the cows did not escape and we found some cool stuff. To this day, whenever I hear an REO Speedwagon song, my mind goes back to the day we had to rebuild that watergap.

Road-Kill

That bridge has remained the same over the years, and more recently caught another impaired driver. It was a clear and cold January morning, with temperatures hovering near the zero mark. Mom and Dad were driving to check raccoon traps set the previous evening. As they approached the bridge, there seemed to be an abnormal number of beer cans in the ditch. This piqued their suspicions of some rowdiness during the night. They parked next to the bridge to take a closer look. Downstream, beer cans were lying flat on top of the creek bank in the grass. There is a rule of thumb for beer cans in grass: Empty cans are light and will settle into any position on the grass, while full cans are heavier and generally lay flat on their sides. Willows growing in the creek also showed signs of disturbance, and right in the middle of the creek bed was a Newton High School parking tag. Tire tracks in the sand confirmed my parents' suspicions that someone had driven off the bridge during the night. Mom and Dad each retrieved a five-gallon bucket out of the truck bed and started picking up the scattered trash and full cans of Busch Light. Several had frozen during the night and exploded. By observing the tire tracks and the footprints in the creek, my parents were able to envision what happened. Multiple high schoolers were traveling west on 400 North when they failed to negotiate the turn onto the bridge. As a result, the driver briefly applied the brakes but was unable to stop the car before he or she ran out of road and plummeted into the creek channel. Based on the tire tracks and lack of broken glass, Mom and Dad assumed that the car did not flip—rather, it landed on the front bumper first and then fell back on its wheels. In all likelihood the kids realized that they would be in a world of trouble if caught with a car full of beer, so they started throwing out evidence up on the creek bank into the grass. In the light of day, the cans were blatantly obvious, but perhaps the cans seemed hidden at night ... or maybe they were just dumb high schoolers. At any rate, the kids managed to remove the vehicle during the night, so they must have had some connections.

Mom and Dad finished picking up the cans around the creek, and they ventured east up the road to pick up the cans that originally sparked their interest. Dad walked along the south side of the road and noticed that less than twenty yards off the road, two coolers were poorly concealed under an autumn olive bush. Both coolers were full of more Busch Light. These, too, went into the back of the work truck.

They continued their mission to check traps and caught two raccoons. When they arrived back at the house, Mom immediately called my cell phone to report on their success. "Hey, Willy! We had good luck trapping this morning."

"Oh yeah?" I asked.

She continued, "We caught two big raccoons, about forty cans of beer, and two road-kill coolers."

Confused by her mixed take, I replied, "What now... What's a road-kill cooler?"

Mom went on to explain, and ever since then the term "road-kill" has been used to describe anything found along the road. We have found more road-kill coolers, wrenches, sweatshirts, and even a ladder.

Chapter 25: Millennium Fence

Nearby the farm was the Prairie Ridge State Natural Area, or just Prairie Ridge for short. Prairie Ridge was a remnant of the prairies that once covered Illinois. Since all of the grasslands were converted to agriculture production during the 1800s, ground-nesting birds, such as the prairie chicken, went from abundant to endangered. The biologists at Prairie Ridge used cattle as a management tool to graze some of the grassland tracts thus mimicking the grazing of bison in pre-settlement times. The light grazing of warm-seasoned grasses helped to create conditions favorable for ground-nesting birds. The Prairie Ridge biologists wanted a new fence built around a tract for grazing. The tract was forty acres with a strong stand of native big bluestem and prairie forbs. It was also located along our usual route to town.

In the late part of 1999, I had just started my first semester of classes at the local community college. I was living at home and commuting to classes Monday through Friday. My brother Bob was commuting to classes at Eastern Illinois University. One day in October he asked me if I would like to help him do a fence project at Prairie Ridge. At first I thought, *How in the hell could we manage that?* Bob must have sensed my apprehension and continued, "We could do it during our Christmas break; we get nearly a month off." How could I argue with that reasoning? Bob and I could knock out a figurative ton of work in a month! Considering this, the project seemed doable. Bob submitted the necessary paperwork, and in a short time, we were awarded a contract to build a five-strand barbed wire fence. The fence would be a mile long by the time we encompassed the whole forty acres. We received the green light for the project in early December and lucky for us the Prairie Ridge staff had already done the first task of fence building; clear out all the existing brush and trees from the path of the new fence. Bob obtained a post-hole digger to mount on the back of our loader tractor and we started by setting corner posts:

1. Layout the arrangement of the anchor post and the corresponding brace posts.
2. Dig post holes for setting corner anchor posts and the corresponding brace posts.
3. Set the anchor post in concrete.
4. Put up the compression beam between the anchor post and brace posts.
5. Set the brace posts in concrete.
6. After the concrete cures, strengthen the entire corner with tension wires that are tightened by twisting the wire with sticks.

Bob and I nicknamed the sticks used to tighten the corners "whapper" sticks, because letting go of the stick while twisting up the #9 wire could result in getting whapped in the face. Luckily we caught some days of really mild winter weather while setting corners. While the rest of the world was worried about the Y2K computer glitch, we were busy setting posts in the ground. We finished setting the last set of corner posts on December 31, 1999. That evening Bob and I listened to the Bare Naked Ladies sing *"Get in Line"* on the radio of his clunky S-10 pickup as we drove home from the job site. I didn't stay home that night. After a quick shower I

164

fired up my truck and headed to a New Year's Party. It was the first time since graduation that I had seen my high school friends. I felt self-conscious about attending classes at the community college. It was a choice based on economics and that choice left me hopelessly isolated. As I walked into the party the song "*All Star*" by Smash Mouth played in the background. My head was swimming with feelings of self-doubt. I didn't have any glamorous stories about going away to a four-year university. My insecurity turned to pride when my former prom date, Abby, first saw me and said, "Will! You got buff!" Apparently, sticking around the farm taking care of the cattle and building fence had put some muscle on me. It could have also been all the pushups and crunches I did each evening in an attempt to stay sane. I was surviving my situation and as I drove home that night, in the new millennium, a song came on the radio called "*Back 2 Good*" by the relatively new band, Matchbox 20. I didn't understand the lyrics, but it sounded good and I was alone, so I sang along at the top of my lungs.

The next day Bob and I unrolled the bottom strand of barbed wire and stretched it between the corners. We were ready to push in T-posts. The next night, it snowed about two inches. Not enough to stop us, but just enough to be annoying. Bob ran the loader tractor that morning while I held the posts that he pushed in the ground with the tractor's bucket. It was pretty repetitive. Every 15 feet I would stand up a metal T post, and then he would drive the tractor up and push the post in the ground about a foot and a half. He would drive and push a lever; I was moving and active. By mid-morning he was shivering and grumpy while I was actually sweating. It took us two days to push in all 350 posts. The snow melted off quickly and the project started moving along again when we were unrolling and stretching wires. The part that took the longest was tying all the barbed wires to the T-posts. One day Mom and Sarah came up to help Bob and I. Sarah played in the tall grass while Mom helped tie the barbed wires to the T-posts. Mom seemed to have a knack of knowing when to take photos. She brought her camera along that day and took the photo below.

By the end of January we finished the fence project by hanging all the gates. My second semester of community college classes had started. Time was moving along, but in my lonely eighteen-year-old mind it wasn't moving nearly fast enough.

Front to back, Sarah, Will, and Bob Gillespie; the photo was taken on a mild winter day in the January of 2000. We were nearly finished with the Millennium Fence project. Notice the "whapper" stick in the foreground.

Chapter 26: Pilling Calves

On the farm, the month of March is synonymous with "mud" and "suffering." Cattle and those caring for them wish for warmer temperatures, more daylight, sunshine, and drier weather. Instead, we are served wildly fluctuating temperatures, rain, snow, sleet, gray skies, and short days. The result in the pasture is deep mud, illness, and seasonal depression for the caregivers. The few days of pleasant weather in March only teases one into believing that spring has arrived in Illinois. Those thoughts are usually followed up by another cold front weather system.

The calves in our cattle herds always seemed to suffer from scours in March. The term "scours" is given to a number of diseases that cause diarrhea in calves. The first sign of scours is normally found on the ground. If we see white-colored calf manure that appears watery, we know at least one of the calves is suffering from scours. Since the disease passes from calf to calf, it's important to find the sick calf quickly and treat it. Like any diarrheal disease, it weakens the host, making the calf susceptible to additional diseases, such as pneumonia. When we detect scours in the pasture, we look for a calf with a messy back end, a hunched back, and droopy ears. If the calf has a mild case of scours, it can usually be cured with something called an Albon tablet. Manufactured by Pfizer Animal Health, Albon contains the active ingredient sulfadimethoxine. Each pill is roughly the size of your pinky finger from the knuckle to the tip— so they're quite large. Of course, no calf wants to take a pill. Like all things with cattle, giving a pill is tricky and messy. First the calf must be caught and restrained. Then the pill must be forced down the calf's throat with a pill-giver or by hand. We always did this task by hand because using a pill-giver could injure a small calf.

During my junior year of high school the March weather was remarkably nasty and scours seemed to hold reign in our pastures. To address the problem, Dad issued Bob and me an entire bottle of Albon pills. He said, "Boys, go out there, and any calf that looks the slightest bit sick or messy in the back end, give him a pill."

I donned my insulated bib overalls and dirty chore coat while Bob did the same. As I stepped outside onto the back porch, I pulled the gloves from my pockets and put them on. The temperature was just above freezing and a light fog hung in the air making it feel especially clammy. I turned to Bob, "You got the bottle of Albon pills?"

He nodded and patted his jacket pocket, "Right here."

We climbed into the work truck and headed to the Bogota pasture. Our mission: to treat as many of the sick calves as we could catch. The catching part would be the hard part, so Bob and I made a game out of catching calves.

We arrived at the Bogota pasture to a miserable scene. The mud in the rutted path back to the hay feeders was ankle deep and the heavy slime tried to pull off our boots with each step. As we neared the cows around the feeders, the mud was even deeper. I whispered to Bob, "Gawd, I wish it would just freeze this mess."

He nodded, "Or actually dry-up."

Dad had moved out a junk bale for bedding the day before. A number of calves were comfortably lying on the pile of old hay. Bob frowned, "Let's try not to scare them off the hay pile if we can help it."

We split up and trudged through the mud around the hay pile. Right away I spotted one that we needed to treat. I motioned to Bob. As he circled around, he spotted two more calves with scours. They all had the typical symptoms. A messy back end, hunched back, and droopy ears. We moved in to catch the first small calf. I would attempt to tackle the calf without drawing too much attention. Bob would help me restrain the calf and force a pill down its throat. A tinge of anxiousness came over me as I slyly acted like I was going to walk by the first calf. In an instant I turned and pounced. The calf tried to squirm and get away, but I had caught him lying down. Quickly, Bob placed a pill between his middle and ring fingers. The calve tried to throw his head from side to side as Bob slid his hand into the calf's mouth and pushed the pill into its throat. Bob and I held the calf for a few extra moments to make sure that it didn't spit out the pill. Success!

Bob nodded, "Ok, Let's let him go." The calf stood up and ran to the edge of the hay pile. Its mother cow sensed the commotion and came over to check on her baby. I could smell the stench of scoury calf manure and looked down. The whitish manure was smeared across the left side of my chore coat. I rolled my eyes, "I got that nasty scours shit on me already."

Bob smiled, "You stink. Let's go catch another one."

I grinned and started my sly oblique approach toward another calf. This one must have seen what his comrade had just experienced and he bolted. I thought to myself, I'll be back to catch you!

Undeterred, I tried for the next sickly calf and made a textbook catch. The trick in wrestling a calf is to get one's body against it immediately so the calf can't kick you. Then knock the calf's legs out from under it. Of course one needs to be forceful, but not violent. Restraining a calf really is much like wrestling. After giving it a pill, Bob and I headed for the west hay pile. Bob handed me the bottle of pills, "Willy, I'll let you pill the next one." The back of his hand was a bit bloody from where the last calf's lower teeth cut him.

We were able to catch and pill another calf at the west hay pile. Then we started slogging through the mud back to the truck. Along the way we encountered a 250 pounder walking around with a messy back end. He was larger than any calf I had caught before, but he needed a pill. Without a word, Bob and I walked up to him. Bob diverted the calf's attention by talking to him in a baby voice, "Hey there big guy, looks like you've got a..." Wham! I dove into the side of the calf and wrapped my arms around his chest. He bucked and I swept my leg under him. I twisted with all my might and we both tumbled into the mud. Bob jumped into the fray and wrapped his legs around the calf's neck. He reached over to my coat pocket and grabbed the bottle of

Albon pills. I grunted, "Hurry Bob, I don't know how much longer I can hold him!"

As I struggled to keep the calf still, Bob quickly grabbed a pill out of the bottle. He slid the pill down the back of the calf's throat and muttered, "Ok Willy, I think we got him."

We released the calf and he walked away a bit wobbly. Then he looked back at us with an expression that said, "What the hell! Why are you monkeys picking on me?"

Bob patted me on the back, "Dang, Willy I didn't think we'd actually be able to pull that one off!"

We were standing in mud and our clothes were smeared with manure, but we were both smiling.

Chapter 27: Barn Wildlife

In all places, history and landscape are inseparable, and in the Midwest, these common themes are joined in depictions of old barn scenes. For years, artists have produced paintings of old barns to elicit nostalgic feelings of "old times" or "country charm." Such paintings appear so frequently that they have become cliché. I disagree with the symbolism of old barns indicating "the way things used to be" or "a testament to the strength of the pioneers." I am not so naïve as to think that rural folks all used to get along and work together. That is not to say that an old barn shouldn't be celebrated. In my view, the barn's role as a livestock shelter warrants the most merit, and even barns that haven't contained livestock for many years still have undomesticated occupants. Where there is life, stories abound.

On our farm, we have three old barns. Each one is complete with a lower level composed of stalls for animals. Between the stalls, the feed-way, which is essentially a big trough, runs the length of the barn. Cattle can stick their heads through stanchions and reach the hay that is thrown down from the hayloft into the feed-way. The stanchions are composed of durable hardwood boards that align vertically with a gap between each which allows a cow to slip her head through and eat. The boards can then be moved in against a cow's neck to keep her from backing up. The hayloft extends from the ceiling of the stalls all the way up to the barn roof. It is typically accessed by ladders inside the barn and hatches on the exterior. When the barns were originally constructed, the hayloft was meant to hold all the hay needed to support the farm's cattle, horses, and sheep throughout the winter. Depending on the date of construction, the hayloft may have been intended to hold loose hay or small square bales. As agriculture mechanized, hay harvesting operations shifted away from small square bales to large round bales and large square bales. Weighing more than 1,000 pounds, both types of large bales require a tractor to move. We produce the large round bales on the Gillespie Farm. For our system, the round bales work better because they can be stored outdoors. Using modern equipment to bale large, dense round bales is faster and less labor intensive than baling and storing small square bales. Due to this modernization, small square bales and the haylofts of old barns have become partially obsolete. However, there remains a niche market for square bales, because during the winter, farmers appreciate having a supply in the hayloft to provide extra feed to cattle that are ill or having birthing difficulties. Also, equestrian enthusiasts tend to like feeding square bales.

The haylofts of old barns are a special kind of place. With the side hatches open, outside light can shine in to illuminate the barn-building carpenter's high level of skill. When the hatches are closed, the lofts are very dim. During the summer a hayloft can be a hot and unbearable place, with stinging red wasps guarding the hatches and doors. Isolated barns with open hatches sometimes serve as nest sites for buzzards. In the winter months, a dry, sheltered hayloft provides habitat for mice and the creatures that prey upon them. Raccoons, skunks, feral cats, and occasionally owls call haylofts home.

174

Down in the stalls, the joists holding up the floor of the hayloft provide habitat for my favorite summertime barn inhabitants: the barn swallows. With curved wings and a forked tail, the birds fly about the pastures and fields, catching insects on the wing. Whenever one lands close enough to be observed, the dark shiny blue color of its head, back, wings, and tail is striking. Barn swallows sport a patch of cinnamon-colored plumage on their faces and beneath their beaks. The breast feathers of the females tend to be white, while the males tend to have more of the cinnamon color on their breast.

The rough-sawn oak joists provide the barn swallows with a place to build their nests. They collect little globs of mud in their beaks from the shorelines of our pasture ponds. Then they fly into the barn and start building their nests by sticking the mud to the side of the joist. With repeated trips for more mud, they build a small shelf. Over the course of a few days, the birds add layers of mud globs until the shelf develops into a half-cup. During the construction process, the bottom layers of mud dry first. A nest in progress has light-colored, dry mud on the bottom and dark, wet mud at the rim. The barn swallows then line their nest with grass and add feathers on top. The female lays three to seven eggs and incubates them for twelve to seventeen days. Once the eggs hatch, both parents make trips to collect insects for the hatchlings to eat. Sometimes juvenile barn swallows from previous clutches even help feed the new hatchlings. I welcome the presence of barn swallows for their "twitter-warble" courtship song and their aggressive predation of insects.

The same joists utilized by the barn swallows for building nests also provide habitat for the commonly-named big brown bat. While the barn swallows feed on insects during the day, bats sweep the skies at night. It can be difficult to detect the presence of bats in a barn. Most of their vocalizations are inaudible to humans. Plus, their small size and brown coloration make them easy to overlook. The trick to finding a bat is to look for its droppings. Big brown bats produce pellet droppings that are similar in size and shape to those of a hamster. Once a scattering of bat droppings is spotted on the floor, look up to find the bat. Male big brown bats tend to be solitary during the spring and summer. During the day, they roost in barns and a multitude of other places, including hollow trees, empty silos, attics, under bridges, behind window shutters, and in picnic shelters. The females are not solitary; they establish nesting colonies. During the winter, males and females hibernate together in well-protected locations, such as caves or mines that are cool, but do not freeze. Big brown bats mate in the fall before hibernating, occasionally during periods of activity in the winter, and again in the spring. The young are born in nesting colonies from late-May to mid-June.

All of the barns at Gillespie Farms serve as bat habitat for periods during the summer. Our most notable bat claims his roosting spot above the workbench in the pole barn.[24]

_____

[24] The term "pole barn" refers to a style of barn construction that

When I first discovered him roosting about a foot above my head, I gathered the family to show them. He was small, with exquisite dark brown fur and neatly folded wings. Mom commented, "I wonder what kind of bat he is?"

I replied, "I don't know... It's a *Batteus batteus.*"

Shortly afterwards, we retrieved a field guide from the house and determined that the bat was a Big Brown Bat or in actual scientific lingo, *Eptesicus fuscus.*[25] Regardless of the correct scientific name, we still called him *Batteus batteus*. It always surprised me that Batteus would return to roost above the workbench because I would commonly tinker on equipment there, pounding with a hammer, running the bench grinder, drilling, sawing, or running the world's loudest air compressor. While all of these power tools were noisy to me, they had to seem deafening to a bat.

One morning about ten o'clock, I was in the pole barn setting up a jig on the table saw. I had the large sliding door

---

became popular in the late 1960's. Originally these barns were built by first setting utility poles in the ground every ten feet as vertical supports. Then, 2"X4" girts were nailed up as horizontal members. Next, factory-made trusses were set on top with the help of a crane. 2"X4" roof purlins were nailed across the trusses, and then the structure was sheathed in metal roofing and siding. Pole barn construction is faster and more economical than construction of a traditional barn. Also, the engineered trusses of a pole barn allow for a wider open-span in the interior. As agriculture mechanized, pole barns became the favored structure for equipment storage.
[25] Schwartz, Charles W., and Elizabeth R. Schwartz. *The Wild Mammals of Missouri*. Columbia, MO: University of Missouri Press and Missouri Conservation Commission, 1959.

open to let in light and a nice breeze. I noticed movement out of the corner of my eye and glanced up to see *Batteus batteus* flying straight at my head. With his wings outstretched flying, he looked huge! He was so close that his leathery wings made a flapping sound as I ducked my head. He zoomed past then swept up suddenly and disappeared between the joists to his favorite roosting spot. My heart raced for a moment, and then I smiled and chuckled. I thought, *Geez, Why am I afraid of a little bat? Although, Batteus Batteus looked much bigger flying; so it's okay that I ducked like I was scared.* I stepped over to the workbench and looked up to see *Batteus Batteus* quietly hanging on the side of the joist. He had shrunken down to his normal size. Apparently he doesn't mind all of the noise and disturbance. He has returned to the same spot every summer for the past six years. We look forward to seeing him in the barn and love watching the bats swoop to catch bugs at twilight.

"Batteus batteus" a Big Brown Bat whose real scientific name is *Eptesicus fuscus.*

While the flight of a bat is intriguing to watch at dusk, it is the visage of a screech owl that instills the most awe. Roughly the size of a pigeon, screech owls make their living by nabbing mice, voles, and small prey of opportunity. At

179

Gillespie Farms, they frequent the barn loft of the east barn, but have also been spotted in the west barn. In early January 2014, we experienced a severe winter storm on the farm. It started on Sunday morning with large wet snowflakes falling until two in the afternoon when the temperature plummeted and the north winds blew at thirty to forty mph. Total whiteout conditions ensued. At the time a very disagreeable cow named Bonga was due to calve. We herded her into the barn while the wind howled and snow drifted across the landscape. By late evening, the temperatures were well below zero, and the wind chill was close to thirty below zero. Fearing that Bonga would give birth, and that the brutally-low temperatures would freeze the calf, we decided to take turns checking on her during the night. If she calved, we would promptly carry the calf up to the warm house. Mom would check her at nine, Dad at midnight, and I would take the three am time slot.

When Mom reported that Bonga was not calving just after nine o'clock, I set my cellphone alarm and settled into bed. I drifted off to sleep. Dad ventured out at midnight and while he was checking Bongo, I laid awake and listened to the wind. I felt sorry for all the animals and wondered how any birds could ever withstand such horrendous cold. Dad returned in a few minutes and also reported no calving activity. I fell back to sleep. When my time to check Bonga rolled around, I was in a deep slumber. My mind seemed to float. I could hear distant "island music." I thought, *Island music, that's odd. I wonder where that is coming from.* Then a rush of consciousness came over me as I remembered setting my cellphone's alarm. I pulled on my heavy winter clothes and grabbed a flashlight. Outside, the intense cold and fierce wind took my breath away. It stung the exposed skin of my face, and the snowdrifts reached up to my knees. When I arrived at the barn, I opened the door to see Bonga calmly chewing her cud. Above her, I saw a flash of movement. I shined my light in that direction to see a bird perched on a beam. It stood about six inches tall, with ruddy-colored feathers, and forward facing eyes. It was a screech owl, staring right back at me. I thought, *Neat! Don't go anywhere, buddy, just stay in here.* Since Bonga wasn't calving, I left quietly and returned to the house. Fortunately, she delivered her calf about a week later when the temperature finally reached thirty degrees.

Unlike the migratory barn swallows, screech owls are year-round residents of Gillespie Farms. They take shelter in cavities and hunt at night. The screech owl I saw in the barn was likely doing both. In the spring, the breeding pairs select a cavity for nesting. Tree cavities are preferred, but screech owls are known to utilize nest boxes and even wood piles. They lay a clutch of two to six eggs. Generally, the incubation period lasts twenty-six days. While the female nests, the male screech owl hunts and brings her food. During the daylight hours, the male screech owl guards the entrance to the cavity. He perches nearby the nest in a location that is well camouflaged yet has a clear view of the entrance. Once, we spotted a large black rat snake slithering across the driveway near the east barn. Enthused by our discovery, we chased the snake to one of the large white oak trees to see it climb up the bark. It climbed steadily, and we stepped in close to watch as it rose higher up the trunk toward an opening. In the blink of an eye, a streak of brown and grey flew in and knocked the snake off the tree. We watched in awe from below and realized that the snake was going to fall on us. We jumped back and looked up to see a screech owl perched near the tree cavity, gazing back at us. His penetrating stare seemed to say, "Why the hell are you driving that snake up to my nest!" He had been nearby the whole time, but we failed to notice him because of his camouflaged feathers.

Sightings of screech owls are not rare, but they're not common either. I can vividly remember stepping into the east barn one fall evening and seeing a screech owl perched at the very top of the hayloft. The last rays of the setting sun flooded in from an open hatch. The owl stood in the opening, with the orange glow illuminating the red hues of its feathers in vibrant glory. From its high perch, the owl watched me. I marveled at how this little owl was so superbly attuned with its setting.

Hearing a screech owl is a more common experience. Screech owls call at night, producing an unmistakable quivering sound. When this sound echoes through the barn lots and oak trees, it harkens back to an earlier era; a time when Illinois was wilderness. We're thankful that screech owls have found a niche on our farm.

The large white oak trees of our barnyard provide more than nest sites for screech owls and other birds. In the fall, they produce acorns, which provide food for many animals including one of the less popular barn inhabitants—the groundhogs. In urban areas, people refer to groundhogs by their other common name, the woodchuck; scientists call them *Marmota monax*. By any name, they find old barns perfect for burrowing under. Their tunneling behavior is troubling because they can weaken the foundations and supporting piers. Despite this, we make little attempt to eradicate them from the old barns. When the white oaks drop their acorns in the fall, the groundhogs feed on them to fatten up for their winter hibernation. They stay in their burrows over the winter and emerge in mid-spring. While Groundhog Day is celebrated on February 2, we never see any groundhogs outside of their tunnels on that day. Rather, they wait until plants begin growing to emerge from hibernation. As herbivores, they feed on a wide variety of vegetation, but tend to be the most frustrating when they raid the garden eating green bean plants. Bad behavior can be unhealthy for groundhogs, but most of the time we accept them for what they are—squat marmots that enjoy a good salad.

The tunnels produced by groundhogs provide habitat for raccoons, skunks, possums, and foxes. These animals have earned my ire by preying on chickens. The chickens can be protected from most of the nocturnal varmints by closing them up tight in their chicken house at night, but this tactic doesn't always work for foxes. Foxes can be active during the day, especially in early summer when feeding their kits. Sometimes the foxes den under the east barn. This location is prime for a fox to dash out and grab a chicken dinner, before the farm SWAT team can respond. During the summer, the foxes hold a reign of terror on the chickens. In the winter, the tables turn when fur-trapping season starts. Those holes under the barns became opportune spots for setting Conibear traps. Conibear is a brand of body-hold traps that quickly kill the animals they catch. During the winter, there is always an overabundance of predators living under the barn. By setting a few traps, we help turn the tables in the chickens' favor.

The west barn is located in the pasture, and it serves as a shelter for calving cows or ill cattle. Ordinarily, the cows and calves are kept out of the barn. Allowing all the cattle to stay in the barn all of the time would result in very messy stalls. We keep the barn relatively clean by selective use. The hayloft is stocked with a few square bales of hay for feeding the ones we let in. As typical with most barns, the west barn's hayloft is accessed by an interior ladder that runs up from the feedway to a hole in the hayloft floor. Most haylofts have a crude frame constructed around the hole to serve as a hand-hold and to keep the stacks of square bales from inadvertently falling through the hole. The west barn lacked electricity; so whenever we climbed up to the hayloft, it was always hard to see. This led to an irrational fear that a skunk would be waiting at the top of the ladder to spray me.

South America

In March 2001, I was attending classes at the local community college. My typical day went a bit like this:
— 6:00 a.m.: Get up and put on my chore clothes. Go out and walk through the cows to look for those that are having

184

trouble calving or any other issues that need immediate attention.

— 6:45 a.m.: Dash back inside the house to forage on cereal, hit the shower, and get dressed in clothes that had not been stained by moop (mud + cow poop).

— 7:30 a.m.: While driving the twenty minutes to Olney Central College scan the radio for "Bent" by Matchbox Twenty. If the DJ's were refusing to play any Matchbox Twenty, I would happily listen to songs by The Goo Goo Dolls, Garth Brooks, Alanis Morissette, Doug Stone, or Tal Bachman.

— 8:00 a.m.: Learn calculus II from a first-rate teacher who also happened to be distracted by his alma mater playing in the Sweet Sixteen basketball tournament. Try not to be annoyed by my friend Nathan's amazing grasp of calculus II.

— 9:00 a.m.: Sit through chemistry class as taught by a monotone professor who was rumored to have a collection of empty booze bottles on his front porch.

— 10:00 a.m.: Try hard to enjoy early American literature as taught by a top-notch professor. Visit with a good-looking nursing student named Sarah, who would eventually become the wife of my friend Ryan.

— 11:00 a.m.: Go to a nearby Subway restaurant for lunch.

— 11:45 a.m.: Find an empty table at the library and work on my most pressing homework.

— 1:00 p.m.: Go to physics class and learn how to apply the math that had been drilled into my head earlier. Benefit from the professor's skillful use of comical physics problems to teach core concepts. Enjoy watching Nathan become frustrated because, for the first time in his life, he actually had to work to earn an A grade.

— 2:00 p.m.: Take care of any parting scholastic questions or visit with friends.

— 2:10 p.m.: Drive home to the farm.

— 2:30 p.m.: Pull into the driveway to the ruckus of cows bawling at me because they want fresh bales of hay and ground corn to eat. Change into chore clothes and start moving hay for the home herd.

— 3:30 p.m.: Drive up and check the feedlot and then the Bogota herd. Feed the cattle and take care of any problems.

Upon arriving home one particular day, I noticed that South America was off by herself in the winter lot. I made a mental note of this and continued with my routine. When I got back to her, I saw that she was calving. I decided to give her some time and check her again after moving out hay.

Moving out hay is not a particularly difficult job, except there were forty-five cows in the home pasture. It was also March which meant that the weather was too cold for grass to grow and the cattle lot was a muddy mess. The cows consumed at least four bales of hay in three days. Unfortunately, they had taken to butting and trampling the bales. This wasting of hay ticked me off. I adopted the tactic of moving out hay when they ran out in all four bale rings. My approach was not to the liking of the cows, and as I moved out new hay bales, the cows butted each other aggressively for rank and tore into the bales while I attempted to cut off the twines. It was rather frustrating because I was mired in the mud with the cows. Then some bitchy cow of higher status would start butting her way to the bale. As the cows of average rank fled, I was in danger of being trampled. When this happened, I yelled and cursed at them until they all backed away from me.

That particular day, I was nearly hoarse from yelling when I finished moving out the fourth bale and parked the tractor back in the barn. I walked out to where I had seen South America earlier. As I approached, she stood up but was obviously wobbly. I walked around behind her to find tiny hooves sticking out. I gently spoke to her, "Alright girl, you've got to go to the barn now." I waved my arms and herded her to the barn. She didn't exactly want to go, but she was a good-natured cow and decided that she would comply. After I latched the barn gate shut, I returned to the house and called the veterinarian. Ken wasn't tied up and could drive down right away. In the meantime, I took the work truck up to the Bogota pasture and made a quick check of the cows there. By the time the vet arrived, it was getting close to four in the afternoon; although, the overcast sky made it seem even later.

Ken and I roped South America to a solid column located in the middle of the stall, and the vet got to work. He took a stainless steel chain and looped the unborn calf's hooves. We both gave a good pull, but the calf wouldn't budge; so I retrieved the pulling jack from Ken's truck. Calmly, he applied a steady tension and started ratcheting. Click-click, click-click, click-click, click-click. South America was beginning to fall over when the calf finally slid out. Ken wiped the slime away from its nostrils and shook his head. The calf was dead.

Ken took his gloved hand and reached into the cow and said, "Yeah, I was afraid of that; there's another one." He repositioned the calf and brought the front hooves up. I

187

removed the chain from the dead calf and handed it to Ken. Once again, he tied it on to the unborn calf's hooves. We pulled together, and the second calf came out. It too was dead. I had messed up. I had let poor South America strain for too long before calling the vet. Right about this time, my dad entered the north door of the barn. I quietly told him what had happened. He nodded and said, "Well, I'll go get the tractor." Ken gave South America a shot of antibiotics to help stave off infection following her trauma, and I unclipped the lasso. She stood still for a while, then walked over to the manger. I helped Ken carry his equipment out of the barn. He took his time to spray down his equipment and get cleaned up. Under the oppressive cloud cover, it was beginning to get dark. When Dad returned with the tractor, I carried the dead calves out of the barn and placed them in the bucket of the loader. Dad drove off through the gate. Somewhere in the pasture, he dug a shallow hole with the tractor and buried them. I stepped back into the barn and checked on the cow. South America was standing silently in the barn with her head in the manger. Her dark brown eyes and white markings seemed dull. She wasn't a tame cow, so I didn't try to pet her. I quietly said, "Let me get you some good hay."

Besides needing something to eat, some good hay would help calm South America while she recovered in the barn by herself. I climbed up the ladder to the dark hayloft, and just as I reached the top rung, a distinct sensation came over me; I was being watched. My fear of being sprayed by a skunk kicked in. Sweat beaded on my forehead as I froze at the top of the ladder. I peered out into the inky, quiet darkness. A few tense seconds passed before, I heard a distinctive "purrrrrrrr, purrrrrrrr, purrrrrrrr." My eyes adjusted to the darkness and focused on another face just inches from mine: It was Garden Kitty; what a relief! She was a very friendly cat with perfectly camouflaged fur. Her eyes were fully dilated, and she had no trouble seeing me. Her face held a pleasant look. I petted her gently, and then crawled onto the hayloft floor. She had apparently been in the hayloft while we were struggling below. I got to my feet and walked over to the south hatch. I found the latch in the darkness and opened the hatch to let in enough light so I could see the bales of hay. It also provided a nice view of the winter pasture, though in March it wasn't much of a view— nothing but muddy cattle lots and gray skies. A few cows looked up at me in the opening. I retrieved a bale and broke it up. I threw several flakes of hay down into the feedway of South America's stall. I would check on her first thing in the morning, and if she seemed okay, I would let her out of the barn. I turned and gave Garden Kitty a few pets before I climbed back down the ladder. She rubbed against my leg in appreciation and then went on about her business, hunting for mice.

As I left the barn, I couldn't help but notice a black cow with a white face looking in. Her name was Snoopy and she was standing right outside the gate. While her markings resembled Snoopy the cartoon dog, it was her tendency to hang around the barn when a cow was sick or calving that cemented her moniker. She was tame so I reached out and petted her face, "Oh Snoopy, what a mess." I scratched behind her ears and followed her gaze to South America, who was still standing motionless by the manger. I patted Snoopy's neck in parting, "Ugh, come on girl, she's feeling pretty rough; let's leave her alone." As I slogged through the mud toward the house, Snoopy stayed and looked on.

Perhaps she was being supportive to her friend or maybe she was just curious. Regardless, Snoopy was a gentle cow that grew to become one of my favorites.

The East Barn

The east barn was larger, but it was no longer used as a cattle shelter. It was also built earlier than the west barn and usually contained more wildlife. It had a wide feedway that ran through the very middle. Over the years that feedway became a storage area for lumber, duck decoys, barrels, and a wide assortment of junk. The hayloft of the east barn had sizeable amounts of hay in it, which had been in the barn for probably twenty years—until the early spring of 2008.

Late summer 2007 was dry, and we were unable to bale all the hay we needed. By March 2008, our stock of large round bales was running precariously low. I happened to have recently liberated myself from engineering work, so I took up the mission of cleaning some of the old hay out of the east barn. This was quite a task because the square bales had fallen apart into a big jumbled heap. Most of the twines holding the bales together were broken. The hay had to be manually forked from the hayloft down to a wagon below. Naturally, my father was against this move. He would say things like, "Oh just keep that hay in there for an emergency." Which directly translates to, "Will that looks like a lot of hard work, why don't you do something else instead." Of course, I enjoyed the hard work, and every day I filled a wagon with loose hay from the loft and took it out to the pasture where I would fork it into a feeder. Much to my amazement, the cows ate the old hay.

One day I was following my normal routine and had nearly filled the wagon when I heard a strange grunting sound coming out of the hay pile I was about to fork. Considering the time of year, I came to the conclusion that this sort of barn wildlife was of the black, white, and stinky variety. I set down the pitchfork and calmly started climbing down to the wagon. I glanced over to the hay pile to see a skunk wriggling out of the hay just before I jumped off the ladder. I had just avoided an encounter that would have left me smelling awful for several days.

Chapter 28: Asleep at the Wheel

March of 2001 was the worst month that I ever experienced taking care of cattle. I lost several calves, I had a cow die, and I pulled a set of dead twins. My only bright spot in that gloomy month was a cute girl with dyed blonde hair named Lori. We met back in November and were frequently going out on dates. I didn't know Lori at all, and that was great. She was from the next county east, and we had no mutual friends. With her, my social status didn't matter, and I didn't care about hers. She liked my affection, and I was so starved for attention that I overlooked some problems. We would meet up and go see a movie, visit a state park, or swim at Lincoln Trail College, where she attended. I was excited— for the first time in my life, it seemed like I had a girlfriend.

Unfortunately, there was always something distant about Lori. There were certain bits of information she seemed to withhold from me. I didn't know it then, but she was struggling to get out of a relationship with her old boyfriend. In early May, I pressed the subject, and when Lori lashed out at me, I gave up on her. I was devastated. To make matters worse, it was summer, which meant that I would be doing farm work in isolation until the fall semester started. I had three months to dwell on all the mistakes that I had ever made.

The thought of being caught up in my head for the whole summer was unacceptable. I needed a plan to keep me super busy and around other people. I decided to get a job off the farm. I recognized that my parents needed my help on the farm, but they saw that I would go crazy without some distraction. The next day, I pulled out the phone book and opened the Yellow Pages. I was pretty good at doing woodworking, so I decided to call some carpenters and see if they needed help for the summer. My first call was to a carpenter named Gery Ochs. I talked with Gery over the phone, and he told me that he needed help. I met with him that afternoon and had a job the next day. I would be working on his construction crew. We started at seven in the morning and ended work at four in the afternoon. During the first week, I busted open two of my fingers, but soon got into the rhythm of things. By the second week I figured out a few of the must-knows for my carpentry job:

1. Electrical tape works better than Band-Aids.
2. During the drive home, a swig of lemon juice from the plastic lemon-shaped bottle in the console of my truck would wake me right up.
3. When roofing, the rough side of the particleboard always goes up.

I liked the carpentry work, and I learned a lot from Gery. Besides being a skilled craftsman, he was the hardest working man that I had ever met. He would roof from seven to four, and then leave his paid projects to go help one of his many brothers fix up a house. He was amazing; the guy worked tirelessly.

Getting home from work at four-thirty was nice because plenty of daylight was left to work on the farm. Despite the wet spring, we were able to get all the crops planted; however, we still needed to harvest wheat and cut and bale hay. As the summer progressed, the jobs were beginning to pile up when Mom noticed that Swimmer Cow and City-on-Her-Back's calves had developed pinkeye. The dreaded disease is caused by the bacteria *Moraxella bovis.* The infection results in a white-colored growth on the lens of a cow's eye. Personally, eye irritations of my own drive me bananas, and I've always felt terrible for cows and calves with infected eyes. Fortunately, the disease can usually be treated with LA-200 (oxytetracycline) antibiotic. Pinkeye is contagious from cow to cow. Cows don't often rub eyes together; flies spread the disease.

After treating the infected cows, we decided the job of mowing the home pasture should be moved up on the priority list. Normally we mowed the pastures in mid-July because by then the grass would be grazed down and the broadleaf weeds could be mowed off before they went to seed. However, mowing the pastures also helps reduce pinkeye infections in an indirect manner. The fescue grass sends up seed heads that ripen in early summer. Those seed heads irritate the cow's eyes as they graze, which can cause their eyes to water, and disease-carrying flies are attracted to watery eyes. By mowing the pastures, we cut off the seed heads and reduced the number of cows with watery eyes. We hooked up the old Case 1070 tractor to the bush-hog mower and moved it to the home pasture. Mowing the pastures would be my after-work job while Mom, Bob, and Dad were out harvesting wheat.

The next day I found myself with the construction crew re-roofing an older farmhouse. It was quite a job, and as

195

the day wore on, it got hotter and hotter. Finally we reached quitting time, and I headed home. The air conditioning in my truck felt wonderful as I cruised along. I caught my favorite Matchbox-20 song on the radio. About five miles away from the house, I started getting drowsy. I took a big swig of lemon juice and grimaced at the sour taste. It woke me right up. When I arrived home, I stepped in the house for a moment and then headed out to start mowing the pasture. The Case 1070 was an older tractor, but it had a cab and working air conditioning. I shifted the tractor into third gear and started mowing. I went bush-hogging down weeds in twelve-foot swaths, back and forth, back and forth... The dull sound of the diesel engine and the rocking of the tractor seemed to lull me. I could feel my eyelids getting heavy. I caught myself drifting off a few times, but then I would shake my head to stay awake. I wished that I had my bottle of lemon juice. I kept mowing.

Suddenly, I fell onto the steering wheel and awoke. The tractor was bouncing in place, with the front wheels dangling over a deep gulch. One of the rear wheels was spinning and digging a hole into the bank. The sound of the engine roared in my ears, and the mower shuddered violently as the blades chopped at the ground. Debris flew from the blades and impacted the back of the tractor. I stomped on the clutch and turned off the PTO shaft that powered the mower. I shifted the tractor to neutral and idled back the engine. I started trying to figure out what had just happened, and where I was. Obviously I had fallen asleep, but with the tractor sloping down, looking at the bottom of a deep channel, it took a moment to realize that I was staring into the washed-out channel that ran along the border between Gillespie land and that belonging to the Kuhl's. When I fell asleep, I must have veered to the left. Then, the tractor drove itself right through the barbed wire fence and through the trees that lined the ditch along our border. I twisted around and looked out the back window and saw that the bush hog mower was caught by two trees. The mower was wider than the tractor. Miraculously, the tractor had rolled right between the two big trees and stopped when the mower got caught. I shut off the engine and struggled to push open the door. Tree limbs pressed against the glass, but I managed to open the door a few inches and squeeze my way out. I climbed down the tractor's steps and jumped onto the sloped bank. Scrambling back up the steep edge into the pasture, I was glad to be out of the tractor.

Now I was wide-eyed from the dose of adrenaline in my bloodstream. My heart was still thumping as I walked around to the right-hand side of the tractor to look for damage. Things could have been much worse. If the tractor would have hit a tree with one of the front tires, it's likely that the front end would have risen off the ground and gone straight up in the air. Then the tractor would have rolled on its back or side. I would have been injured. If the mower had missed the big trees, then the tractor would have fallen into the deep gulch. Again, it's likely that the tractor would have rolled over.

I had escaped unscathed. As I looked over the tractor, it appeared to have dodged a bullet also. All of the

197

windows were still okay, but tree limbs were pressed hard against them. Simply pulling the tractor backwards would cause more pressure on the glass and probably break two of the windows. I looked at the fence. All four strands of barbed wire were broken, and two fence posts were snapped off at the ground.

I considered myself lucky that the tractor and I had escaped severe damage. However, with the fence broken and tractor stuck, I had a situation to correct. Dad, Mom, and Bob were out harvesting wheat, so I had to deal with things on my own. I groaned and thought, *You idiot. Taking a nap would have been more productive. Now you've got to fix all this.*

With a list of supplies compiled in my jittery brain, I walked back to the pole barn. Thankfully, the cows were out of sight and possibly grazing on the far east side of the pasture. I definitely did not need any curious bovines sniffing around the disaster area. At the pole barn, I piled a log chain, some fence posts, a wire stretcher, tying wire, fencing pliers, leather gloves, a chain saw, and a pair of loppers in the bucket of the loader tractor. As I drove the loader tractor out into the pasture, I thought, *Well, I guess that since I'm working off the farm I can't do everything I used to. At least I haven't thought about Lori in the past thirty minutes. Damn it, I just did!*

The first order of business was clearing away the limbs against the tractor windows. Amazingly, the chainsaw decided to work with me, and the engine started on the third pull. Limbs beyond the reach of the chainsaw were trimmed back with the loppers. I hooked the log chain onto the back of the bush-hog. With the loader tractor in the lowest gear, I pulled the tractor backwards—slowly. The stuck Case 1070 rocked from side to side, then it rolled back into the pasture. I breathed a huge sigh of relief. I walked around the 1070 and inspected it for damage. The only problem I found was some of the rubber gasket around the right side window had pulled loose and broken. I thought to myself, *Wow! This could have been a lot worse.* Considering the tractor was thirty years old, we probably wouldn't worry about fixing that.

With the tractor extracted, I started fixing the fence. Using the bucket of the loader tractor, I pushed the two new fence posts into the ground, spliced the barbed wires, and tied the strands to the fence posts. I stood back to admire my work; truthfully, it didn't look like much had happened there. With my hands resting on my hips, I considered my options, *Well I could start mowing again ... Nope! I'm calling it a day.*

I put away the loader tractor and all the tools before the rest of my family returned to the house. I parked the Case 1070 and the bush-hog up in the winter lot. I'd start mowing pastures again the next day. I walked up to the side porch of the house to meet up with everybody. I asked, "Well, how did things go for you guys?"

Dad replied, "We got finished with that field. How did you do today?"

I answered, "Work was fine. We put a new roof on the old Clapp place. But I had some trouble this evening."

Mom set her shoes by the door and looked at me with one raised eyebrow.

I continued, "I drove through the fence and into the ditch between us and Kuhl's."

Dad inquired, "What happened?"

I rubbed my forehead and admitted my guilt with a sigh, "I fell asleep."

Now, you might be thinking that I was going to get in trouble. That's not what happened. I was nineteen years old, trying my hardest to help out. Mom and Dad could see the big picture, so when I described the incident, Mom gave me a hug and insisted that from then on I would take a break when I got home from roofing all day.

At the supper table that night, our conversation soon turned to other mishaps from mowing pastures. On the surface, mowing a pasture seems straightforward: drive the tractor back and forth mowing down weeds with the bush-hog. However, the pastures are notoriously rough and steep. Sections of the pasture are intersected with drainages that sometimes wash out or stay wet. While rough terrain is an obvious hazard, plenty of other problems lurk around, unexpected. For example, male white-tailed deer shed their antlers in early spring, and those antlers lay points-up on the ground. Accidently driving over one can result in a punctured tire. Changing out that flat tire on uneven ground leads to more risk. Mowing pastures is dangerous, and it's not the first problem that injures someone, it's the second or third

complication caused by the initial problem. Ironically, my initial problem was a cute girl with dyed blonde hair.

Ragweed

Yet another unexpected hazard is the noxious weed commonly known as ragweed. Fortunately, I am not allergic to ragweed pollen, but it is kryptonite for my brother, Bob. Because of that, the award for most miserable pasture-mowing mishap goes to him.

Hobart lived just north of the Bogota pasture. He had a few horses, sheep, cows, chickens, guineas, peacocks, cats, and a dog. If you are envisioning a neat, tidy little farm, switch to the polar opposite of that. Hobart's place was a disaster. He had an old barn that was barely standing; parts of the structure sagged precariously, as if waiting to fall on an unsuspecting victim. His garage was full of junk and smelled like old cat pee. The disheveled chicken house had no floor and served as a smorgasbord for varmints. The chicken pen was accessed by a door that was really a repurposed wire bed frame. The fences around his pasture sagged with broken, rusty wires. Only the electric fence kept his animals from roaming the countryside. The one nice building on Hobart's place was a pole barn with stalls for the horses, but even it was a mess on the inside. Once, as a favor to Hobart, Bob and I set traps for varmints in Hobart's chicken house. After we had set the traps, we walked over to the horse barn to visit with him for a minute. While he was talking, a huge rat went running across the beam behind his head. I glanced over at Bob, and he returned a half-smile, indicating that he, too, had seen the giant rodent. Hobart continued talking, completely oblivious to the barn wildlife behind him. Only one unique feature redeemed Hobart's place: He kept goldfish in the horses' watering tank. The water stayed clear, since just a few horses drank from the 150-gallon tank. Located in a shady corner of his barn lot, the tank was a sort of naturalized water garden, with bright green algae and lazy orange goldfish that were six inches long!

Hobart was older than dirt, and he had been so old for so long that I couldn't picture him as a young man, even if I tried. We farmed his crop fields for him, and since he was the landlord, we did all we could to keep him happy. He took advantage of this and asked us to move out hay for his animals on the coldest day of the year and bale square bales on the hottest day of the year. It was toward the end of July when Hobart called with another request. He told my dad that his old John Deere tractor had broken down. Hobart couldn't mow his own pastures and wanted us to do it for him. We weren't particularly surprised—earlier in the day, Dad had noticed that Hobart's tractor was up in the yard, partially disassembled. Mowing his pasture land was above and beyond the duties of someone that rented his farmland, but we obliged. Dad was busy moving off hay bales, so he sent Bob to mow Hobart's pasture. Unfortunately, Bob couldn't use the larger Case 1070 with a cab and air-conditioning to mow, because Hobart's gates were too narrow for the twelve-foot bush-hog to pass through. Bob had to use our older Allis-Chalmers D-17 tractor with a four-foot mower. The D-17, a relic from the 1960s, was an open tractor with a four-cylinder gasoline engine and a wide front

202

end. While the machine was crude by modern standards, it still ran like a top.

Bob drove the D-17 over to Hobart's place. He started mowing around the messy barn lot. The pastures had sprouted giant ragweed, which was pollinating. As the dull blades of the bush-hog mower shredded the plants, copious clouds of yellow pollen floated up into the air. Bob's body reacted like it was under attack. Mucous plugged his sinuses, and his eyes began to swell and fill with thick, yellow liquid. Despite all his suffering, Bob's sense of stubborn pride kicked in, and he powered through his weakened state. He was determined to finish mowing Hobart's stupid pasture. He noticed that the sheep were running back and forth from the patches of tall ragweed into the mowed areas. Bob slowed and let the sheep escape. His eyes were nearly swollen shut, and he sensed that soon he would be unable to see. He decided to hurry up and finish the job. He jolted forward, and the front tire of the tractor ran over a lagging sheep. As the front tire bounced back to the ground, Bob clutched the tractor and shut down the machine. The sheep struggled to its feet and ran off like nothing happened.

Ashamed, Bob walked up to Hobart's house to tell him about the sheep. Hobart met Bob at the door and recognized that something was wrong with the teenager. Bob's eyes were nearly swollen shut, and his entire face was puffed up in an allergic reaction. Hobart called and got in contact with Mom. She rushed to pick up Bob. Mom had suffered from allergies all her life, so she was no stranger to reactions like this. As they returned to the house, Mom took stock of Bob's symptoms. He looked terrible and was unable to see, but his lungs were clear and he wasn't breaking out in hives. She gave him some antihistamine medication and led him to the shower. When Dad arrived home from hauling hay, he was in serious trouble with Mom for sending Bob to mow Hobart's ragweed-infested pastures. She was also ticked-off at Hobart for taking advantage of us. Dad drove back to Hobart's pasture. He finished mowing and checked on Hobart's sheep. Apparently, the run-over sheep was fine—when Dad and Hobart walked through the flock, they couldn't tell which one had been run-over. As for poor Bob, it took hours for his symptoms to subside, but eventually his eyes cleared and his face returned to its normal size.

Chapter 29: Work Trucks

Simply checking the cows doesn't require much of a vehicle. Something that can haul two buckets of corn and some rudimentary veterinarian supplies does the trick. A few neighbors use imported Japanese minitrucks. These funny looking things have a tiny cab that sits over the engine. The engine runs on diesel fuel, and the steering wheel is on the right side of the vehicle rather than the left. The truck bed is tiny, but it just meets the requirements. Some farmers like them because they save fuel. However, any time one needs to haul cattle, pull something out with a chain, jump start a tractor, or make a quick trip to town, a full-sized pickup truck is needed. We always called this truck the work truck. A cattle farm's work truck has a hard life. It gets used every day of the year. It drives back dusty roads during summer, snowy roads in the winter, and muddy roads in March. On any given day, the work truck's cab could contain: an assortment of gloves, a pump-action shotgun, screw-worm balm, hooded sweatshirts, a marking crayon, binoculars, a tire jack, empty soda cans, a lasso, a flashlight, receipts, spare change, a rifle, stocking hats, a pipe wrench, stray shotgun shells, machetes broken baler parts, tying wire... Meanwhile the bed of the truck could contain: buckets of ground feed, fencing supplies, sacks of protein supplement, mineral blocks, boxes of twine, a tool box, a newborn calf, corn stalks, flat tires, muddy boots, a grease gun, a backpack sprayer, seed corn, ... the list goes on.

With the image of all that stuff being loaded and unloaded or just hauled around, imagine the weather changing from blazing sun to pounding rain to blowing snow.

A picture begins to emerge: The work truck gets beat to hell. This was most definitely the case for my dad's old green truck. It was 1978 when that Chevy Scottsdale rolled off the assembly line. Back then, it was a thing of beauty, with a green and white two-tone paint job, an automatic transmission, two gas tanks, and a 350 engine. My first memories of that truck date back to sometime in the late 1980s. The truck had aged considerably and had a distinct smell that translated to burning oil. The body had suffered some damage, and the bed was more rust than metal. Its role had switched from primary work truck to a different fate—it was the go-to truck for jobs deemed too abusive for the work truck Dad depended on every day.

During the winter, it was used for cutting and hauling firewood. Dad drove it out into the woods over limbs, brush, ditches, and stumps. When he came to a dead tree, he stopped the truck. The family piled out of the cramped cab. Dad cut up blocks with the chainsaw while the rest of us would load them in the truck. As a child, I wasn't always strong enough to get a chunk of firewood all the way up into the bed. I could almost get it there, but then I would run out of steam and let it fall down the outside of the bed. Scrapes in the paint from these mishaps weren't an issue with this truck. Dad didn't care. During the spring planting season the truck was loaded way past capacity with bags of seed beans. Each bag weighed sixty pounds, and we piled them high. You could almost hear the green truck's leaf springs and axles groaning as Dad drove it to the field. In the summer, the truck was used for hauling hay. We had a custom-made gooseneck trailer that Dad pulled behind the green truck. The trailer held eight large round hay bales. During the hottest part of the summer, that rig made countless trips back rough roads to the hayfields for bales and then back to the barn lot to be unloaded. With all of this abuse, the green truck's condition deteriorated, but somehow it still managed to function like an old soldier.

In the winter of 1995, the green truck took on a major role hauling silage feed for the cows. We backed up the truck to the trough and shoveled the silage feed out to the hungry cows. The cows rubbed up against the truck and further damaged the exterior. The acidity of the silage rusted more of the truck's bed, and mud from the cattle lots got splashed over every square inch of the truck. It was in very rough shape, and we suspected it would blow up at any time—so we nicknamed it the Green Bomb. After its tour of duty as a silage hauler, the Green Bomb spent a number of years quietly resting in the east barn. We simply didn't use the truck anymore; we didn't cut firewood because we had upgraded to a gas furnace, we didn't pull the bale trailer with the truck anymore because we had bought a bigger bale-hauler, we didn't even use the Green Bomb to haul seed beans in the spring. Unintentionally, the old truck sat in the barn and provided habitat for barn wildlife. However, looking back I now realize that it was actually just waiting to go out in a blaze of glory. The Green Bomb got its chance in 2004.

Fall 2003 marked the beginning of a new era for my family; Mom decided to build a new house. Since home building requires so many decisions, Mom wanted a carpenter who would work closely with her to construct exactly what she wanted. Mom and Dad decided to hire the carpenter Gery Ochs, who I had worked for a few years previously. Having spent the summer working on Gery's crew, I recognized that he was perhaps the hardest-working individual I had ever met. Gery's son shared his father's work ethic. We sold the Green Bomb to Garrett Ochs. We deemed him worthy.

One Saturday, Garrett hauled the old truck over to his shop on a flatbed trailer. He had a big job ahead of him. The Green Bomb needed a new battery, a carburetor cleaning, some oil, and new fuel. After a few hours of work, Garrett turned the key, and the truck awoke from its slumber. It coughed, sputtered, hissed, shuttered, groaned, and then roared; the old engine still ran. Next on Garrett's job list were a whole slew of modifications. First, he removed the exhaust system and replaced it with a series of eight pipes that ran straight up from the engine's exhaust valves and out through a cut in the truck's hood. He trimmed back the rusted sheet metal around the truck's wheel wells. Then he removed all the glass from the truck and took out the radiator. He re-directed the coolant lines from the engine to a chest of ice he strapped in the passenger side of the cab. Finally, he welded the doors shut and painted the driver's side white. The Green Bomb was ready for battle.

Garrett entered the Green Bomb in the demolition derby at the 2004 Jasper County Fair. I wasn't around to see the event, but I've been told that the truck roared in the muddy rink. It shot flames from the straight pipes when

Garrett revved the engine. The Green Bomb rammed into every opponent there. The old truck took hits from every angle and kept running strong. Garrett was hoping to win the derby, but it wasn't meant to be. The truck got sandwiched and lost a back axle. Garrett ended up in fifth place, and the Green Bomb was sent to the scrap yard, where it was crushed and recycled. I like to imagine that the steel from the Green Bomb was used to make another truck, and somewhere out on the road today, somebody is driving that truck. They may not know it, but that vehicle has the heart of a warrior!

Shiny New Truck

In the early 2000s, Dad traded in our old blue work truck for a brand new Chevy 2500 truck with a 350 engine, which was the epitome of a work truck. Two weeks after it arrived on Gillespie Farms, we had to load up fat calves in the trailer for the trip to the sale barn. Like most things on the farm, this was always an ordeal. The first round of business was sorting the calves. The feedlot contained about forty calves. Normally, when we hauled calves to market, eight were selected. The problem was getting the selected calves separated from the herd and then loaded onto the trailer. The process had many steps:

1. Drive the young feeder calves out of their lot into a small holding pen.
2. Drive the fat calves out of their lot into the smaller feeder calf lot.
3. Evict those calves that were not being hauled off to Salem.

4. When only the selected calves were left, herd them into the barn.
5. Back the cattle trailer up to the barn.
6. Drive the selected fat calves up into the trailer.
7. Close the door on the trailer and haul the calves off to market.

In this particular instance, there was a variation in step 2. We happened to have an older foundered calf in the pen with the feeder calves. The term "foundered" is used to describe cattle with a condition, acidosis, that occurs when a bovine's rumen becomes out of balance. In the feedlot, this happens when a calf consumes more grain than it should. The excess of grain begins to rapidly ferment in the rumen and produces more lactic acid than the digestive system is able to buffer. This results in water from the calf's circulatory system permeating into the rumen and leading to dehydration and other problems. The most severe cases can cause death, while the mild cases are hardly noticeable. The permanent damage to a calf is known as founder. A foundered calf has difficulty walking and develops long, spade-like hooves. These cattle don't reach their full potential. We had a heifer that had foundered when she was first released to the self-feeder. She was also quite tame. While she should have been released into the larger feedlot with the rest of her class, we kept her in the feeder-calf pen because she had a calming influence on the young, hyper calves. This also allowed us to keep better tabs on her condition. She had trouble getting around, and from time to time, we would let her out of the pen into the barnyard to graze on the grass. There was no threat of escape from this calf. A person could literally crawl faster than she could move. It was her slowness that caused us to leave her in the lot while we backed the cattle trailer up to the barn. She wasn't leaving the feeder calf lot, so why take the time to drive her into the holding pen with the rest of the feeder calves? She appeared content at the hay feeder, so we left her alone.

While we were in the barn pushing and shoving to load the calves into the cattle trailer, the foundered heifer ambled over to the new Chevy. The pewter-colored truck was far shinier and cleaner than anything she had ever seen. She wandered closer to the truck while we were preoccupied loading the fat calves destined for market. Inside the barn, we yelled, "GET ON UP THERE!" We waved our arms, pushed, shoved, and swore to get those calves in the trailer. The foundered heifer was out in the lot staring at the truck when she saw a calf on the side of the truck staring right back at her. Not to be outdone, she shook her head at this new calf to assert her dominance. The calf in the side of the truck simultaneously shook her head right back. The foundered calf decided that this rookie needed put in its place, so she slammed her head into her reflection on the side of the truck. Her head-butting produced a strange "DONK" sound, and after two good butts, she backed up in surprise to see that her rival was gone! In its place was a huge dent. Our Chevy 2500 had not stayed new for very long. While the dent detracted from the truck's cosmetics, its utility was still very much intact. Its 350 engine proved itself useful when pulling the cattle trailer down to the sale barn in Salem.

Over the years, that truck kept running strong, but the doors began to sag. Those sagging doors became a pet peeve of mine. The annoyance was intensified when Dad drove the truck without closing the doors completely. It irked me because we had a good truck and the sagging problem became worse when he drove the truck without fully closing the doors. Often, I found myself in the passenger seat of the work truck with Dad driving. He rarely got his door fully latched, so I would ride along listening to it rattle. I gritted my teeth trying not to say, "Slam that damn door shut!" I would buy new bushings for the door hinges from NAPA, install them, and almost get the doors to line back up. Then Dad would drive the truck around awhile with the doors barely latched, and they would be hopelessly sagging again.

With barely functional doors, the truck was still running like a top when it was traded for a new truck. This time, Dad decided to mix things up a bit and he bought a Dodge. The Dodge truck had great doors, plenty of power, but a major design flaw: The truck bed sat way too high. Back in the not-so-distant past, if one needed something out of the truck bed, he or she simply leaned over the side and picked it up. The bed sides of the Dodge truck rose up to the tops of my shoulders. This meant that anything not accessible with the tailgate had to be retrieved by climbing into the truck's bed. Conversely, any items that need loaded into the front part of the truck bed also require climbing. Dodge should have seriously considered providing a Sherpa along with their

212

trucks. Unfortunately, all the major truck manufacturers are making their trucks taller now. Considering this, those Japanese minitrucks are beginning to look more appealing.

Chapter 30: Falcon

Falcon was not a cow; he was a duck. He wasn't just any duck either. He was the greatest mallard drake that ever lived. His story is intertwined with that of the cows. Falcon came into my life during the Southern Illinois University spring semester in 2002. It was finals week. The weather had turned warm and humid. I opened the windows of my second-story dorm room to let in the spring air and the chorus of frogs from the nearby Thompson Lake. That evening I studied my chemistry notes in preparation for the upcoming final, and I was just about to close the books when I heard someone outside call my name, "Hey, Will! Are you up there?"

I whirled around from my desk and looked down to see an attractive girl from chemistry class named Amy. I replied, "Hi Amy!"

She continued, "Didn't you tell me that you grew up on a farm—with ducks?"

"Sure did! What's up?"

Amy lifted her cupped hands and said, "Well, I was just walking back from the parking lot, and I found this baby duck in the middle of the road."

I ran down the staircase to meet her. She held a duckling that had gotten separated from his brood. We chatted for a minute and figured out a plan of action. I would take the tiny mallard duckling and keep him warm during the night. The next morning, I would walk around the lake and try to find the brood that he came from and return him.

Against all dorm regulations and game laws, I wrapped the duckling in an old, soft sock and placed him in an open shoe box with my desk light on him. He enjoyed the warmth and fell asleep. I thought to myself, *Well, he'll be lucky to make it through the night*—mortality is pretty much a sure thing with isolated ducklings. The next morning the little duckling was very much alive. I fed him some tiny pieces of bagel soaked in water and packed him in my messenger bag. I walked around the lake and found three broods of mallards. I couldn't find any ducklings as small as him. I even tried to return him to multiple broods. Each time, the duck hen would hiss and shun him. I looked at the duckling and said, "Well, baby, it looks like you're going home with me." I had two more days of final exams before I could return to the farm for the summer. During that time, I fed the young duck algae I pulled out of the lake, breadcrumbs, and bits of milk-soaked cereal. The few dorm residents that I let in on the little secret were huge fans. I returned to my dorm room after my last final to find my roommate's friend, Bonk, in the middle of the floor, lying flat on his back with the little duckling sitting on his chest, eating bread. I was so pleased. It can be hard to get ducklings to eat. Bonk had no idea what a great job he was doing.

The drive home from college was about two-and-a-half hours. The duckling was nestled in a shoebox with some soft socks on the passenger seat of my truck. Sometimes he would cry, "Eeep, Eeep, Eeeep, Eeeep!" I put my hand in his

215

box, and his cry would change to the happy peeps of a duckling at ease. Such a wonderful sound!

When I arrived on the farm, everyone was excited to see the cute little duckling. At Gillespie Farms we're all fans of little ducks. I entrusted the duckling's care to Sarah and Mom. I would be gone during the day at my summer job, working for the Illinois Department of Transportation as a construction inspection intern. Days spent out on the job site monitoring construction workers seemed long, but when I returned home, the reward was petting the little duckling and enjoying some farm work before darkness fell.

Sarah and Mom developed a special ritual with the duckling. Every morning at ten, they took a walk down to the pasture woods to check on the cows. They carried the duckling with them, and when they arrived at the creek crossing, Sarah would let him muddle around the riffle— under close supervision. He loved the creek. Together they would find lots of good things for a duck to eat. Sarah turned over rocks to find insect larva, worms, tadpoles, tiny frogs, or anything else aquatic that moved. The duckling gobbled up all of the good things that Sarah found. It usually took thirty minutes for Mom to count and check the cows then return to the creek. Sometimes she would bring a horsefly or two that she swatted off a cow's back. The young duckling loved horseflies, too. Duck food was plentiful, and he grew at an amazing rate.

Midway through the summer, we had the joy of introducing the duckling to swimming. Luckily, on the farm we have a big pond that offers relief from the summer heat. In the middle of the summer, farm work slacked up a bit, and we took this opportunity to head down to the pond for a swim. The duckling always went with us. He didn't like the deep, open water, which is understandable since deep water can be dangerous for little ducks: snapping turtles and large fish gobble up ducklings that venture out too deep. To mitigate the danger, the duckling caught rides on our backs or stomachs. We floated out in the deep, clear water together, and whenever a floating patch of algae brushed by, the duckling sieved it with his bill. He would happily sit on our stomachs while we pulled over bits of algae for him to eat.

Falcon catching a ride on Bob while floating in the pond.

We gained all sorts of new insights from our pet duck. For example, the body temperature of a mallard is right around 105 degrees Fahrenheit. This means two things: The duckling had an extremely high metabolism rate and needed to forage constantly, AND whenever he pooped on you while swimming, it felt burning hot! Oh, the lessons learned from ducks.

As we entered late summer, anticipation grew for the day that the little duck would fly. We watched as his wings grew long and flight feathers started to fill in. He knew the day was coming, too. He would stretch his wings out and flap, then jump off the ground just enough to get some air, but not enough to really show off. It was around this time that the duckling earned his name. Ducks dislike being held. Even the tamest duck dislikes being confined by one's grip; however, they do like being close. We found that the little duckling would stand on a flat, outstretched hand quite contently. It is a striking pose to stand up straight with your hand outstretched, providing a seat for a proud duck. You've seen such images, but instead of a duck, it's a falcon standing on the falconer's gloved hand, which is why the duckling was named Falcon.

Excitement is seeing your little duck fly for the first time. Falcon started with short flights down the driveway and back. Then he flew down to the pond. Along the way we noticed something very interesting happening: Falcon had the ability to fly, yet he preferred to walk places with his barnyard counterparts. At the time we had six Rouen ducks. They look just like mallards, except they're much larger, slower, and unable to fly. As Falcon grew up, the Rouens became his new friends. He went everywhere with them, through the cattle

218

lots to the pond, around the chicken yard, and into the chicken house for a safe spot to spend the night.

We were glad the other ducks accepted Falcon. It was a natural progression, although it was still sad when he quit swimming with us. Regardless, he still possessed the ability to make us smile. One hot afternoon in late summer, my family was down at the big pond enjoying a swim when we noticed the ducks dabbling up in the shallow end of the pond. We called out to Falcon, "Falcon, Eeeepppeep, Eeeepppeep, Eeeepppeep!" Much to our surprise, he flew out of the group and landed amongst us. He happily swam with us for several minutes before returning to his domesticated comrades. Falcon had found his niche, but he still held some allegiance to the humans who raised him. He stayed with Rouens and us that winter when all the other wild ducks migrated. Over time, the Rouens started falling prey to a fox. Luckily, Falcon was far more agile and wary than the Rouens. He escaped the fate of his friends, and eventually he ended up alone. Ducks are gregarious creatures, and when Falcon became the sole survivor, we knew that he would soon move on.

In pure Falcon style, he waited until everyone was around for a family get-together. It was just the beginning of fall and corn harvest would start shortly. Knowing that we would soon be very busy, my family took some time to go fishing and relax. We were walking down to the pond with all of our fishing gear when Falcon performed a fly-over and landed on the roof of the house. Bob called out, "Falcon, you silly duck. What are you doing on the roof?" We didn't know it at the time, but Falcon was saying goodbye. Falcon took off and swung wide out around the pond. We could hear him call, "Phrraaack, Phrraaack, Phrraaack" like mallard drakes do. He was off to explore his world, and we counted ourselves lucky to have known him.

Falcon as a grown mallard drake; what a stunning lad!

Chapter 31: Dodge Ramcharger

My internship with the Illinois Department of Transportation took some of my time away from the cows. It was an easy job, but, as I had learned from caring for the cows, there is always something that makes life more difficult. During summer 2002, the overpasses and bridges on Illinois Route 50 from Lawrenceville to Vincennes were being replaced. It was a large construction site, and the Illinois Department of Transportation assigned three construction inspection interns to join the full-time staff on the project. I happened to be the intern who lived the farthest from the job site, and considering the logistics, IDOT assigned me a state vehicle, a ten-year-old Ford Escort station wagon that was near the end of its life cycle. Since I was assigned a vehicle, it also became my job to pick up the other two interns on the way to the site. Unfortunately, the first intern on the route was the one who made life more difficult. She had wavy black hair, beautiful dark eyes, and a petite yet athletic build. Her name was Ashley, and she knew that she was very attractive, popular, and of a much higher social status than I. On our first day of work, I attempted to carry on a conversation with Ashley, but she tipped her hat over her face and went to sleep while I drove to the construction site. This became her routine: Get in the car with Will and fall asleep. Fifteen minutes after picking up Ashley, I would pick up Carl. He was a nice enough guy, but he was quiet by nature, and we had little in common. We normally would have a short conversation, and then he, too, fell asleep in the car.

This arrangement became very frustrating. I would leave the farm at six-thirty in the morning, pick up the other two interns and arrive at the job site just before eight. The drive was long and dull. I tried listening to the radio, but Ashley turned it down. My passengers offered no help in keeping me awake and alert. Once at the construction site, we surveyed, measured, painted lines, filled in forms, collected samples of concrete, and watched to make sure the contractor was not cutting any corners. Whenever there was down time the job became very educational for me. The general laborers complained about their evil ex-wives. The union carpenters bragged about their sexual conquests. The steel workers told drinking stories, and the pneumatic drillers killed 30-point bucks and caught 12-pound bass. All of this exhaustive bull-shitting was followed by a drive home with both of my passengers catching up on their sleep while I struggled to stay awake.

Toward the end of that summer, Carl left his IDOT position two weeks early to travel before the fall semester started. While this streamlined the commute, it also meant more silence for me to endure. A few days after Carl left, something wonderful happened while driving the Ford Escort home from work—the electrical system went haywire. The car would still drive, but none of the gages or lights seemed to work. This meant that the Department of Transportation garage would have to assign me a different vehicle. Woohoo! The next day, I drove the dying Ford Escort to the state garage and was issued a Dodge Ramcharger of 1989 vintage. It was a sport utility vehicle of sorts. Mine was white and looked a bit like O.J. Simpson's white Chevy Bronco. It had a pristine interior and appeared to have been driven very little over the preceding ten years. It lacked air conditioning, but that was just fine with me. Having the windows down helped keep me awake. During the drive from Effingham back to the job site east of Lawrenceville, I had seventy miles worth of time to test out the vehicle's features. While driving on Route 50 just past Red Hills State Park, I turned on the cruise control. It worked, but the vehicle had a tendency to decelerate quickly when I took my foot off the gas pedal. Then when the cruise control engaged, the engine surged until it brought the speed back up. When it reached cruise speed, the engine idled and the vehicle rapidly decelerated. I played with this feature until I learned that this condition could be exacerbated if I engaged the cruise control when coasting down a hill. Needless to say, a few iterations of the cruise control surge-and-lurch game could make the most accomplished fighter pilots carsick.

I now had a tactic to get even with Ashley. She didn't know it yet, but her condescension toward me was going to earn her an awful case of carsickness. I considered the route into work, and I knew exactly where to turn on the cruise control. The next morning was just like any other. I picked up Ashley, and with the usual snobbish demeanor she quickly went to sleep over in the passenger side. I was awake and alert, anticipating deployment of cruise control surge-and-lurch. About forty-five minutes into the trip, I turned south on Illinois Route 1 and brought the Dodge Ramcharger up to speed. I glanced over to ensure that Ashley was still sound asleep. She appeared to be quite unconscious. As we started down the first decent hill, I set the cruise control. The Dodge Ramcharger didn't disappoint. It coasted to the bottom of the hill, then the engine revved, and we charged forward. The surge even surprised me. It lasted for fifteen seconds, and then the engine returned to an idle, and we both slumped forward in our seats as the vehicle decelerated. Ashley still appeared to be asleep through the second surge and lurch. On the third acceleration, her eyes opened she took shallow breath and gulped loudly. I kept my eyes firmly on the road and wore my best poker face. Finally, she spoke up, "Are you doing that?"

I responded, "Huh?"

She continued, "Are you revving the truck?"

I responded, "Oh, no. I just set the cruise control, and it seems a little rough."

The Ramcharger surged again. Ashley sighed audibly and looked straight ahead. A few awkward seconds passed. She was starting to look pale. I asked with feigned sincerity, "Do you want me to turn that off?"

Her voice exemplified the contempt she had of the lesser being driving the vehicle when she replied, "Uh, yeah."

I turned off the cruise control and rode out the last surge. Ashley was still a bit pale when we finally arrived at the construction site. I parked the Dodge Ramcharger near the workers' trucks. Ashley made her way to the Porta Potty, and I walked up to the job site. The union carpenters were crass, like usual, and started razing me, "Shit, they gave you a Dodge Ramcharger! You were probably porking her in that thing."

I shook my head no and replied, "Nah, but she might be a little carsick."

One of the older general laborers cracked a wide grin and fired back, "Or PREGNANT!"

The author, on the last day of his summer job, posing with his state-issued Dodge Ramcharger. In the background sits the broken-down Ford Escort Station Wagon.

Chapter 32: Slimer

It was a typical March day; the winter lot of the home pasture was muddy, and the weather was cold and gray. I was making the evening rounds, checking the cows when I came across a newborn calf that was feebly walking around the muddy lot bawling and looking for her mother. With black fur and clear eyes, the calf was apparently healthy, but the cow that birthed her was nowhere in sight. I hadn't realized that any cows were due to calve. The newborn wobbled through the mud from one cow to another, looking for an udder to nurse. Each time it touched a teat, the cows kicked it away. Disgusted by this, I picked up the calf, and we went looking for her mom together. I slogged around the hay pile with the new calf held against my chest. I looked for a cow that could have just calved. *No luck.* I carried her over by the Calm Pond to see if it could have been one of the cows resting there. *None of those cows.* When I set the calf down by the last suspected cow near the garden gate, I watched the newborn get kicked away and I thought, *Screw this! Let's just give this calf a bottle, and put her in the barn. Maybe her damn mother will start looking for her!*

I carried her to the barn, set her in the cozy box stall and then headed to the house. Mom met me at the door and asked, "It sure took you a while to check the cows. Is everything alright? "

I shook my head and said, "No, I've got a new calf out there, and no one is claiming it."

With a surprised look, Mom replied, "That's weird. We better give it some colostrum." She went to the chest freezer on the back porch and pulled out a frozen package of colostrum that had come from the Kaufmann's dairy farm. When the package of colostrum thawed and warmed up, she poured it into a bottle and screwed on the nipple. Dad arrived home and we headed out to the barn to give the calf the bottle. Inside, the young calf was standing in the corner. I approached her and petted her back while dad picked up the calf's chin and put the nipple in its mouth. Immediately, she started nursing. The next morning, we fed the calf a bottle of mixed powered milk replacer. Over the next few days, we had hopes of finding the calf's mother. We walked through the lot looking for a cow with a large un-nursed udder and bloody membrane from afterbirth on her tail. We came up empty-handed. None of the cows were looking for a missing calf either. A week passed and still no momma-cow came forward to claim the calf. We accepted the fact that the new calf would have to be raised on the bottle. This was a strange situation—typically cows are motherly to a fault!

Regardless of her abandonment, the young calf was strong and healthy. She soon earned her name by nursing the bottle so aggressively that milk foam and slobber would drip down her chin. When the bottle ran out, she would chase the bottle-holder around the barnyard demanding more milk! If one stuck around and petted her, she would rub the milk slime all over our clothes, hence the name Slimer. She grew quickly, and by mid-summer it became apparent who the mother was. They shared the same look, even though Slimer was black and her mother was light gray. The day we made the connection, that cow lost a great deal of my respect. In my mind she became, Slimer's Mom—the ultimate white-trash cow.

Slimer's Mom was just a heifer when Slimer came along. For reasons unknown to us, she failed to claim her first calf. Somehow, she calved and recovered so quickly that we completely missed the birth. The second time around, Slimer's Mom did an excellent job raising her calf. Every calf after that was also raised without a problem, and so over the years Slimer's Mom improved her reputation. But, like any cow, she still had the ability to pull classic stunts. For instance, a few years back, we had a little plum tree that was right along a paddock that we rotationally grazed. The lot was not well-fenced; two sides had only electric fence, while the other two sides were older woven and barbed-wire fencing. The tree was loaded with plums that were nearly ripe. We were about ready to pick them one Saturday morning but decided to let them ripen another day. We went on about our chores and noticed that the cows really wanted out into the paddock. Knowing that we would be nearby all day, we opened the gate and let them graze the paddock. Very casually, Slimer's Mom walked over to the plum tree, reached across the fence, and started eating the plums one after another. We chased her away, but not before she had eaten half the fruit on the tree. Knowing that she would return, we picked the rest of the plums. Slimer's Mom was such a typical cow.

While Slimer's Mom was allowed to stay in the home herd and repair her reputation; Slimer experienced a different fate.   Since Slimer was so tame and had a gentle temperament, we wanted to keep her as a cow. So like all heifers, she was sent to the Slack pasture to mature. Eventually, she graduated and was sent to the Bogota herd to be bred and become a cow.

Unfortunately the Bogota herd shunned Slimer, and we watched helplessly as she was ostracized from the herd. By late summer, we were hoping that the bull had at least bred Slimer. Heifers tend to come into heat every twenty-one days. While this condition is not readily apparent by looking at a cow, it's easily apparent by their behavior and the behavior of other cows and the bull. The cow in heat mounts other cows, those cows mount her, and the bull is right there in the mist of the silliness. He repeatedly sniffs her backside, and then curls up his upper lip and scrunches his nose. With Slimer, we considered that the herd of cows might not accept her, but the bull will surely smell when she's in heat and breed her. If she had a calf, then she could stay in the Bogota pasture and eventually work her way into the ranks. Fall and winter passed, and we suspected that Slimer was not pregnant. I hated the thought of this; if she wasn't bred, she would have to be sold.

One March day, I walked back to the hay pile to check the Bogota Herd. A chilly, hard wind blew from the west. I counted the cows and noticed that Slimer was missing—as usual. She would be just outside the herd somewhere. I looked around the perimeter of the herd and spotted Slimer

229

grazing on short grass 150 yards away. She was on the crest of a hill with the wind whistling around her. I thought to myself, *Poor girl. I wish she would stay with the herd.* I decided to walk over and see my pet cow. As I approached Slimer, she looked up as if to greet me. I petted her face, scratched behind her ears, and teased her, "Slimer you need to be friendly with the Bulla." I had turned and started walking away when I noticed an odd shadow over me. Out of the corner of my eye, I saw Slimer's nose, then I felt her knees on my shoulders. Slimer was trying to ride me! I bolted, and she dropped her front hooves to the ground with a solid, thud. I had escaped but was taken aback by the quickness of her advance. I hadn't heard her approach because the wind was roaring in my ears. From a few yards away, I glanced at Slimer with wide eyes, thinking, *You could have crushed me!* Slimer returned to grazing and was acting like a perfectly normal cow again. In retrospect, I should have gone back to the hay pile and then herded the bull over to Slimer. Maybe she would have gotten bred then.

By summer, it was clear that Slimer was not going to calve, nor would she get bred. We loaded her up into the cattle trailer with a few other cows that we considered culls. When we arrived at the sale barn, Dad backed the trailer up to the offloading chute. I hopped out of the truck and opened the trailer door. Reluctantly, the cows stepped out of the trailer. I herded them down the chute and into the raceway. The raceway narrowed until the cows could only pass through in single file. In the narrow section, the staff glued ID stickers on each cow's back. After the last cow was marked, the workers opened and closed a maze of gates until the cows were driven into a holding pen. As Dad finished the paperwork at the marking booth, I returned to the truck. He started the engine and asked, "You wanna carry in a bucket of feed for the old girls?"

"Yeah, we ought to," I replied.

Dad drove the truck and trailer around to the other side of the building where we could park out of the way of the other cattle haulers. I quickly stepped out of the truck and grabbed a bucket of ground feed from the bed. As I walked back to the holding pen I had to step aside to let some workers drive a bunch of fat calves to their holding pen. I found our cows and dumped the bucket in a small trough next to their water tank. While the other cows aggressively took their place at the trough, Slimer simply stood by and looked at me with her dark brown cow eyes. I stepped over to her and petted her head. I said, "Goodbye, girl," and left the pen. I pulled my hat down low as I walked down the center aisle of the sale barn back to the work truck.

Chapter 33: Proud to Run

My parents made a point to teach me how to deal with an aggressive cow at an early age. It's quite straightforward, really; if a cow is simply picking on you, hit her hard and let her know that you won't be pushed around. However, when dealing with humans, they taught me something entirely different. Mom and Dad always insisted that physically fighting was never the right thing to do. They expressed that kids who fought lacked self-restraint and were weaker inside. This was hard for me to understand, but I abided. I was taught to run from physical altercations with human opponents, and for some reason, I grew up with many opponents. I was born in 1981, the same year that a bumper crop of kids were born in my school district. My peers and I overloaded the schools, and along the way, many of them grew to be mean-spirited. So many kids were malicious that it tainted the entire personality of my class, the class of 1999. I worked at surviving high school and even enjoyed participating in the annual musical production. But as a seventeen-year-old graduate, I was bitter and unprepared for many social interactions. My social skills became particularly weak in my interactions with girls.

After high school, I earned my associates degree at a nearby community college. I attended classes in the morning and came home to care for the cows in the afternoon. During this time, the number of cattle on Gillespie Farms peaked. The cows became my primary responsibility. Before, they had been Dad's responsibility; however, in 1999 he had started working off the farm managing a state park, so my part-time college job became caring for eighty cows. While I enjoyed caring for the animals, times turned dark for me as a sense of deep isolation set in.

In late summer 2001, I loaded up my truck and left the farm for college at the Southern Illinois University in Carbondale. Upon my arrival, I learned a huge new lesson: *There's nothing wrong with you; normal people like you.* This was such a relief— I realized that my past interactions with malicious kids and the isolation of the farm had badly impacted my outlook on life. I made friends and enjoyed life. I still had difficulty in my dealings with single girls, but at a university known for its college of engineering, there were many more male students than females. As gloomy as that may sound, I wasn't the only guy who couldn't get a date, so I didn't feel so bad.

It amazed me that I could go from a situation with enemies around every corner to living life surrounded by friends instead. Still, I carried a nagging feeling that if I had fought back against my opponents and let my anger out through my fists, I would feel more pride in myself. Little did I know that my ability to follow Mom and Dad's lesson would soon be tested to the max.

During the summer of 2003, I was enrolled in the Southern Illinois University Archeology Field School. Going out into the field and working on excavations was a dream come true. The crew was an eclectic bunch of anthropology majors who openly accepted a civil engineering major into their world. When we returned from the excavation site to campus on Friday, July 3, I packed up some clothes, fueled up my truck and headed north. I had a party to attend. My roommate for the past two years had just graduated with a degree in computer science. Phil and I had become friends, and I was thrilled when his parents invited me to the graduation party they were throwing for him. They lived in Springfield, Illinois, which is located about 170 miles from Carbondale. The party was on Saturday afternoon. I decided that I would drive to the farm on Friday evening to see my family. The next day, I would help with chores around the farm in the morning, and then I would drive up to the party in Springfield.

Early on Saturday morning, Dad and I moved off hay bales that he had rolled-up the day before. Once we finished that job, Mom and I decided to take a walk down to the pasture woods and check the cows of the home herd. It was just after ten in the morning, and the day was sunny but not hot. As we left the house, we went through the garden gate and walked past the Pekin ducks dabbling in the muddy pond south of the house. We crossed over the metal pipe gate and walked around the big pond. We always kept the cows fenced out of the big pond so it would stay clear for fishing and swimming. A soft breeze picked up, and blew ripples across the pond's surface that broke up the reflection of the bright blue sky. At the far end, a great blue heron lifted off from the shore. Mom and I crossed at the stile behind the pond and continued into the cows' summer pasture. The fescue grass was healthy and green with seed heads up to my knees. Evidence of the herd grazing was everywhere: cow pies over there, nipped grass all around, and bare soil paths in the heavily traveled areas. The cows had recently grazed in the bottom, and all the paths led back to the pasture woods. We crossed the creek at a riffle as tiny frogs jumped to escape our feet. As we approached the pasture woods, bright sunlight made the trees appear a deep, dark green. A few deer flies buzzed around our heads as we crossed the grassy hills before the woods. Typical of all pastured timber, the south woods was distinctly open on the ground. The cows had eaten all the saplings and any leaves from tree limbs they could reach. The openness of the pasture woods gave it an airy feel. The canopy was held high by the large oak and hickory trees. The shade of the trees and the gentle breeze made the air noticeably cooler than the grassy area we had just left. The cows were enjoying the most peaceful part of their day. As expected, they were all lying down, quietly resting. Many were asleep. Having grown accustomed to our presence over the years, the cows let Mom and me walk among them without stirring. Mom counted the cows to make sure they were all there, and I visited some of my old friends. Silage Cow was happily chewing her cud with her young calf nearby. She leaned her head against me as I scratched behind her ears. She gently rocked her head as if I was hitting the itch that had been bothering her all morning. Good Gray Cow was nearby, lying by the bull. I petted her neck and continued through the herd. I stopped to see Red Rip, City-on-Her-Back, Little Red Cow, Snoopy, Julia Gulia, Slimer's Mom, Swimmer Cow, and South America. Mom finally spoke up and said, "Well, let's head back to the house and get some lunch. Then you better get on the road."

235

I nodded and flashed a grin, "Yeah, I don't want to miss the party!"

Mom gave me a sideways glance and struck a serious tone, "Will, you seem happier nowadays."

I let out a little chuckle and shrugged, "Well, everybody is nice to me down at college."

I decided to drive my family's Pontiac Grand Prix instead of my pickup truck in order to burn less fuel. I would be returning to the farm on Sunday morning, so it would be an easy switch back into my truck. I left the farm, near Newton, at two o'clock, and I decided that my route to Springfield should go through Charleston.

Passing through Charleston on my way to Springfield was not the quickest way to the party, but it wasn't too far out of the way, either. I happened to know a girl from Charleston. Her name was Megan, and she lived on the third floor of my dorm at SIUC. We had a tight-knit community around the dorm, and we often found ourselves in the same groups at the cafeteria, ball games, and the college bars. The only things that I knew about Megan were that she liked to party and she was from Charleston. Before leaving for summer break, I asked her for her phone number just in case I was in Charleston sometime later. She willingly gave me her number and I thought, *Cool, maybe I've got a chance.*

I had mustered up the courage to give her a call at the beginning of my road trip. I picked up my cellphone, and she answered on the second ring, "Hello?"

236

"Hi, Megan. This is Will from SIUC."

And so our conversation started. I explained to her what I was up to and asked if she would be willing to hang out a bit when I drove through Charleston. She said, "sure" and gave me directions to meet her at her parents' place. I was thinking, *Things are going pretty good.*

Megan's parents were college professors that lived in a large house just west of Eastern Illinois University in Charleston. I knocked on the front door, and Megan greeted me and invited me in. Her mom was there, and we visited for a bit until her mom suggested, "Why don't you two go get something to eat?" I thought to myself, *Wow her mom is cool!* Megan agreed with her mom's suggestion, and we went to a Mexican restaurant not far from her house.

Megan and I ordered some food, and then started regaling stories from the dorm. We recounted the comical wrestling match between my roommate, Paul, and Megan's friend, Vincent. Paul stood about five-foot, four-inches tall and weighed 130 pounds. Vincent was six-foot tall and weighed close to 300 pounds. Both had been wrestlers in high school and loved to joke around. Sometimes they would have a half-hearted match in the hall of the dorm. Of course the outcome was predictable; except for one time Paul managed an amazing maneuver that pinned Vincent and left foot prints shoulder-high on the side of the wall. We were enjoying a good laugh when a big group of girls with a couple of guys came walking in. Our conversation abruptly stopped. The girls were all preppy-looking dolls with blond highlights, tight clothes, and painted nails. They all knew Megan, so she greeted them as they passed by our table, but then she looked a bit nervous. Our stories resumed for a few minutes. I told Megan how I managed to avoid a fire drill one morning. Then one of the guys stood up suddenly and stormed out of the restaurant. He swaggered out to his truck and drove off like a bat out of hell. Megan became visibly nervous. Naively, I asked, "What's up?"

She replied, "Well, those are some of my boyfriend's friends, and he is a really jealous guy who hates everything to do with Carbondale."

My first thought was, *You have a boyfriend?* I asked Megan, "So, um, maybe we should get outta here?"

She nodded, and I dropped a twenty on the table for the food.

We made our way to the door and quickly walked to my car. On the drive back to her house, I did my best to maintain a conversation, but soon that gave way to an awkward silence. I dropped her off, and she briskly walked inside. Then, just as I started to drive away, I saw a white Dodge Dakota Sport pickup truck with a brush guard on the front come to a screeching halt in front of the house. A guy got out of the truck and went running up to the front door of her parents' house. I shook my head at the craziness and thought, *See ya, I'm gone!*

Once back on the road, I started to enjoy my road trip again. I really didn't expect much out of my encounter with

Megan. She was always nice to me, but she partied so hard that picturing her as anyone's committed girlfriend seemed like a stretch. Instead of being disappointed, I was looking forward to Phil's graduation party. I glanced at the clock and realized that I would soon be running late. I shrugged off the thought—after living with Phil for two years, I knew that he was a night owl, and the party would still be going on when I arrived.

I drove away from Charleston on Highway 16 and continued through Mattoon. Eleven miles away from the craziness, on the other side of the next town, I looked in my rearview mirror and spotted a familiar white Dodge Dakota Sport pickup truck closing the distance behind me. I could hear the rumbling of his truck's exhaust pipes as the driver aggressively drove up inches behind my car. Inside the truck were three guys all giving me the finger. I checked the mirror again in disbelief. *Wow, what in the hell is wrong with these guys?*

Highway 16 clears out of the west side of Mattoon as a straight two-lane road with corn and bean fields on each side. As I analyzed the situation, it dawned on me that these guys didn't drive all that way over here to simply to give me the finger. In the full sunshine of four o'clock in the afternoon on the Fourth of July, they pulled into the oncoming lane and drove right alongside me. I kept my eyes glued straight ahead and didn't bother acknowledging their aggressive gesturing. Then their truck started crowding over toward my car. I thought, *What the hell! They're trying to run me off the road!* The situation was getting worse. My muscles tightened and I

239

resolved not to let them run me off the asphalt. I kept the car on edge of the pavement and refused to look at them. It became apparent that if I didn't keep ahead of them, they would end up pulling in front of me and blocking my escape. At this point, I decided that I should call 911.

The dispatcher answered, "Nine-one-one, what is your emergency?"

I urgently replied, "I've got a couple of guys who are trying to force me off the road."

"Okay, sir. What is your current location?"

I answered with precision, "Just west of Mattoon on highway 16."

The dispatcher paused and then I heard her ask the others in the room, "Hey, where is Mattoon, Illinois?" I felt my stomach knot up. She returned and asked, "What county is that in?"

Out of the corner of my eye I could see one of the passengers in the truck gesturing and yelling. Any sound was drowned out by the rumbling of the truck's exhaust pipes. The white-colored passenger door was little more than six inches away from my side mirror. I racked my brain to remember what county Mattoon was located in. Sweat began to bead on my forehead. My call had connected to the dispatch center where I bought the cellphone plan, 150 miles away from my current location.

I managed to reply, "Ummm, it's the county next to Coles County."

She curtly asked, "SIR, are you traveling at a high rate of speed?"

I glanced down at the odometer and noticed that the needle was beginning to pass by the ninety mph mark, "Um, I don't think you understand."

The dispatcher cut me off in a perturbed voice, "YOU NEED TO SLOW DOWN."

In the moments I lost focusing on the bossy and unhelpful dispatcher, the pickup truck pulled ahead of me, as I feared. Right before my eyes, the driver pulled a maneuver I had only seen in movies. The aggressor whipped his truck sideways in the road. His tires screeched as the truck slid down the middle of the highway and blocked my path. I stomped on my brakes. The dispatcher came back on the line, "Sir, I am going to contact the county's sheriff's department. I will give them your number, so be expecting a call from them."

Then the line went dead. I dropped the phone and made a decision; *those guys will never catch me. Not today, not tomorrow, not ever. I'm in a faster car, and if this chase goes off-road and they wreck this car, they'll have to chase me on foot.* I took a breath and thought, *Good luck catching me.* Considering all the miles I ran for exercise, I was confident that they could never catch me—I am a runner.

I shifted the car into reverse and started backing up as fast as I could. I covered a quarter mile at forty mph in reverse, but I had to stop when traffic from Mattoon began to approach. I faced forward to see the Dodge Dakota Sport barreling toward me, also in reverse. Thirty yards ahead of me, the driver whipped the truck across both lanes again, but he failed to completely block my lane. I shifted the car into drive and pulled off onto the shoulder and the ditch. Rocks and dust flew as I blasted past his rear bumper. I didn't hold back. A sense of calm came over me as I pushed the accelerator all the way to the floor. *He would never catch me.*

I was willing to speed, but not endanger others in my escape. I slowed down when I approached some traffic in the next small town. The driver of the Dodge Dakota Sport pickup truck didn't care about others and drove like a maniac to catch up with me. He attempted to repeat his crowding maneuver a second time. Then, I heard his truck's tires screech abruptly. Megan's jealous boyfriend and his buddies must have decided to end their chase right outside the county line.

My cellphone rang, "This is the Shelby County Sheriff's dispatch, are you in need of assistance?"

I told the dispatcher of the chase, and she directed me to meet a law enforcement officer at the Casey's Gas Station in Windsor, Illinois. I can remember thinking to myself, *At last, help is on the way.*

I pulled into the gas station and watched two patrol cars scream past with lights and sirens blaring. They were heading to intervene. Unfortunately, they were a few minutes too late; I had already made it out of the fray. I exited the car and sat down on the curb. I felt hyperaware of my surroundings. I suspected that everybody around me was friends with those guys. I felt vulnerable sitting still. A few moments later, a patrol car pulled up next to my vehicle. The officer knew immediately that I was the one in trouble. He took my statement. I wrote down every last detail. People filed in and out of the gas station and stared at us. I could feel them judging me.

I checked over the car to make sure that it wasn't damaged. Everything seemed fine. Apparently, the Grand Prix was made for speed. The officer half-jokingly asked, "So, are you going to see that girl again?"

I shook my head and replied, "Absolutely not."

He cracked a thin smile and said, "Well, you're all right now. Drive safe to Springfield."

I called Phil to let him know why I was running late. Then I called my brother and told him what had just happened and that I was fine. I needed to confide in him. I asked Bob not to tell Mom and Dad because I would tell them about the ordeal later, and I didn't want them to worry. However, a few minutes after getting off the phone with Bob, I received a call from Mom— I suppose that I was asking a lot for Bob to handle a call like that. I was glad to hear Mom's voice.

I arrived in Springfield much later than anticipated. Phil's graduation party had completely wound down. Phil and his parents wore looks of shock when I explained to them what had happened. Phil's dad exclaimed, "Oh, I'm sure glad you didn't stop and try to fight those guys." His comment struck me as odd because the thought of fighting with them never even occurred to me during the ordeal. The next morning Phil and I went out for breakfast and met up with his girlfriend, Melissa. She gave me a huge hug and said, "Phil told me what happened, I'm so glad you're okay!" I retold the story at breakfast and left for the farm afterwards. On the drive back, I considered every last detail. By the time I pulled into the driveway of the farm, excitement and thrill had worn off and full force anger had kicked in. *How unfair is it that I had to be the one to run? Why do things blow up in my face every time I try to pursue a girl? Why wasn't Megan upfront with me? Why is it that girls with boyfriends or husbands like me, and single ones avoid me like the plague? What the hell is wrong with me?*

I parked the car and opened the door. I pulled out the floormat and threw it on the driveway. I handled my anger the only way I knew how—I did pushups. Around the sixty mark, I started getting winded and switched to sets of twenty. When I reached 165 pushups, I collapsed on the mat and closed my eyes. Sweat poured from my forehead, and my ears started ringing. An intense feeling of calm came over me.

Returning to College

When classes resumed at SIUC that fall, things finally started going my way. A group of freshmen girls moved in just down the hall from me. They found me to be a bit of an enigma. I broke several stereotypes they held, and I enjoyed it tremendously. I was the first "country boy" they had ever met who:

1. Didn't chew tobacco.
2. Didn't drive a <u>loud</u> truck.
3. Didn't talk with a hick accent.
4. Didn't act cocky.
5. Ran for exercise.
6. Helped fix their car.

If it wasn't for item six and the farm pictures on my desk, I think they would have seriously doubted my farm credentials. I welcomed their attention, and I felt like my life was moving forward.

Then one night, the past summer's car chase came back to haunt me. It was a Friday night, and a huge group from my dorm was going out to Fred's Dance Barn to party. I had never been to Fred's before, but I decided to go because everyone seemed so excited about the night out. The only thing complicating the night was that Fred's was about ten miles away from Carbondale, and the group was short designated drivers. Since I was a "responsible" senior, I volunteered for the duty. I ended up with two Ambers and a Jessi in my truck. One Amber had a boyfriend, the other was of no interest to me, and Jessi was very much into one of my friends. So this was shaping up to be a less than spectacular Friday night. We arrived at Fred's Dance Barn and paid the cover. Inside, the intense smell of cigarette smoke and loud music dulled my senses. The tables around the dance floor were filled with loud college students celebrating their newfound country-ness. I scanned the dance hall to see where my friends were sitting and recognized someone on the dance floor. Right in the center of the crowd, I saw Megan dancing close with her boyfriend. A surge of anger came over me, and I thought, *Now we're even buster, your friends aren't anywhere around.* My fists clenched, but I held my anger and reconsidered, *Will, you never got a good look at the guy, that might not be the same guy because she could have a different boyfriend! Will, you don't want to get arrested! Will, you have to drive these damn girls home! Will, things are going good for you, don't screw it up!* Knowing that I was on the verge of exploding, I strategically backed away and placed myself at a table near the exit. I sat there for thirty minutes, considering my plight. *Will, you can just leave and the girls will find another ride home. Will, why are you the one who is suffering here? Will, why are you sitting here thinking when you should be having fun? This is completely unfair!*

While lost in complete crisis mode, two arms wrapped around me in a huge bear hug and lifted me off the ground. My initial shock gave way to relief when I realized that it was my good friend, Jessica, "Will, I haven't seen you in sooooo long!" Jessica and I had met the previous year. She was tomboy who dominated the girls' rugby team. When she set me back down on the ground, I explained my situation, and she yelled, "LET'S KICK HIS ASS!"

I busted up laughing.

She grabbed my arm and said, "C'mon, you're hanging out with me and my girlfriends tonight."

That night ended with me telling cow stories to drunken rugby girls, and I couldn't have been happier. I fulfilled my duties as the designated driver, and I found out later that Megan was with a new boyfriend. If I had started a fight, it would have been with the wrong guy. It was twice now that my parents' lesson paid off. My view was changing; I was proud to run.

Chapter 34: Blinding Snow

The winter season typically brings snow to all of Illinois. Normally, the northern areas of the state—near Chicago—catch the first dustings of the season. Then as winter progresses, cold fronts from the Canadian Rockies clash with warm humid air masses from the Gulf of Mexico to produce widespread snowfall. The white blanketing lifts the spirits of many anticipating Christmas and the holidays. Snow is a travel inconvenience, but for those with cattle, snow can mean much bigger problems. Adult cattle and healthy calves are able to cope with the snow and cold weather. However, calves born on snowy ground rarely survive without quick intervention. When a wet newborn drops out of its mother and lands on snow, it quickly loses body heat. If the calf is born on a hay pile, it will generally survive.

During winter, cattle producers address this problem in two ways: First, by stepping up how often they check the cattle, and second, by providing bedding. If a farmer notices that a cow is soon to calve, he can corral her in a shelter during the snowfall or while snow is on the ground. If no shelter is available, the cow can be corralled in a pen with extra hay for bedding. After the snow stops falling, the farmer can move out some junk hay bales to provide extra bedding for the animals. Despite our best intentions over the years we have lost many newborns born on the snow. These losses have forever prejudiced my view of the white stuff used to make snowmen.

Checking the cattle early and often during snowy periods can result in a life-saving intervention. One Saturday in the winter of 2002 Mom made the rounds in the morning to check the cows at Bogota. Her forty-eighth birthday was in November, and gray hairs had rapidly begun replacing the brunette strands of her youth. She wore her heavy coveralls over her favorite blue jeans and sweatshirt. She also wore some wrinkles on her face. Dad was away at work, and she feared that the light snowfall overnight and the extreme cold could mean trouble for the cattle. While driving the work truck up to the Bogota pasture, she listened to 95.7 WCRC. The radio station out of Effingham played old country songs and reported a temperature of five degrees with the wind chill well below zero. The clouds that produced the snow were gone and had been replaced by a cold northerly wind that blasted the landscape. It was the type of cold that pierced right through Mom's coveralls. Being a thin woman, she definitely felt the chill.

She opened the gate and instead of dumping a couple of buckets of feed in the trough, she drove the work truck back to the hay pile to check the cows. With temperatures that cold, she didn't want the cows to leave the hay pile for corn at the trough. The cows and calves were huddled together with beads of snow frozen in their fur. They stoically chewed their cuds while the smallest calves nursed for extra energy. She counted the herd once and came up with thirty-four. She counted the herd a second time and the number didn't change. She needed thirty-five, one cow was missing.

Mom trudged a quick circle around the hay piles to make sure one was not out of view yet in close proximity. No luck. She walked down the trail to the watering hole in the
249

creek and still came up one cow short. Her fingers inside the thin jersey gloves ached from the cold. She climbed back into the cab of the truck and decided that maybe the missing cow could be spotted from the north road along the pasture.

While driving slowly along the north border, Mom peered out the driver's side window, looking for her missing cow. Her breath fogged up the cold glass, so she had to roll down the window. About halfway along the border, she neared the bridge over the creek. From this vantage point she looked up into the bluffs and spotted the missing cow. The yellow Charolois was fifty yards off the road, behind a large oak tree. Mom parked the truck, crossed the barbed-wire fence, and walked up to the cow. In the exposed roots of a pin oak tree lay a newborn calf, shivering. Mom considered her options while the cold north wind blew drifting snowflakes against her face and caused her eyes to water. *If the boys were here, I would have them carry the calf to the truck. There's no way I can carry him or lift him into the cab of the truck.* Mom returned to the truck and grabbed a grungy sweatshirt from behind the seat. While the mother cow patiently looked on, she rubbed the calf vigorously, then covered him with the sweatshirt like a blanket. She left for the house knowing that the calf needed some warm milk.

Back home, she quickly warmed up some frozen colostrum. She put four pints in a bottle, and capped it with a nipple. As she headed out the door, she also grabbed the esophageal tube just in case. On the drive to Bogota, WCRC played the classic Tammy Wynette tune "Stand By Your Man," then reported that the temperature had risen to a whole ten degrees with the wind chill hovering between zero and minus five degrees. Mom turned off the radio.

Before she stepped down from the cab of the truck, Mom slipped the bottle into the front of her coveralls to keep the milk warm. She slid the esophageal tube into the back pocket of her coveralls and walked up the hill to the calf. The mother cow looked on as Mom held the calf's head and placed the nipple in his mouth. Mom spoke to the cow, "It's okay girl, I'm trying to help him. I'm sorry you had him last night." The calf's slobber felt cold. She worked with the calf for a few minutes, trying to encourage it to nurse. Mom feared for what she had to do next. The chilled calf wouldn't nurse a bottle, so she had to use the esophageal tube.

The esophageal tube is an attachment to a bottle composed of flexible hose with an eighteen-inch section made of stiff plastic pipe. When newborn calves are unable or unwilling to nurse a bottle, the plastic tube is slid down the calf's esophagus, and milk is routed straight to the calf's rumen. It is most unpleasant for the calf and not without risks because if the milk spills into the trachea, the calf drowns. Like so many tasks on the farm, one simply must grit their teeth and do it.

Mom felt her gut tighten; she had never fed a calf via an esophageal tube on her own before. She'd held calves while Dad, Bob, and I used the tube on many occasions. She had also seen calves die when things went wrong, but with the situation at hand she didn't have a choice. She mimicked what we did by using her legs to hold the calf. She carefully slipped the tube down the calf's throat until its lower teeth matched up with the previous bite marks on the tube. She held his head with one arm and raised the bottle with the other. Warm milk started flowing into the calf's stomach. He let out a gurgled bawl, and she nervously said, "It's okay little guy, just a bit more." When the bottle ran empty, she lowered his head and slowly pulled the tube back out of the calf's throat. He coughed and ran his tongue around his mouth. Mom vigorously rubbed the calf and said, "That wasn't so bad, now, was it?" She retrieved an empty feed sack from the back of the truck and laid it on the snowy ground under the calf as a barrier. She placed the sweatshirt back atop the calf and headed home. She had done all she could do without help. She didn't know it at the time, but her actions had just saved that calf's life.

Alive

Dad returned home from work that frigid afternoon. His job away from the farm was managing Sam Parr State Park. The park was composed of 1,180 acres with a 183-acre fishing lake, hunting areas, camping, hiking, and picnicking. The community made good utilization of the park and kept my dad busy. During the spring, summer, and fall, there were always events happening: high school cross country races, archery shoots, family reunions, weddings, fun runs, fishing tournaments, dove hunting, and youth conservation day. Things slowed down in the winter, and the park staff focused on building nest boxes for wood ducks. When Dad first stepped into the house, Mom laughed and said, "Go outside and shake off. You are covered in sawdust!" He stepped to the edge of the porch and brushed off. Dad hadn't noticed the thick layer of dust in his bushy mustache. As he turned to come back in the house, he nearly ran into Mom pulling on her coveralls. She said, "We've got to go pick up a calf at the Bogota pasture."

They drove around the north side of the Bogota pasture and parked near the bridge. Dad walked up the bluff to pick up the calf. Mom stayed at the truck and gathered up the pile of empty Diet Coke cans that rattled around the passenger-side floorboard; they needed that spot for the calf. She had just finished throwing the cans in a feed bucket in the bed of the truck, when Dad returned with the calf and placed him on the newly cleared floorboard. Mom slid her feet down beside it. When Dad climbed back in the cab, he said, "Brrr! It's still really cold out." He turned the truck's heater on high and headed back toward the house.

That night, Mom and Dad kept the newborn bull calf in the warm, dry basement. Before bedtime Mom looked in the bathroom mirror and noticed that her face was badly chapped from the cold wind. She wondered how the newborn calf had survived out in that intense cold for a single minute.

The next morning, the calf was noticeably stronger, and he nursed a bottle. The winds had calmed during the night, and by noon the temperature rose to twenty-five degrees. The outside air felt distinctly warmer. When Dad returned from work that evening, they took the calf back to the pasture. This time they called the cows to the trough and corralled the calf's mother. Dad poured some ground corn in a pan for the cow. The yellow cow hungrily chowed down on the corn and allowed Dad to walk the calf over to her udder. He took a bottle half-full of milk and let the calf nurse it for a few moments. Then he took the bottle away and pushed the calf's head to the cow's nipples. With a little coaxing, the calf started sucking on one of her nipples. While working with the calf, Mom noticed that its eyes appeared cloudy. They had suspicions that the calf might have been blinded by the cold wind.

Over the next few days, Mom and Dad made a point to feed the little calf a bottle of milk whenever they checked the Bogota herd. As he grew stronger, their fears were confirmed—the calf was indeed blind. The intense wind and cold temperatures had frozen his eyes and caused permanent damage. A blind calf can be raised by the cow to be perfectly healthy, but such a calf is difficult to herd, corral, and load into a trailer. Furthermore, once the calf is grown to full size, it cannot be driven around the show ring at a sale barn. Essentially, a blind calf won't fetch a fair price.

Soon, the young calf became known as "Blindy." While at first we had no intention of naming him, the descriptive moniker streamlined daily conversations, so it stuck. Since Blindy lost his eyesight at birth, he seemed to manage pasture life better than those cattle that lose their sight later in life. Blindy learned to follow the sounds of other cows, and his mother proved to be a top-notch cow; she always found him when it was time to nurse. The calf also stayed tame. Whenever we checked on the Bogota herd, we

254

made a point to pet Blindy and talk to him. His ears became well-tuned to listen for footsteps, and he welcomed human voices by facing their origin and shaking his head, begging for petting. As we petted his back, Blindy would turn his head toward us and lick the knees of our overalls. It was a sign of affection from a little calf that we were lucky to save.

We were worried when it came time to wean Blindy. His mother needed time to gain weight and fat reserves for her next calf. While Blindy had done well in the pasture without vision, we feared that weaning him might be easier said than done. We approached the challenge of loading him in the trailer by leading him. Mom walked in front of Blindy and called to him while Bob quietly walked behind. Whenever he stopped, Bob would gently push him. It was an unconventional tactic, but it worked. They loaded Blindy in the cattle trailer first, and then herded in the rest of weaning-age calves. When they opened the trailer and let the calves out into the feeder lot, Blindy walked out of the trailer last and gingerly followed the sound of his comrades' hootsteps over to the trough. Blindy would do just fine in the feedlot.

It's Blindy

We knew all along what would happen to Blindy. It was accepted that bull calves would be weaned, castrated into steers, fed out in the feedlot, then loaded into the cattle trailer and hauled to the sale barn. This wasn't sad—it was simply fact. We raised beef cattle for profit, and if no one ate beef, I would have never had the chance to know so many wonderful cows. Dad realized that if Blindy was taken to the sale barn, cattle buyers would bid very little for a blind fat-calf. Their reluctance to pay full price was simply due to the difficulty in herding blind calves and not because of any problems with the meat. We decided that rather than be insulted by a low-ball price, we would have Blindy custom butchered at a local processor. Then we could keep some of the beef, and my aunt and uncle's family could buy some.

In rural areas, butchering one's own farm-raised calf is a common practice—except for my family. Dad was an avid hunter, and he had raised all three of his kids to be effective with a gun and bow. Every year we hunted the deer that inhabited our property. Normally, we harvested several deer and filled the freezers with "farm-raised" venison. We didn't eat the cattle because doing so would be eating into our profit. Anyway, we had plenty of deer. In addition to hunting deer, we also hunted squirrels, doves, ducks, geese, rabbits, and turkeys. In the Gillespie household, it was completely normal to have fried squirrel for one meal, followed by roast deer for the next, followed by baked goose legs, followed by duck fajitas, followed by turkey and dumplings, followed by fried rabbit, followed by grilled doves. It was all considered meat, and we didn't discriminate against the source. The only time we ate beef was at restaurants.

As it turned out, the blind calf provided beef for many great meals. One meal was particularly memorable. During the spring semester of 2004, I started dating a very special girl. Laura was not a country girl. She grew up in the suburbs of St. Louis and Chicago. While I had a good grasp on all things rural, she was used to a more urban setting. I liked that she was adventurous and not afraid to try new things.

256

Whenever Laura visited the farm, she loved seeing all the cows, chickens, ducks, and cats. She even welcomed the hunting. She asked lots of questions and absorbed all of this new knowledge with an open mind. In August 2004, Laura came up to the farm to visit for a couple of weeks. It was the perfect season for a farm visit because the workload was light, and I had plenty of time to show her around. Laura arrived at the farm just before lunch on a blue-sky Saturday. When she approached, she noticed that the pole barn was open and honked the car horn as she pulled in. I left whatever I was working on and ran out to meet her. We went up to the house. Mom had cooked a beef round roast that was sliced thin to make roast beef sandwiches. We sat down at the table, and Laura innocently asked, "So what kind of meat are we having? It smells delicious!"

Mom nonchalantly replied, "Oh, it's beef."

Laura assumed that we commonly ate beef for lunch because we raised cattle. She jokingly asked, "Which one is it?" Her expectation was that we would shrug and not know. Au contraire!

Mom quietly answered, "It's Blindy."

The smile on Laura's face dimmed and she squeaked.

I laughed heartily and teased her, "I don't think you were prepared for that answer!"

Chapter 35: Ruffler

My girlfriend's understanding of farm life grew by leaps and bounds the first few months that she dated me. However, anyone with such a limited exposure to farming is bound to make some rookie mistakes. One of Laura's first mistakes resulted in some hilarious consequences. Since she was spending a few weeks on the farm, I had several small projects planned that I thought would be fun for us to work on together. One of these projects was bringing the pet tomcat from the barnyard at home up to the feedlot to catch rats at the corn feeder. I thought it would be a straightforward mission:

1. Pick up the lazy pet tomcat while he snoozed on the patio.
2. Place him in the cab of the work truck and drive to the feedlot.
3. Carry the tomcat out to the corn feeder where the bold rats would climb up and taunt me while I did chores.
4. Release the tomcat to attack the rats like a lion takes down a gazelle.
5. Leave the tomcat to his work for a few hours.
6. Pick him up from his new lazing spot and place him in the cab of the work truck.
7. Return him to the barnyard of the house.

Perhaps it was naive of me to think any cat would go along with a human's plans, but our tomcat, Ruffler, was quite used to being handled. Also he always seemed to enjoy meals that he caught. The first step of the plan was easy. Ruffler barely seemed to notice that we had picked him up. He purred loudly up until the moment that we closed the truck doors. At this point, Ruffler's eyes opened wide, and he climbed up to the top of my headrest. His anxiety worried me, but he was trapped in the truck, so we proceeded with the plan and drove to the feedlot. He sunk his claws deep into the head rest and scarcely moved for the five-mile trip. Occasionally, he would let out a long, "Maaaaooooooo!" but mostly he just stared outside at the moving scenery. Once at the feedlot, Laura had to remove him from his perch. Something about a female's touch seemed to calm Ruffler, and we continued with the plan. Laura carried him out to the corn feeder while I drove the CaseIH 2294 and disk over to a small plot in the former feedlot. We planned to plant it to wheat that fall. I had been tilling the ground for about fifteen minutes when Laura came running out into the field waving her arms. I throttled back the engine, hit the clutch, and shifted the tractor to neutral. I climbed down from the cab to meet Laura. She was breathless but managed to say, "I got shocked, and Ruffler ran away." The look on Laura's face told me that I should be concerned, but the absurdity of the situation struck me as funny.

"What?" I asked while suppressing the urge to laugh.

Laura filled in the details: When she took Ruffler over to the feeder, she set him on the ground and the rats froze in place. The tomcat must have been unclear on the mission because he was oblivious to the motionless prey. He pranced over to some shade by the fence and lay down. Laura noticed the brazen rats and was devoted to the plan, so she pursued the tomcat. She reached over a singular wire and started petting Ruffler as he rolled over by the woven wire fence. At that moment, the inside of her forearm touched the electric fence. The current shot down through her arm to her fingertips, through the tomcat, and into the ground. Neither Laura nor Ruffler had ever experienced an electric fence before. The shock is startling and painful for a large animal. It's even worse for a 100-pound woman and a nine-pound domestic cat. Ruffler let out a "MEEROOOOOOWWWWW! HISSSSSS!" and ran from Laura into the nearby barn. She immediately began to worry that Ruffler would end up lost at the feedlot forever.

I was able to contain my urge to laugh and instead consoled Laura, "Don't worry about that tomcat, he'll be fine!"

Looking at her arm, she said, "See, Will, there's a red line going down to my fingertip." With a good measure of sympathy I assured Laura that she was just fine, and we walked over to check on Ruffler in the barn. We found him easily because he was still vocalizing his displeasure at the situation, as cats do. Hunched in the corner, his hair was sticking up at odd angles, and one eye seemed more fully dilated than the other.

My better judgment took over and I said, "Why don't we leave him alone for a while."

Laura climbed up into the cab of the tractor with me and rode while I finished disking the field. We checked on Ruffler again. He was the same so we headed back to the house. Our plan was to retrieve Ruffler from the feedlot during our evening chores.

We returned to the feedlot at six o'clock. I filled two buckets of corn and carried them out to the trough for the feeder calves. Meanwhile, Laura went to find Ruffler. She didn't have to look very far; over by the fat calves' corn feeder, Ruffler was eating a rat. The mission's objective had indeed worked, despite some setbacks. We waited for Ruffler to finish his meal; then we picked him up and jumped in the truck. Ruffler spent the duration of the ride clinging onto the truck's headrest for dear life. When we arrived back at home, I got out of the truck and expected Ruffler to run out. Instead he very slowly and sheepishly clawed his way down the seat. Then he jumped out of the truck and ambled away nonchalantly.

Icefishing

A few years later, we had an especially cold spell in January. This was difficult for the cattle, but it enabled us to enjoy a rare winter activity in south-central Illinois: ice fishing. In the southern half of the state, weather dictates that we are only able to go ice fishing a few times every two or three years. It's a pretty novel activity: chop a hole in the ice, drop down a baited hook on a line, and pull out a fish. In the smaller ponds found around farms, ice fishing can be incredible if the conditions are right. You can catch a fish, unhook it, re-bait the hook and catch another fish in rapid succession. That particular year I took Laura with me down to the pond. Ruffler followed behind us, thinking that we must be up to something interesting. We walked out onto the ice, and I chopped a small square hole with the axe. While I got our gear ready, Ruffler lapped up cold pond water from the new hole. Then he must have realized that his paws were freezing and sticking to the ice. He climbed right up the outside of my overalls and coat. Thankfully, my thick winter clothes withstood the claws and shielded me from getting scratched. He stood on my shoulders, keeping his paws off the ice below.

A few minutes later, Laura caught a fish. It was a nice bluegill, about eight inches long. When it came flopping out of the hole and landed on the ice, Ruffler jumped off my shoulders and dashed over to the fish. Laura scolded him and put the fish in the bucket and sat on it. The tomcat then started an intense campaign to guilt us into giving him the fish. He paced by Laura and meowed repeatedly. We continued to fish, and Ruffler simply would not stop. He jumped on Laura's lap and protested loudly until finally she stood up, and Ruffler jumped in the bucket. She sat back down and trapped him. In a few moments crunching noises came from inside the bucket. We sat in a comical silence while imagining Ruffler devouring the bluegill. Soon, I caught another fish. I unhooked it and threw it out on the ice. The fish flopped in the powdery snow and then began to freeze. The snow stuck to the fish like cornmeal breading sticks to a fillet. Laura caught another fish, and we soon began to feel bad for Ruffler, who was still trapped inside the bucket. She stood up and started laughing. She grabbed my arm and said, "Look, Will! He ate the fins off the fish." I looked in the bucket expecting to see a half-eaten fish, but instead, there was a bluegill in pristine condition except for the missing fins. Apparently Ruffler was not paying attention when his momma cat taught him how to eat a fish.

Squirrels

The next summer, Ruffler took a great interest in the fox squirrels that inhabited the yard trees. The squirrels barked at Ruffler incessantly. Ruffler slept most of the daytime, but every now and then, he would try to ambush a squirrel. We dismissed his efforts as futile and sided with the squirrels. One day, Mom came home from work to find a squirrel tail in the front driveway. In true cat style, Ruffler had eaten most of his catch and left the tail where we would spot his trophy.

But Ruffler had not won the battle unscathed—back near his tail was a large squirrel bite. We dismissed it as minor, but as time went on, the wound became infected. It seeped fluid constantly, and Ruffler started to get ill. I teased him that the yard squirrels were venomous. Mom, Sarah, and Laura all spoke up for Ruffler and insisted that we take him to the vet. Dad rebuffed their insistence and advocated that Ruffler would get over this infection on his own.

One day I drove into the barn lot and found him lying in the driveway. At first, I thought he was dead. I decided that I would take him away and bury him, so I climbed down from the truck and walked over to him. He weakly turned his head and looked at me. I was upset. I thought to myself, *Why did we let him get this sick? He may be a barn cat, but he is a great pet.* This situation was simply unacceptable. I had to do something for our pet cat. I took Ruffler up to the house and gently set him in the yard. I rummaged through our medical supplies until I found some tiny hypodermic needles that were intended for allergy shots in the distant past. I then looked through the leftover cattle medicine that we kept in the refrigerator. Behind an old jar of jelly, I pulled out a bottle of LA200[26] that had been prescribed earlier for a calf with pneumonia. A bit was leftover from treating the calf, so we just kept the bottle around in case we needed to treat another calf. In this case, I was going to treat a cat. I looked at the label. No guidance was provided for dosage to cats. I shook my head at the ridiculousness of the situation, and I called our cattle veterinarian. "Hi, Joe, this is Will Gillespie. I'm embarrassed to ask this, but we've got a damn barnyard tomcat that has got a gangrene infection. I've got some leftover LA200 in the fridge. Could I give him some of that?"

Joe chuckled, "Why, yeah. Try giving him one cc a day for three days, and see what happens."

Now I had a plan. I asked for volunteers to help me hold the tomcat still while I gave him an injection. Sarah and Laura were standing nearby, ready to help. I found a pair of leather gloves for each of them and said, "I don't think you'll need these, but I've never given a shot to a cat before, and I don't want anyone to get scratched by Ruffler."

We stepped outside and found Ruffler in the shade where I had left him. He was unable to walk or even hold his head up. He looked inches away from death. Sarah and Laura held him while I administered shots under the skin on both sides of his neck. Ruffler was so sick that he didn't even seem to notice. We set him back down in the shade and left him in peace. I didn't expect him to recover, but a few hours later

---

[26] LA200 is a broad spectrum antibiotic called Oxytetracycline. It is produced by Pfizer animal health.
http://www.pfizerah.com/Print_Friendly.aspx?drug=lq&country=us&lang=en&species=da&s=/product_overview.aspx

we returned to see a noticeable difference in Ruffler. There was more light in his eyes, his wounds were rapidly draining, and when we petted him, he would weakly call, "maaaooo, maaaooo". On day two we repeated his injections. Ruffler let out a weak "rrraaaoow" when I injected him, but made no attempt to squirm. His condition continued improving—he even began to eat again. This was a good thing, except he had become incontinent and was making an awful mess in the yard where he was sleeping. He was still unable to walk, so we moved him to a new shady spot away from his mess. On day three, we repeated his injections. This time, Ruffler clearly was not happy about the situation. He was more vocal and attempted to squirm away.

The medicine worked wonders for Ruffler. Within a few days, he was able to move around a bit by dragging his back end. Every day he continued to eat and grow stronger. Sometimes the squirrels would cut nuts in the tree above Ruffler and bark at him. I teased the squirrels and Ruffler, "You fluffy-tail freaks, quit giving him a hard time. As for you Ruffler; just leave the squirrels alone. We feed you plenty of kitty food." The squirrels disregarded my scolding and continued barking at Ruffler. It took weeks and weeks for Ruffler to fully recover, but by that winter, he was back to his old antics.

Chapter 36: Pasture to Bean Field

In the summer of 2004, I took a road trip to Willow Springs, Missouri, for a job interview with the Missouri Department of Transportation. The small town is located about eighty miles east of Branson. From my apartment in Carbondale, Illinois, it was a 223-mile drive. I left Carbondale at four-thirty in the morning and drove three-and-a-half hours before I rolled into Willow Springs. As planned, I arrived early, and located the MoDOT office. Then I drove to a nearby restaurant to eat some breakfast and relax. At nine-thirty, I met with the MoDOT engineers and had a good interview. Afterwards, one of the engineers drove me out to see their latest project. It was a major reroute of US-63 around the southwest side of town. As he pulled onto the wide four-lane road, I couldn't help but notice an old white barn nearby. The entire side of the barn was painted with black bold text that read something like, "MODOT STOLE MY LAND TO ROUTE AROUND DOWNTOWN BUSINESSES!" The engineer noticed me reading the barn and arrogantly commented, "That whole family has been nothing but troublemakers on this road project. Apparently they don't understand..."

I nodded as he continued blabbing away, but thought to myself, "Please stop talking. I understand this type of conflict all too well."

When we arrived back at the office, the head engineer and the human resources director handed me a letter. It was a job offer. I thanked them for the interview and expressed that I would respond to the letter in the next couple of days. I walked out of the office to my truck, and then started the long *drive back to Carbondale. Along the way I had plenty of windshield time and I began to think about my family's own roadway conflict.*

R.O.W.

In areas of the Midwest where property lines were laid out by the General Land Office, a township consists of a six-mile by six-mile square. Those that live within the township elect a board. A portion of the property taxes is allotted to the township board, and this money is used for maintenance of township roads. Every four years, an election is held for township road commissioner. This individual is paid a salary to maintain the township roads. Duties of the position include replacing washed-out culverts, running a drag on gravel roads, mowing the grass in the road ditches, clearing trees that fall on the road, filling potholes, clearing snow in the winter, replacing road signs that become too bullet-riddled, and posting signage for construction or closed roads. It's a long list, but when those duties are spaced out over the course of a year, it's not a difficult job.

In April 2001, the people of Smallwood Township elected Max Smith to the position of township road commissioner. He replaced the longtime incumbent road commissioner, Melvin Birk. Some residents felt that Smith would be a good road commissioner because they claimed he'd get things done. In retrospect that kind of thinking now makes me cringe. Smith farmed a little, did carpentry a little, rode horses a lot, and loafed at the welding shop a lot. In the run up to the election, he seemed to be constantly hanging out at the welding shop. A member of the township board ran it, and over the years his shop had become an old roosters club of sorts. Hanging out at the welding shop was easy campaigning for Smith and he won the election. We didn't know it then, but Max Smith as the township road commissioner was bad news for us and the cows of the Bogota pasture.

The township road 400 North runs east-west along the north side of our former Bogota pasture. In the two-and-a-half-mile stretch from the Bogota-Wakefield blacktop to the township line, the road served three residents and provided access to several farm fields, including the north side of our pasture. It was a quiet gravel road that crossed over Wolf Creek just before the stream ran into our Bogota pasture. Besides being a trap for catching drunk drivers, as described in an earlier chapter, the creek also had a tendency to flood and wash gravel off the road. In the spring of 2002, the weather was abnormally wet. The dank, humid air smelled of mold because day after day heavy showers came and flooded the farm fields. All the runoff gathered in the ditches and flowed into the creeks and rivers, causing them to rise beyond their banks. When Wolf Creek overtopped the bridge, it washed away some of the gravel, and formed gullies in the road. Smith addressed the damaged road by hauling in some more gravel and smoothing the surface with the road grader. While doing this work, he noticed that some willow trees had sprouted in the creek channel just downstream of the bridge. Sandy sediment was building up in the willow sprouts, and he decided that removing the willow trees would improve the conveyance of water under the bridge. He reasoned that if conveyance was improved, perhaps the creek wouldn't overtop the bridge again and wash out the road. He approached my dad and asked if he could remove the willows with his backhoe. The willow trees were right along the road's right of way and most likely on Gillespie land, too. We didn't have a problem with his plan, and we moved a section of the water gap so that he could take out the willows.

While the willow trees were being removed, the Gillespie Farm was in full-on scramble mode. The heavy rains had finally ceased enough that we were rushing from field to field evaluating which areas needed to be completely replanted. It was depressing; so much of our first planted seeds simply rotted in the ground. A few fields could be salvaged by touching-up the thin areas with more seed. Bob was working on that task by patching up the cornfields. Dad and I were scouting for the next least-sodden field to replant with soybeans when we happened to drive along 400 North. Smith was excavating the sediment and the willows with the backhoe and had the road blocked. He climbed down off the backhoe, put on his cowboy hat and walked over to talk with my dad. With a strong nasally whine he said, "Jim, I would like you to move that fence on top of that there hill so I can take it down with my road grader."

Dad hesitated and then responded, "Max, we can't deal with that right now. We're doing all we can just to get our crops replanted. Let's talk after planting season when we've got some time to do fence work."

As we drove away I noticed that Dad was visibly annoyed by Smith's request. Moving a well-built barbed wire fence is no easy task. We would have to completely remove the fence: untie the wire clips (four per post), take off the first string of barbed wire and roll it, then the next and the next, until all four barbed wire strands were rolled up. Then we would have to pull several posts and pound them back in the ground just a few feet further away from the road. Once the posts were set, we would have to unroll each string of barbed wire, tighten it, and tie it back to the posts. All this would probably have to be done on the hottest day of the year while we would be wearing leather gloves and tough blue jeans for protection against cuts. Also we'd be fighting off the biting deer flies we called "green-eyed bastards." Moving the fence would most likely cost us two days. We didn't understand why Smith was so concerned about grading down a hill along such a minor road.

Dad wiped his forehead on his shirtsleeve, "What the hell, Will. Only three folks live along this road. I just don't get it."

With all the worries on Dad's mind, the last thing he needed was two days devoted to doing fence work for a road project that wasn't all that necessary. We moved ahead with replanting the corn and bean fields, applying nitrogen fertilizer, mowing hay, and doing all the millions of tasks that need to be done on the farm in the spring and early summer seasons. During this time, Dad was also working off the farm managing a state park, I was working for the Illinois Department of Transportation as an intern, Bob was working

270

for the Forest Service, and Mom was teaching school. My sister Sarah was only fifteen years old, in high school, and more than ready for the school year to end. To say that we were busy was an understatement. When June rolled around, we harvested wheat and planted beans in the stubble. By the last week of June, we had nearly caught up on our work when, unbeknownst to us, Smith drove his road grader from the township garage over to 400 North. He proceeded to scrape away the soil along the 200-yard stretch of fence that he asked us to move earlier. That evening after Mom had been checking cattle, she met us "boys" at the door. The frantic look on her face told it all. In the steepest areas, he actually removed the soil beneath the fence, destroying its structural integrity. He had made no attempt to contact us after the earlier conversation. We were taken completely off guard.

The damaged fence was along the twenty-two-acre section of the pasture we called Earl's hills. Fortunately, it was linked to the main fifty-one-acre pasture by a gate. We shut the gate and were able to keep the cows away from the damaged fence. Closing off this pasture was sad to us because less than seven years ago, we had completely rebuilt the fence around Earl's hills and added it to the cow's pasture. Back during the winter of 1995, it seemed like every weekend had been spent working on that fence. We had worked together as a family to remove all the old fencing and build a strong new fence. Even my brother's new girlfriend helped out. At only seven years old, the Earl's Hills section of pasture was encircled by a fence that was still shiny, and now we were forced to keep the cows away from it because of the road commissioner's actions. We immediately contacted Smith and asked him to stop. His reply was belligerent. Mom called the county sheriff and asked what could be done to stop the destruction of our property.

It was a frustrating situation; it seemed that the road commissioner had started a project with no written plan, no research into road right-of-ways; and, more importantly, he had alienated a landowner who would have worked with him. Mom contacted the township board secretary and asked that "Fence Damage along 400 North" be placed on the next meeting's agenda. All five of my family members attended this meeting because we had worked so hard as a family to build that section of fence. The meeting was held on the first Tuesday evening of every month in a small building that resembled a one-room schoolhouse. An hour before the board met, a severe thunderstorm rumbled through the area and knocked out power to much of Smallwood Township. As a result, the township building was nearly dark when we entered. The open door allowed in just enough dim light to distinguish the faces of the board members. Quiet murmuring passed around the room as we sat down in the chairs along the wall. The room was tense as they began their meeting. The normal business items on the agenda lasted twenty minutes. When the board finally came to "Fence Damage along 400 North," Mom and Dad described what happened. They expressed that a portion of our fence no longer had any structural integrity because the soil beneath the posts had been removed. We also told the board that the road commissioner's actions were vandalism of private property. Their reply was not surprising; the oldest board member named Floyd piped up, "Why don't you understand that we need this road work done?" Some of the board members insisted that the removal of soil was not vandalism and that the road commissioner had acted appropriately. We knew that the meeting was a lost cause when another board member brought up an unrelated grievance. We left the meeting with a sinking feeling that this problem was only going to get worse.

Mom and Dad had no idea what to do next. Dad wanted to avoid any conflict; however Mom was ready to take some kind of action. She arranged a meeting with the Jasper County State's Attorney. Our fence had been damaged and it didn't seem fair to us that no one could be held responsible. Dad wasn't able to attend the meeting with Mom. Between farming and managing the state park, he didn't have a minute to spare. Mom figured that he was using the "busy card" to avoid dealing with a confrontational meeting. Either way, Bob went along with Mom instead. After the meeting I heard all about the encounter. Mom expressed that although the State's Attorney reiterated Smith's opinion that our land along the road must be graded down in order for the road project to proceed, the State's Attorney was open to considering our concerns. As we sat around the supper table that evening, Mom said, "At the end of the meeting I was just engaging the attorney in conversation, when I said that her job had to be a difficult one, always dealing with conflict. She had replied, 'Oh, I love it.'"

Ironically, no one could show us a plan for this road project that everyone seemed to mention. Then, on September 2, 2002, we received a letter from the county state's attorney indicating that we had ten days to move the fence along the 200-yard stretch that Smith had previously undercut with the road grader. There would be no reimbursement for damages because the road commissioner had claimed the fence line was in the road's right of way. As threatened, the 200-yard section of fence was bulldozed out. Then, on September 12, we received a second letter from the county state's attorney expressing that the entire stretch of fence from the bridge east was going to be removed. This was the entire north boundary of the Earl's hills section. We were furious. The fence had been the boundary for the previous 150 years. As promised the fence along the entire north boundary of Earl's Hills was pushed out with a bulldozer and hauled away. One side of the Earl's Hills portion of the Bogota pasture had been removed. We had worked so hard to build that fence. Watching it torn out for a plan-less road project without any kind of compensation was simply exasperating.

On November 5, we contacted Connor and Connor Surveying to get the road right-of-way surveyed. This was a step that the road commissioner should have taken before even starting the project. The surveyors called the county engineer to locate records for the road's right-of-way. The county engineer told the surveyor that there were no records for 400 North. It seemed that Smith had removed the fence without any knowledge of where the road's right-of-way was located.

Road Improvement?

The fence and excess soil excavated from our land was hauled away. Oddly, the soil and fence posts he removed did not end up being used on any township road projects. Instead, that material ended up in Smith's horse pasture. As the weather turned cool in late fall, Smith graded some of the newly excavated soil out into the road, and then spread crushed stone over it. The weather turned rainy and the un-compacted road bed turned into mud. The road became impassible. The few residents along the road were furious and called the road commissioner to fix the situation. Smith dumped more gravel on the road in an attempt to keep it passable, but the freeze and thaw of winter only turned the road into a quagmire. One night Mom got a call from one of the road's residents. The lady screamed, "Patty, my child is sick, and I can't get him to the emergency room because I'll get stuck on this road! If you would have taken that fence out like the road commissioner asked we wouldn't have this problem!"

Mom suspected the call was really just harassment. She slipped into schoolteacher mode and calmly replied, "I'm sorry to hear that your son is sick. We have a four-wheel-drive pickup truck. I will be right up there to pick you both up and take you to the emergency room."

The lady stuttered saying, "N-No, we don't need that!" and slammed down the phone.

Smear Campaign

One day I walked into the Wakefield Mill and noticed that the bench of loafers fell silent as I approached the counter. Kelly, the mill's owner stood up from his desk and cheerfully asked, "Hi, Will, what do you need today?"

I casually replied, "Well, I'll start with four bags of protein supplement for grinding feed, and a little bag of peanuts for me."

As I set the money on the counter, the silence of the loafers grew awkward. I could feel eyes burning into my back. Finally, I looked over my shoulder to see Smith's face scowling at me from the end of the bench. I slowly turned forward and noticed Kelly's eyes look to the door as he met my glance. He cheerfully continued without hesitation, "The supplement is out in the feed shed. I know you can load it, but I'll give you a hand. I think that I left some mineral tubs in front of the pallet." Kelly and I walked out of the store and headed toward the feed shed. He glanced behind to make sure the door was closed and offered some consolation, "I have a feeling you know a lot about what was being said in there."

I let out a sigh and nodded my head, "Yeah I do."

The Real Purpose

We feared that soon Smith would decide to remove the fence along the entire north boundary of the larger fifty-one-acre portion of the Bogota pasture. With Bob and me busy off the farm, we had no time to construct new fence. Most importantly, even if we could, where would we set it? Since the township road commissioner acted without documentation of the road's right-of-way to begin with, what would stop him from claiming a wider setback in the future?

We thought that our frustration had peaked, but then mid-winter Dad got a call. It was Dick Dickerson. Dick ran an excavating business and had built several ponds for us over the years. He loved to coon hunt during the winter, and I had gone with him a few times. We considered him a friend. In his gravelly voice Dick said, "Jim, the road commissioner asked me to do some dozer work, and I just wanted to call and find out more."

Dad replied, "Ugh… What's going on?"

Dick continued, "Smith wanted me to figure an estimate for opening up an old road along your narrow forty-acre property, east of your pasture. He told me that where the fencerow and trees are now was once an old township road that was never closed. Now, Jim, you've let me coon hunt over that way, and I know that the fencerow through there is grown up in big old pin oaks. Hell, if it's a road, it sure hasn't been driven on in at least fifty years. Are YOU wanting that road opened up?"

Dad sighed and responded, "Oh, boy. Well, I'm glad you called because we definitely don't want that opened up." Dad proceeded to explain the situation on 400 North.

Dick replied with understanding, "Well, that's a shame Jim. Tell you what; I've got plenty of work lined up and I would rather coon hunt back there than build that damn road."

Dad's face turned pale as he said, "Sounds to me like you better get back there and coon hunt that fencerow. Dick, I appreciate your support; thank you for the call."

Then the next day Ray, a family friend and neighbor, stopped by the house and delivered some news:

Jim, I didn't want to tell you this, but yesterday I overheard something at the welding shop that I think you need to know. I went in there to see if my log-splitter was fixed yet. It's still not done, but anyway, the usual loafers were sitting around and they were saying something about bulldozing out a fence-row to build a road. I was only half-listening until I heard old Floyd laugh and say, "Yeah, that would sure piss-off Jim Gillespie and we'll just pay for the dozer work with the township road fund!" Now I don't know exactly, but I think those guys were talking about building a damn road right through that fencerow and woods along your land that you call the narrow 40."

This new scheme was way over the top. Max Smith was seeking to use township funds to bulldoze an area that we valued as wildlife habitat and a place to hunt. Essentially he was looking to use public funds for the purpose of intimidation. We were shocked at the blatant bullying. Mom and Dad eventually reasoned that Smith had no real intention of opening the old road. Instead, they believed it was his intention to spread the word of opening up the old road just so the rumor would get passed along to my family and cause us anxiety. If that was true, his ploy worked.

Cause and Effect

However, maybe it worked a little too well. Every action is followed by reaction, and we came up with a plan. Step one involved hiring a lawyer. We located a lawyer in Flora, Illinois, who agreed to take the case. On June 3rd, 2003, we hired Coble and Milone to sue Smith and the township board. We hated doing this, but we had been pushed way too far. Gary Milone worked quickly to file the paperwork before the statute of limitations ran out. On June 13th, we filed suit against the Smallwood Township Road District and Max Smith. The lawsuit was necessary to recuperate damages caused to our land and to make a statement that the Gillespie family could only be pushed so far before they struck back. We felt betrayed. Also, in our view, those employed by the community should perform their duties in an ethical manner. Bullying is definitely not ethical; so the battle began.

The day that letters were served, we were on full alert. Mom and Dad checked over the property several times to make sure no retaliatory vandalism was happening. While our lawyer fired letters at the township's lawyer, we made plans for the inevitable next step: selling the Bogota herd. The township's lawyer advised Smith to cease any roadwork along 400 North and informed our lawyer. Because of this, we felt more secure that the north fence of the main Bogota pasture would not be removed until the lawsuit was settled.

We hoped to keep the cows through the winter and planned to sell them in spring 2004. Typically, brood cows bring a better price in the spring, and we had plenty of hay to feed the cows. The thought of seeing the pasture empty made me sad, but we anticipated that the road commissioner would remove the rest of the north boundary fence. We contacted our cattle agent and told him the news. He expressed sympathy for our situation and told us that he would call some folks looking to buy good cows. The more potential buyers of brood cows at the sale barn could mean better prices. It was a small but appreciated consolation.

Meanwhile, the lawsuit moved forward. Our lawyer contacted us and indicated that the township board and Smith had proposed third-party mediation to sort out the matter. This was a typical tactic because court costs can be so expensive and the outcome so unpredictable. We considered our options. Obviously, I wanted Smith and the township to pay out the nose for the malicious conduct of the road project, but we also wanted to move on with life. Mediation was set for March 10, 2004, at the courthouse in Louisville, Illinois.

It was a Wednesday morning, and I drove up from college to join Mom and Dad at the courthouse. I felt that they needed my support and that my analytical skills could come in handy. As I parked my truck next to theirs at the town square, I couldn't help but notice how much older they looked. Dad was wearing a pair of khaki pants and a button-up shirt; but the dress clothes didn't hide his gray eyebrows and tired eyes. He hated conflict and the entire ordeal wore on him terribly. Mom also had no love of conflict either, but she had zero tolerance for those who sought to hurt her loved ones. She wore a look of intense focus, but smiled when I approached. Together, we walked up the stairs into the courthouse. Just inside the entrance, I spotted Max Smith and a member of the township board, Floyd Halloway. Smith looked away, but I didn't. As I walked across the rotunda of the courthouse I stared down the cranky old trucker, Floyd. I telepathically told him, *You're a couple of vindictive assholes and now you're going to pay.* Mom, Dad, and I sat in a small conference room with our lawyer. He indicated that the township wanted to remove the rest of the fence along the Bogota pasture. We knew that this was coming and included it in our cost structure that I had calculated in a spreadsheet. Our suit was outlined to include land acquisition for the right-of-way, damages to the land, construction of new fencing, and punitive costs. Our lawyer took the outline to the mediator. He returned with a possible settlement; it was a sum of all the items except for the punitive damages. We had won and rightfully so. However, the stress and anxiety caused by the entire ordeal was tremendous. We also felt that punitive damages should have been included due to the deliberate unethical misconduct of an elected government official.

Afterwards, Mom, Dad, and I visited outside the courthouse. It was a pleasant day for March—the sun was shining and the air had warmed to the mid fifties. We felt some relief. I should have been happy, but I kept remembering the day I saw Max Smith at the mill. Because of a road commissioner drunk with power, we had suffered tremendously for two years. The stress had visibly aged my parents, and inside of me I felt the kind of anger that doesn't go away.

Goodbye, Old Girls

Two months later, on a gorgeous spring day we started the morning by feeding the Bogota cows at the trough in the southeast corner of their pasture. The cows noticed that the entire Gillespie family came back to check them, and this was odd. But since there was ground corn in the trough, they happily munched away, oblivious to the events at hand. We closed off the gate to the pen around the trough. As the cows finished eating, we herded them into the corral. We loaded up the cattle trailer and hauled away eight cows at a time. Several trips later, the Bogota pasture was empty.

Once the cows were all hauled away, Bob brought out the Case IH 2294 tractor with the no-till drill. We filled it full of roundup-ready seed beans and began planting the old pasture to soybeans. That was the only time that I have ever seen cow manure on the closing wheels of a no-till drill. Two days later, all the grass was sprayed with glyphosate. On the third day, a light rain fell on the new planting. The fescue grass turned brown, and little yellow soybeans began emerging from the ground. To our relief, we ended up with a beautiful stand of soybeans. However, Floppiness, Timid Cow, and all the other cows of the Bogota herd were gone forever.

Driving Back from Willow Springs

My thoughts returned to the present and the drive back to Carbondale from Willow Springs, Missouri, seemed to drag on. Along US-60, the land was beautiful, with big rolling hills covered with forest and little farms nestled in the valleys. However, a combination of too little sleep, an arrogant engineer's comments, and memories of my family's conflict brewed a toxic environment of negativity in my brain. I was frustrated and in no state of mind to make a decision about accepting or declining a job offer. I passed by the little towns of Winona and Fremont, and then I decided to take a break. I exited US-60 at VanBuren and drove down to the canoe launch along the Current River. I parked my truck and stepped out to stretch my legs. At the water's edge, I considered, "if I take this job as a highway engineer, I'll be part of the very thing that has caused so much pain and anger for me and my family." I knelt down and looked into the crystal-clear water. I cupped my hands together beneath the surface, leaned forward, and washed my face. The cool water and the open air seemed to wash away my emotions and leave a sense of peace. I thought to myself, I don't have to accept this job— besides, the pay is pitiful. I blankly gazed out at the swiftly flowing water for a moment, and then washed my hands again. The clear water of the rock-lined stream felt wonderful. I rubbed my eyes and washed my face a second time. By now, I could feel eyes watching me. I figured that it looked odd to see a man, wearing a suit, washing his face in the Current River, but I didn't care. I stood to return to my truck and saw a pleasant-looking family watching me from the other side of the parking lot. I had just made my decision to decline the job offer. That fall, I returned to Southern Illinois University as a graduate student. My major was Civil and Environmental Engineering with a water resources specialization.

Chapter 37: Fourth of July Feedlot Exodus

Summer of 2005

During graduate school I dearly loved my summer job. I worked as a trail crew leader in the wilderness areas of the Shawnee National Forest. We built trails beneath the shady canopy of tall oak, beech, and poplar trees. The shade was countered by the humidity. Sweat drenched our clothes as we chopped, sawed, hacked, dug, carried, and marched in the southern Illinois heat. Building trail is hard and dirty work, but it's rewarding. Each morning, I would park the green Forest Service truck at the trailhead. We shouldered our packs and hiked in to our project area. After working we hiked out on that day's segment of our newly constructed trail.

That year the Fourth of July fell on a Monday. I left Carbondale on the preceding Friday evening and headed up to the farm. That long weekend was full of the best farm activities: swimming in the pond, playing with Falcon the duck, hauling hay, eating watermelon, and checking the cows. On the Fourth a front blew through and brought a shower, overcast skies and cooler temperatures. It was a welcome respite from the heat. Late in the afternoon that day I said my goodbyes and started driving south. I had to work the next day, and I was looking forward to it. We were starting on a rocky section of trail that needed a switchback; this segment had some serious aesthetic potential. As I drove back to Carbondale, I gripped the steering wheel with my calloused left hand and smiled all the way. It seemed that each small town along the route was shooting off their fireworks show as

285

I passed through. It made the drive fun, but just as I arrived at my place I got a call on my cell phone. It was Mom and her voice sounded frazzled, "Will, the fat-calves got out!"

Mom's account of the events which led to the phone call:

That evening was so cool and pleasant that we delayed having supper and instead Jim and I went on a drive to look at our crops. The corn was nearly at the tasseling stage with glossy leaves, and the beans were knee high. While we were out and about, we stopped to feed the calves at the Bogota feedlot.

I stepped out of the truck and looked over the fat calves and spoke to them like I always did. I had fed them every morning for several months. The past winter when the calves were first weaned, I'd fed only one bucket, then I gradually increased the buckets so that by July I had been dumping bucket after bucket into their trough in an attempt to bring them up to full feed. The calves knew that an approaching truck meant feeding time, so they'd come running and stand by the gate waiting. Often I would pick a bunch of grass and hold it across the gate. They would stick out their long tongues and take the bundles of grass from my hand. A couple of the fourteen calves were too shy to take grass from me, but at the trough they weren't shy at all. They would crowd around me to get the first mouthful of grain. I always petted them a little bit. I'd rub the wiry thick fur of their necks. By

July, lingering at the trough between these rather tame 800 pound calves wasn't a good idea. I was risking getting squeezed or a foot crushed every time I fed them. Considering this, Dad and I decided that it was time for me to stop bucket-feeding the calves and time for them to start self-feeding at the gravity-flow feeder. As one would expect, I was still driving up to check on them most mornings.

That Fourth of July evening I decided to risk dumping a bucket in the trough just to pet a few of the calves. They came merrily running up to the gate when I filled a five gallon bucket with feed, and called "Sook Calvies, Sook!" I opened the gate and started toward the trough with the first bucket of corn. Behind me, Jim filled another bucket of corn and let the gate swing open a bit as he stepped inside the feedlot with the second bucket. The calves were ambling over to the trough and I mentioned to Jim that I wished all the kids could have been home for a weenie roast or something on this beautiful evening. Suddenly some sound alerted me and I turned to see the calves heading out the wide open gate instead of following me to the trough. That instant I knew that I had to get around them and turn them back as fast as I could, but running and trying to clear the hotwire and climb the fence to get in front of them would take too long. So I calmly and briskly walked through the center of the herd. When I got out front, I turned and waved my arms and yelled. I was able to turn back three of the ten calves. The seven others just kept going. Jim also slipped out of the lot and tried to cut them off, but to no avail. The three calves I had turned joined the four calves still at the trough. Apparently those calves had been caught unaware of the group's decision to make a break for it. Jim closed the gate to keep them in.

I turned and followed those seven very big, very valuable, and very free calves down the gravel lane. They were joyfully kicking up their heels and galloping along. We tried to catch up with them; we needed to get ahead of the group and turn them around. I knew that wildly chasing after the calves was pointless because that would spook them and make them run helter-skelter. These calves were running out of joy and excitement, not out of fear or being wild.

I slowed down and tried to catch my breath. The calves veered west and started down the lane towards the old Bogota pasture. I thought to myself, "If the calves end up in the old pasture and we might be able to catch them there." Then I remembered that the fence along the north road of that pasture had been removed by that damned road commissioner over a year ago. Even if the calves went through the open gate into the old pasture, they still wouldn't be contained. I panicked and ran after the calves down the lane. The calves paid little mind to me and just kept kicking up their heels. At the end of the lane they bunched up for a moment and then turned south, thus avoiding the open gate gap. They galloped through the knee-high wet soybeans. I went running after them. I had just slipped on some flimsy tennis shoes when I had left the house and now after running half a mile those shoes were wet and tearing at my heels. About that time Jim yelled to me, "Patty, just stop, wait. I'll go back for the truck."

He knew that it was futile to chase after those calves. I knew it too. The sun had set and it was already starting to get dark. When Jim returned with the truck's headlights on, I realized just how dark it already was.

I clambered into the truck, and Jim sped out into the bean field. The calves were now just dark shapes in the bean field south of us.

I yelled at him, "You're running over our beans, Jimmy." As we bounced along in the truck, he shook his head and forcefully replied, "We gotta catch up with those calves." He pulled the truck in front of the calves, and we jumped out waving our arms going, "Whoa, now. Calvies. Hold On." The calves just shook their heads playfully and went around us. They just kept parading on to the south.

We turned around and drove out of the bean field and then we went to the hard road. Basically we circled a mile and three-quarters around to the south *side of our farm. Jim spotted the calves as they were approaching the County Road 300. He turned on his warning flashers and stopped the truck right where the calves were headed to. We jumped out of the truck and ran toward the calves, waving our arms. The calves stopped. Thankfully we were able to turn them back. They slowed down a bit and went back the way they came.*

Mom and Dad had a huge problem. Basically escaped fat-calves are every producer's worst nightmare, and to make matters worse it was the Fourth of July. People would be driving up and down the roads late into the night. If those calves ended up out on the road somebody could hit them; and hitting an 800 pound feedlot calf is a bit different than hitting a 150 pound deer. Obviously their vehicle would get totaled, but somebody could also get seriously hurt or even killed.

Of course besides the obvious problems of calves indiscriminately destroying crops and possibly getting out on the road, there was another problem. We had just gotten the calves up on full-feed.[27] If we weren't careful they would

---

[27] In the feedlot, calves are fed a diet rich in grains and hay. The digestive tract becomes accustomed to this diet, but when the calves escape, they tend to eat large amounts of green vegetation. This influx of different food can unbalance the calf's rumen. When the calves are captured and returned to the feedlot, they sometimes over-eat grain, develop acidosis and founder. Foundered calves never reach their full potential and sell at lower prices. For a producer to work through all the steps of raising a calf from the brood cows to vaccinating and implanting to weaning to

founder whenever we captured them and returned them to the feedlot. Mom continues:

> Jim and I climbed back into the truck and just sat there for a moment. We didn't know what to do, but we had to make a plan. There was no way to catch the calves in the dark and trying to catch them would only serve to scare them. We needed to keep the calves off the roads during the night and we'd try to organize some help to catch the calves in the morning. The calves were heading north and were about a half mile away from the busy Bogota-Wakefield blacktop road. Considering that they had already run more than a mile, we really didn't know how far or where they would go.

Nightfall

The calves had escaped, it was getting dark and it was just you, Sarah, and Dad on the farm, what happened next? Mom continues:

> Well, we decided to make a quick trip to the house (about three miles away). Jim would drop me off and I would make some phone calls to our neighboring farmers that had cattle. On the way home, we passed by Jerome's place. His driveway full of trucks, they were having a Fourth of July party. We didn't really want to stop, but considering that the calves could end up trampling across Jerome's land,

the feedlot and then have something go wrong when the calves are so close to being sold, it's absolutely demoralizing.

we knew that we had to. When Jim and I pulled in the driveway everyone stared at us. It was awkward, but Jim stepped out of the truck and explained our situation. Jerome agreed to help us catch the calves first thing the next morning. We continued to the house.

Sarah was there and very concerned because we had been gone from the house much longer than expected. This was before Jim and I had cell phones, so we couldn't just call her to let her know what was going on. Will had already left, and Bob was down at Cape Girardeau. Jim drove back up to make sure the calves weren't getting out on the roads.

We figured that I would call some of our neighbors who had cattle. Maybe a few would help us recapture the calves, although when I picked up the phone I called Will and Bob first.

I remember Mom's call. As she described the situation over the phone, my gut tightened. I was stuck between a rock and a hard place; my supervisor with the Forest Service was the only other person who could take out the trail crew if I was not there. Unfortunately, my boss was away on a work detail at the National Folklife Conference at the Smithsonian Institute in Washington D.C. If I didn't show up for work on Tuesday morning, there would be a leaderless trail crew. I was the only person on the crew certified to drive the Forest Service truck. The crew would be forced to spend the entire day goofing off around the shop instead of going out in the wilderness area and building trail. I couldn't let that happen. I hated it, but I had to tell Mom that I couldn't come up to help.

Mom continues:

> Bob didn't answer his phone. I left him a message that the feedlot calves had gotten out. Then I called Ray, Terry, Wayne, and Gary. Let me explain why this was important: I didn't know where those calves would be going during the night. Would they keep walking across country? Would they settle down someplace? Whose land would they cross? Would they get on one of the roads? We had no idea what to expect and we needed to be prepared for the worst. I wanted to let the neighboring farmers know that our calves were out. Also, I figured that the farmers with cattle could be good help for corralling the calves. I can particularly remember calling Terry. He was in poor health, and he seemed tepid on the phone. He replied, "Patty, I really don't know what I could do to help?"
>
> I responded, "Could you block a road with your pickup tomorrow morning?"
>
> His voice perked up a bit, "Why yeah; I could do that."
>
> It was pitch-dark. Jim had driven back up and parked his truck on the gravel road near the curve in the Bogota-Wakefield road. Then about every fifteen

or twenty minutes he would drive around and make sure the calves weren't walking down the road somewhere. I had probably spent twenty minutes making calls and then Sarah and I drove up and started patrolling the roads like Jim was. I believe that sometime around midnight Sarah and I went back to the house because I was about to fall asleep driving.

Cape Girardeau, MO

In Cape Girardeau, Bob checked his voicemail. Then, he called home but couldn't reach anyone. This was before the era of widespread cell phones and Dad, Mom and Sarah were all out of the house, patrolling the roads for the renegade calves. After a quick husband-wife discussion, they decided that they could both call "off work" the next day and they would leave Cape for the farm immediately. However, when Bob and Mylinh looked outside of their apartment window to the street below, they saw a problem; the entire downtown was packed with cars and people set up to watch the fireworks show set on the Mississippi River. Along the river, Water Street was filled with lawn chairs. Driving out of Cape Girardeau was impossible until the party people called it a night and cleared out of the streets. Bob and Mylinh decided to wait until after midnight to depart. In the meantime they would try to catch some sleep.

Bogota-Wakefield Blacktop

Back at the farm Dad sat in his truck next to the township gravel pile and watched the digital clock switch from 10:42 to 10:43 pm. Thus far, the calves had not appeared on the road. Hopefully they would stay away from the speeding pickup trucks and cars. Best case scenario; the calves would mill around in one of our prairie patches or woodlots until morning. However, the behavior of hyped-up feedlot calves is unpredictable. Dad was just about to start the truck and make his rounds again when the headlights of a car approached on the main road. It slowed down and pulled alongside his truck in the dark gravel lot. It was a deputy sheriff. He rolled down his window, "Hi there Jim, is everything alright?"

Dad was relieved when he recognized the deputy as the one that had helped with some unruly campers at the state park he managed. "Well, I had some cattle get out this evening, and I'm just keeping watch to make sure that they don't get out on the road."

The deputy turned off his cruiser's engine and leaned back in his seat, "Where are they at?

Dad pointed, "Right at dark they were about a half-mile west of here." He paused, "They're feedlot calves, so who knows what they'll do."

The deputy nodded in agreement, "It sounds like they're pretty far off the main road though."

Dad wiped his brow, "Yeah, but considering it's the Fourth of July, I know there will be tons of people out tonight. I don't want anyone to get hurt because of my damned calves."

The cruiser radio suddenly crackled and the deputy cocked his head to listen. He reacted with a sigh and continued, "Well be careful. I honestly doubt if just one in ten of these cars on the roads tonight have sober drivers. I'll be out all night; so don't hesitate to call in if you need some help." With that, he started the cruiser's engine and drove off into the night.

Kinmundy

It was just after midnight when Bob and Mylinh had settled into their Prius and started their drive north. The downtown Cape Girardeau bars were still full of inebriated people enjoying their Fourth of July, but the streets were mostly empty. Bob drove across the bridge and turned left onto Route 3, north toward home. It was going to be a long night. They stopped along the way and Bob got a soda to stay energized. He exited off of Interstate 57 near the little town of Kinmundy. He was feeling wired from interstate driving when he drove through Kinmundy's First Street at forty miles per hour. A local police officer clocked him in a thirty-five-mile-per-hour zone and decided to conduct a traffic stop. It was three in the morning. Bob looked in his rearview mirror and saw the red and blue lights. He muttered "Shit" and pulled over. The officer reported the Missouri license plates back to dispatcher then approached the vehicle. Bob had both hands on the steering wheel when the officer shined his flashlight in the car. He asked, "What are you up to?"

Bob looked over and said, "Officer, we have a bunch of feedlot calves that got loose last night on my folks' farm up by Newton. We're driving back from Cape Girardeau to help them get the calves back in."

The officer must have understood the gravity of the situation and sensed that Bob was honest. He nodded and said, "Ok. Go ahead, but be careful driving and don't speed through my town."

The Kitchen

Bob and Mylinh finally made it to the farm shortly before four am. They quietly slipped into the house and dropped off a few bags. It was probably close to four am when Mom heard the stirring in the kitchen. She tiptoed down the stairs and found Bob and Mylinh. Bob cracked a sly grin and said, "Mom, if you wanted us to come home you could have just asked us instead of turning loose the feedlot calves!"

She was sure glad to see them but felt guilty that he had driven all night to come up. Furthermore, Bob and Mylinh were both going to miss work and after the ordeal, they would still have to drive three and a half hours back to Cape.

On the Loose

During the night the calves browsed through the bean field and then continued into one of our prairie plantings. In the darkness they wandered west through the adjacent woods and eventually crossed onto the neighbor's land. Cool morning air had pooled in the bottomlands, and the calves bedded down near the creek to rest. In truth, the calves had picked a pleasant spot to spend the last few hours before dawn. Mom continues:

> *The eastern sky was just beginning to lighten when Bob and I drove up to the feedlot. We drove back our western lane and started walking to the last place that I had spotted the calves before dark. It was just light enough for us to follow the trail. Although, let me be clear, I don't really mean a trail per se, but just the evidence of squashed plants, some manure, and the occasional track. Since the sign was still fresh, it was pretty easy to follow. Heavy dew had fallen during the night which meant that in no time our pants were wet from the waist-down. The calves had gone west out of the bean field into a prairie patch. They had gone all the way to the west boundary and crossed onto Richard's ground. They were down the hill, bedded down in the cottonwood trees by the creek.   The calves looked so peaceful and content when we found them. One didn't have to use much imagination to picture them as woodland bison relaxing in a grove of trees in presettlement times. Once we had located the calves, Bob walked out to the nearest road to let Dad know what was going on and figure out a way to capture the calves.*

Our Neighbors

Dad leaned against his truck, pulled up his binoculars and glassed across the broad bean field to the north. He scanned the Ash Grove woods beyond the field. Somewhere out in that section Bob and Mom were trailing the calves.

298

While only a half hour had passed since they set out, it seemed they had been gone for hours. Dad heard a vehicle approaching on the gravel road and turned to see Ray's blue Ford pickup. Farther down the road, Dad could see a dirty silver-colored truck approaching. Dad glanced back at the woods and breathed a sigh of relief when he saw Bob step out of the brush line. Ray parked his truck behind Jim's and put on his ball cap. He stepped out of his truck and took a couple of long lanky steps over to Jim, "Still looking for the calves this morning?"

Jim motioned toward Bob in the distance, "I think that we've got them located."

Ray replied, "Surely they didn't go too far."

Jerome rolled his truck up beside Jim and Ray, cut the engine and spit out a stream of chewing tobacco juice from the truck's open window. "Hell of a way to celebrate the Fourth by having your fucking calves get out "

Jim managed to return a groggy smile and replied, "Yeah, no kidding. Bob and Patty started trailing the calves at first light, and Bob's walking out right now. I figure that they've found them."

An awkward silence passed while the three men watched Bob grow nearer.

Dad hollered, "BOB, DID YOU FIND THEM?"

Bob looked up and yelled back, "YEAH, THEY'RE DOWN BY THE CREEK."

"Whew", Dad sighed.

Jerome spoke up, "At least you found them. Why, hell Jeff down the road had his bastard cattle out for a month before he found'em."

Ray crossed his arms and chuckled, "I don't think that Jeff ever looked very hard!"

Jerome looked down while he cut open the seal of a new Skoal can, and muttered, "Yeah, that's for sure."

Another truck rolled up and parked behind Ray's. It was Wayne. He took one last sip of coffee and then stepped out of his truck. He walked with his natural bow-legged steps up to the group, "Morning. Find the calves, Jim?"

Jim replied, "Yeah." He motioned toward Bob, "Bob and Patty went out to trail them at first light."

Wayne asked, "How many got out?"

Dad set his binoculars back on the dash of the truck, "Seven."

Bob approached the group, "We found the calves down by the creek. They're just west of our line on Richard's ground. I don't know the best way to get them back. I guess we could try to drive them back onto our land and get them in the old corral on the far end of the Bogota pasture." Bob paused then turned toward Ray, "They're not all that far from your place, Ray."

Dad spoke up, "Ray, would it be alright if we tried to drive them into your cattle lot instead?"

He replied, "Well sure. I sold my last calves in the fall, so that lot is empty."

Dad thoughtfully nodded, "You've got good fences, and the gate opening is positioned toward where the calves will be coming from.

Bob looked to Ray and pointed down the road, "Isn't there a gate gap on the far corner of Richard's land?"

Ray replied, "Yeah it's across the road and not far from the entrance to my lot. If Richard would let us drive the calves through there, we would just have to get them driven down the road a bit and turned into my gate and then they would be caught."

"That might work," Dad paused. "I really don't have any other good ideas for catching them."

Bob commented, "That will be the closest good fence; any other direction fences are nonexistent."

Dad stepped toward his truck, "I better go ask Richard if he is alright with us driving those calves across his ground."

Ray walked around the truck and said, "I'll go with you, Jim."

Dad started his truck as Ray ducked into the passenger side.

As they rolled away, Bob turned to Wayne and Jerome. "I'm hoping things will come together like we're planning. You guys might as well come with me to help drive the calves.

Jerome hesitated before tucking a pinch of chew in his lip, "Yeah, I can drive those sons-of-bitches." He continued muttering something indistinguishable as he started his truck and backed it up out of the way.

Bob thoughtfully pressed the back of his hand against his mouth, lowered it, and spoke, "Wayne, you know, Mom has been feeding those calves. Maybe she ought to walk ahead of them with a bucket of feed."

Wayne chuckled, "Well, since she's been feeding them, I bet they're pretty tame."

Bob hesitantly nodded, "They're tame around her, but knowing our luck they'll act like damn idiots this morning."

Wayne offered, "Yeah, that'd be about right!"

In a few minutes Dad and Ray returned. Richard had given them permission to drive the calves across his land. Bob grabbed an empty bucket from the back of Dad's truck. He dumped a little feed in the bottom of the bucket from a full bucket in the truck. He lifted the bucket. He spoke to

Dad, "We can have Mom lead the calves with this bucket of feed. But, I don't want the bucket to be too heavy. Mom will have to carry it the whole time."

Dad nodded to Bob and turned to see another truck pull up. It was Terry. Dad motioned him to drive up to the group. He rolled down his truck window and looked out with tired eyes and quietly said, "Morning, Jim."

"How you doing, Terry?"

Terry replied, "Oh my back is not very good, but I'm still trying to get around."

Dad motioned over toward Ray's land, "We're hoping to drive the calves through Richard's and get them in Ray's pen over there."

Terry nodded, "Okay."

"Could you block this road for us?"

Terry asked, "Where should I park?"

Dad pointed to a spot over by the gate gap, "Just this side of that gate gap."

Terry shook his head, "Jim, I'm sorry that I can't do more, but my back is just no good."

"Terry, I need someone to block this road. I'm glad you came."

Bob, Mom, Dad, Jerome and Wayne started the walk back to the creek bottom where the calves were still enjoying a lazy morning.

Driving Those S.O.B.s

Amongst the cottonwood trees that lined the creek, the calves were at ease and watched with curiosity as Dad, Jerome, and Wayne circled behind them. Bob and Mom were more direct; they walked up to the calves and roused them up. The calves rose and stretched their backs. Mom made a point to show them that she had a bucket of feed. With a bit of coaxing from the men behind them, the calves started moving. Mom walked ahead of the calves, she called to the calves quietly, "Sook calvies, come on, sook calvies."

The calves followed behind her just as intended. The group filtered through the cottonwood trees with Mom in the lead, the seven calves behind her, and Bob, Dad, Jerome, and Wayne spread in a broad line bringing up the rear. Everyone was quiet except for gentle voices reminding the calves that men were behind them, "Hey on, hey on, hey on."

Mom reached the open bottomland field and led the calves along a mowed path at the edge. The calves, being basically lazy, gladly took the easy mowed path behind her. The morning sun filtered into the bottomland. Mom looked over her shoulder to see the presently well-behaved calves following along, not far behind. As she started up a gentle hill, the calves became more inquisitive about their surroundings. The men coaxed the calves forward by softly waving their arms. The convoy kept moving forward.

Mom crested the hill and looked back to see the calves still following her. Ahead she could see the gate gap. It was the next obstacle. They had to get the calves through that narrow opening in the yard fence. She noticed Ray was smashing down the weeds to make the opening in the fence appear more inviting. Mom kept walking ahead. The calves crested the hill and jostled around a bit, excited to be out in an open field. The men stepped up their pace but didn't hurry toward the calves for fear that they would spook them. Then unexpectedly, the calves began to run. The steers were galloping away from the fence opening and Ray's corral. Ahead was the yard and then a broad bean field with no fences or any kind of structure that could be used to capture the calves. At that moment, Jerome took off at a fast, level run to the far left of the calves. He slipped around them in the nick of time and stepped out onto the gravel road waving his arms widely. Fortunately the calves turned toward Ray's corral. Mom called frantically, "SOOK CALVES, SOOK CALVES, THIS WAY!" They walked along the yard's edge with Mom in the lead. Up ahead Ray and Terry had positioned trucks to block the road. Ray stood beside his truck and stepped forward to help urge the calves south through his gate gap.

Mom stepped into Ray's lot with the bucket in hand. The calves followed nervously. The big barn loomed ahead of them. Beside the barn was a lush pasture with a wide open gate. Mom walked through the opening and made a show out of dumping the bucket of grain into a trough strategically placed just within the pen. The calves watched and anxiously paced in Ray's driveway. They were unsure of this new development. Bob, Dad, Jerome, and Wayne moved forward and waved their arms more forcefully. Mom called to her calves and one turned toward the feeder. Seeing this, the others followed. Bob hurried forward and swung the gate closed behind the calves; they were captured.

With the seven calves safely captured in Ray's pasture lot everyone breathed a sigh of relief; but they weren't home yet. Jim quickly thanked our neighbors for coming out to help with our fiasco. As the help left, Dad and Bob retrieved the work truck and the cattle trailer. Loading the calves out of Ray's pasture went smoothly. Within half-an-hour the calves were back in the feedlot.

LaRue Pine Hills

During all this excitement I was in far southern Illinois, 115 miles away from the farm. I was working with my trail-crew in LaRue Pine Hills. We were cutting side-hill trail about three-quarters the way up a 400 foot slope. The tall beech and oak trees shaded the forest floor. Rocky soil and tree roots had made the job of digging trail difficult.

I looked at the watch on my belt and then straightened my back. I called out to the rest of the crew, "Anybody ready for lunch?"

My crewman Paul muttered, "Yeah, since we got here."

I laughed, "Me too!"

I tossed my pick mattox on the uphill side of the trail. I followed my crew as we walked back down the trail fifty yards to where we had left our backpacks. I sat down on the hard packed earth and took off my hard hat. Water dripped from the sweat band. I pulled my backpack over to me and noticed a tick crawling on the shoulder strap. I picked off the tick and set it on the trail between myself and Paul. Without a word Paul leaned forward with his lighter and struck a flame about a quarter-inch from the tick. The heat caused it to balloon up and burst with a satisfying "pop" sound. I chuckled, "It never gets old watching ticks die like that!"

Paul leaned back and lit a Marlboro. He took a drag, then exhaled, "And there's a never- ending supply of them too."

I opened my backpack and dug into my lunch; a deer burger sandwich, apples, some cookies, a mozzarella cheese stick, and some tortilla chips. As I eagerly munched away, I felt a sense of guilt; here I was enjoying my day with the trail crew when my family had been struggling with the escaped calves. *How did they fare? Were they able to catch them?* I wished that I could have been there to help.

As always happened, lunch passed quickly and we went back to work. It wasn't a particularly hot day, but as the afternoon wore on the humidity became intense. I repeatedly wiped the sweat from my brow and wondered; *Were the calves still out? Did Bob make it up there? Did anyone help?* When four o'clock finally came, I gathered the crew and we started hiking out of the woods. We loaded up in the Forest Service truck and headed back to the ranger station. I drove Route 3 north through the Mississippi bottoms and then turned east on Route 149 toward Murphysboro. Once at the ranger station, the crew cleaned, sharpened, and put away the tools while I took care of some parting paperwork. At quitting time, I pulled out my cell phone and called home. Mom groggily answered. She told me that the calves were back in the feedlot and that Dad, Bob, and Mylinh were catching up on sleep after spending most of the night awake. I didn't press her for details; I would let her nap and listen to the rest of the story later.

Chapter 38: Nuisance

After graduate school, I took a job at an engineering firm located a long hour's drive away from the farm. The firm was quite small, with a professional engineer as the president, myself as a project engineer, two surveyors, and a secretary. (Of course, the secretary kept the whole mess in order.) The firm was in the process of moving to a new building when I started. They were seeking to grow into a larger business. This meant that they needed each and every dollar that we could earn. We worked on all kinds of projects, and we worked long hours. During the same period, my mom retired from teaching high school science. It was a much-needed retirement for her because the circumstances of teaching in the local public school were becoming unbearable. School administrators called frequent staff meetings to inform the teachers of all the newest laws and regulations. My mom saw this as school administrators simply covering their own backsides and weaseling out of their responsibilities. New regulations covered every aspect of teaching from discipline, to testing, to educating learning disabled students. Nearly every student was being labeled with some kind of disorder that prevented him or her from taking responsibility for learning. Teachers were not allowed any latitude in teaching style. This made teaching a lab class nearly impossible. Since being a worksheet and video teacher was not my mom's style, she jumped at the chance to move on from wrangling petty individuals to wrangling cows and calves. She found the latter to be pleasantly honest and direct. A cow cannot threaten to sue the teacher for a lazy kid receiving a failing grade.

There were only eighteen cows on the farm then, and Mom made the most of it. She fed them buckets of corn every day and generally made pets out of the entire herd. When it came time to wean calves, Mom already had her eye on the heifers that she wanted to keep as cows. One in particular was all black and had an amazing attitude. This black heifer always held her head up high. When others picked on her, she didn't back down or ever lower her head. It was as if she was saying, "I don't give a damn if you don't like me!" Mom dearly loved this heifer. Here was a bovine that exuded the type of mantra that she always wanted but never could perfect. As a schoolteacher, she had to be poised and civil in a small town.

The heifer calf was weaned with the first class of calves who graduated under Mom's care. Once moved to the feedlot, this particular calf kept her style and grew into a large black heifer with amazing muscle structure. We could tell that she was special. It was a late-summer weekend when Mom decided that she wanted to move three heifers from the feedlot back to the pasture to become brood cows. I was tired but happy to be loading up the new heifers for the pasture. Turning out new heifers into the pasture is comparable to three pretty college girls moving into a co-ed dorm mid-semester— much drama ensues. Mom, Dad, and I took the work truck up to the feedlot. We hooked onto the cattle trailer and turned our attention to selecting the heifers to keep. In the past we had always waved our arms and herded the selected heifers into the barn. This time around, the heifers were much tamer and decided that corn in the trough was more important than the humans waving their arms and yelling, "Hey-on!" Mom found this funny and suggested that we wait until they finish their corn then just walk into the barn with a bucket. Through corn conditioning, she had taught them to follow her with a bucket. We lacked the time to do taming like this before, but Mom's retirement had allowed her to spend much more time with the cows. I volunteered to carry the bucket. As I started across the feedlot to the barn, Mom's favorite calf started playfully butting me and kept it up all the way to the barn. I was naturally irritated and asked, "Are you sure that you want to keep this one?"

Mom's reply was full of endearment, "Oh she's a good girl!"

I laughed and said, "She's a nuisance, that's what she is!" I had no idea that I had just named my mom's soon-to-be favorite cow.

Nuisance and two other heifers were turned out into a pasture that contained seventeen cows, one bull, and a previously established cow hierarchy. The new heifers were first attacked by the lowest tier of the cow hierarchy. These poor cows at the bottom weren't about to let any new heifers join the hierarchy above them. While the lowest cows asserted their slim margin of superiority, the bull visited the heifers to see if any of them were in heat. Fortunately for that group of heifers, none of them were in heat that day.

The following day, we checked the cows in the usual manner. We honked the horn of the work truck to announce that it was feeding time, and then we dumped two buckets of corn in the feed trough. The cows came running and trotting up to the trough. Somewhere in the mix was Nuisance. She ran right up to the feeder fearlessly, got about two mouthfuls of corn before Slimer's Mom slammed her head against Nuisance's ribs and knocked her away from the feeder. Nuisance wasn't stupid; she knew that going up to the feeder would result in her being butted, but she did it anyhow. She was remarkably bold and wouldn't be intimidated; traits that my mom so respected.

It wasn't long before Nuisance came into heat. The Bull at that time was a big lazy black Limousin. He put little effort into anything other than eating or belloring at the bull across the road. During his peak of laziness, Bulla was almost reluctant to pursue cows in heat. Needless to say, there was no courtship. Bulla took a sniff of Nuisance's backside curled his upper lip as if to say, "Hey there, heifer, you're in heat. Wanna get it on?" Knowing Nuisance, she probably appreciated his forwardness and complied. Either way, my mom was very happy when Nuisance did not come back into heat in a month. She knew that her favorite heifer had been bred. She counted nine months and marked the calendar when Nuisance would be expected to calve.

While Mom was enjoying her retirement and taking care of the cows, I was working at the engineering firm. I rose out of a deep slumber at five-fifteen in the morning. I spruced up and ate some breakfast, then left the house thirty minutes later. I'd drive to Mt. Carmel and hope to arrive before seven. I worked on my projects by making calls, drawing in AutoCAD, filling out permit applications, sending emails, meeting with clients, and all of the other little tasks that engineers do. I would usually begin to get weary between four-thirty and five, and if nothing unexpected was happening, I could leave work and make the hour drive home. However, there was always something unexpected happening. The surveyors would need points created from plans and imported into the data collector for their surveying equipment, or we would need a set of plans completed for an upcoming meeting. During the summer, I could usually make it back to the farm before darkness fell. In the winter I wasn't as fortunate. Most days I would arrive home just before dinner. Mom always seemed to say, "Oh, I've got a good story for you about Nuisance."

Somehow, Nuisance knew how to work the system. She was always nice to my Mom, but she would give anyone else a good butting if given the chance. Mom would report on Nuisance, "Well, I was moving out hay today and Nuisance was already on the hay pile when I moved out the bale. Just as I set down the bale with the tractor, Good Gray Cow came up and butted Nuisance out of the way. Nuisance didn't look the slightest bit bothered by Good Gray Cow, and instead of sulking off the hay pile, she just moved over a bit and kept on eating." Nuisance moved up the hierarchy in this manner. It wasn't through fighting or making friends; she simply did her thing and always held her head high.

Mom was thrilled when Nuisance had her first calf. It was a coal-black bull calf with Nuisance's strong features. We were hopeful that the calf would be tame like Nuisance, but he was much the contrary. What he lacked in tameness, he made up for in vigor and spirit. He reached the 200-pound mark quickly and was constantly playing with the other calves. With her first calf, Nuisance established a reputation as a good mother.

Here, Black Nuisance soaks up the morning sun on a cold day. Her motto was, "You don't intimidate me. I'm eating corn at the trough too!"

Chapter 39: More Observant

Sarah walked into the library and found a spot to study next to Dejon. She unpacked her laptop and started it up. Dejon smiled to her. Sarah had noticed that he spoke English well, but seemed self-conscious about his accent. He had grown up speaking a tribal language, but had been taught English when he entered school. He had trouble pacing the syllables to match the Midwestern dialect. It was so different from the English taught in Ghana. Sarah smiled back and asked, "So are you guys ready to win tomorrow night?"

Dejon glanced up, "We've been practicing, but they are a tough team. So maybe." He looked back to his computer and typed in an instant message to his family. He added, "You'll be there with the band?"

Sarah nodded and said, "Yeah, I'll be playing the trombone." She entered her password and started working on a report for her literature class. She glanced over and noticed Dejon frowning. He sighed and pulled a textbook out of his backpack.

"Their internet's down again." Dejon complained.

Sarah quietly replied, "Hmmm. It seems to be working on my laptop."

"No, No. I mean in Kumasi." He added.

Sarah whispered, "Oh, I'm sorry! I thought you meant here at the library."

Dejon shook his head and started reading. When Sarah looked back at her computer screen, she considered the subtle clues in their conversation and thought; *He traveled across the globe to attend college on a basketball scholarship. We're about a month into the season. I bet he's homesick.*

Sarah's power of perception rivals the best. Her skill has been honed over the years. As the youngest sibling, she patiently waited while we worked on farm tasks that she was too young to help with. Enumerable times the very young Sarah would have to entertain herself while the rest of us were busy changing a flat tire, moving out hay, fixing fence, treating a sick cow, or addressing any other problem. Mom would find a safe place for her to play and watch us, and then Sarah observed and created. She drew the scenes on any piece of paper around her: seed bean bags, receipts, or if she was lucky, a notebook. Her creativity didn't stop there. The setting provided her with corn shucks, feathers, and tree leaves; everything she needed to make her own toys when our five-minute jobs of fixing equipment would turn into an hour-and-a-half long frustration fest. While we ignored her, Sarah learned to notice the colors, textures, lighting, and sounds around her.

As Sarah grew, her drawings became more refined. She had a knack for depicting action. Extra lines in just the right areas of a drawing would turn a cow into a running cow. These appeared without instruction; she observed and created. School started as a challenge for her. Even in elementary school Sarah's class was overrun by girls bent on popularity. While Sarah didn't fit in with that crowd, her

317

teachers and classmates recognized that she was very skilled at drawing. More importantly, she didn't shy away from attempting a difficult drawing, and if it didn't turn out like she intended, Sarah would keep working on it.

Throughout high school she kept producing art. Inspiration came from the world around her. Sarah knew how to observe and see the beauty in her surroundings. She had been doing it for years. Mom and Dad encouraged her to pursue a career in art. That is exactly what she did.

Now Sarah was sitting in the Olney Central College library, midway through classes for her Associates degree. She turned toward Dejon and asked, "I've seen you studying in the library and over at the gym practicing, would you like to get away from the college a bit on Saturday afternoon?"

He nodded, "That would be very nice."

Sarah offered, "How about I pick you up on Saturday about three o'clock, and you can have supper with me and my family out at our farm?"

Dejon smiled and chuckled, "Oh. That sounds good. Thank you... but, promise that you won't make me play basketball."

Sarah laughed, "Ha, we've got plenty of cows but no basketball hoops."

On Saturday, Sarah drove into campus and picked up Dejon. She had to adjust the passenger seat of the Grand Prix back so that Dejon could fit his long legs inside her car. He was close to seven feet tall, much taller than any of the Gillespies. During the twenty minute ride from campus to the farm, Dejon spoke with Sarah about his home in Ghana. During supper, Mom asked Dejon how he ended up at Olney Central College. He described the selection process for the basketball scholarship. Dejon mentioned the grade standards and the athletic level needed to be considered. Midway through dinner, my family realized the high level of focus and dedication Dejon maintained in order to attend college in the US. Despite Dejon's humility, it was clear that he was one of the best and brightest. Dejon also described his Uncle's farm outside of the city. It was a place that he enjoyed visiting.

After dinner Dejon, Sarah, and Mom took a walk out through the cattle pasture. It was late fall, the ground was dry and the cows were enjoying the cool evening. Mom was unsure how the cows would react to Dejon. He was very tall and dark; much different from anyone else the cows had ever seen. In the past, our cows had reacted fearfully to strangers in the pasture. They would hold their heads up high and act like they were about to stampede. However, Dejon walked amongst the herd with a slow easy-going gait. Instead of a fearful reaction, Mom's cows barely paid any attention to the stranger. It was obvious to Mom and Sarah that Dejon had spent some time out at his Uncle's farm in the countryside of Ghana. He knew how to act around cattle. When Sarah drove Dejon back to campus that evening, he mentioned being a bit homesick. Her perception was spot-on.

Eastern Illinois University

Sarah graduated from OCC and transferred to Eastern Illinois University. At EIU her creativity and artwork kicked into overdrive. Art classes taught Sarah new methods for producing art. While enrolled in an oil painting class, she started a series of paintings that were inspired from the farm. Sarah saw the beauty in the rural setting that most art aficionados overlooked or shunned. Her series consisted of 4 paintings; the last one was titled *Hungry*.

Hungry's Mother

Sarah's painting had a back-story; many, many years ago, we mistakenly took a bull calf to the feedlot that we had forgotten to castrate. By the time Dad recognized the problem—evident by the bull calf's thicker neck and growing scrotum—it was too late. Unbeknownst to us, he had already bred one of the heifers. Nine months later she gave birth in the feedlot. Lots of problems result when a very young heifer gives birth. It's not a good situation for the mother or the offspring. Dad was doing the normal morning chores when he spotted the newborn out in the muddy feedlot. He muttered, "Oh shit!"

Fortunately, the small calf was as sound as a pound. The calf's mother was a tannish-orange heifer with some white on her face. She was also very wild. Somehow, Dad was able to herd her into the barn and then haul the pair down to the home pasture. She proved to be a good mother and was named Feedlot Cow out of convenience. In a few years the flighty Feedlot Cow became the homeliest cow on the farm. She had long hooves, a thin neck, and wild eyes.

Repeatedly we would intend to cull her, but she would give birth to a healthy calf just before hauling off the cull cows. Year after year we would say, "Oh, we'll haul her off next spring." Over a time span of twenty years, she raised healthy calves despite her dreadful appearance.

About the same time Sarah started attending college at Eastern Illinois University, old age caught up with the Feedlot Cow. The old cow began losing weight. Once again, she gave birth to a healthy bull calf in late winter. Mom was worried about Feedlot Cow's failing health, and anticipated that the old girl wouldn't produce enough milk for her calf. Mom intervened by often feeding a bottle to the new calf. The old Feedlot Cow did not seem to mind Mom feeding her calf. The calf loved the extra milk and would run across the winter lot like he was starving to claim a bottle. His eagerness to nurse a bottle, earned him the name, Hungry. In truth, Feedlot Cow was producing enough milk for her calf, but Mom continued bottle-feeding the calf for fun of it. One day Mom and Sarah were feeding Hungry in the barn when Sarah observed an image that she wanted to paint. Sarah created her rendition on a forty-eight by twenty-four inch panel with oil paint.

In late summer of 2011, she entered *Hungry* into a visual arts exhibition at the Cedarhurst center for the arts in Mount Vernon, IL. When the art jurors viewed the exhibit, Sarah's painting earned first place.

Hungry Oil on 48"x24" panel by Sarah Gillespie. While the calf was well fed, he never turned down an extra bottle from Mom.

Chapter 40: Nothing in the Feeder, Preppy Cows

Since cutting back on the number of cattle, we only had twenty cows left at the home pasture. In this smaller herd the cows' individuality and social hierarchy became readily apparent. The social structure wasn't pleasant to see. A few very aggressive cows had become the top tier, and they ruled over the feed trough like a tyrant with an iron fist. This group included Nuisance, Bonga, and Square Face. They asserted their dominance by running to the feeder ahead of all the other cows and then butting away any of the lower tier cows that tried to approach the trough. Their behavior triggered memories of the preppy kids I knew in school; backstabbers that would use any means necessary to keep their place in the hierarchy. Witnessing the subjugation of the lower tier cows on my own turf caused the revenge segment of my brain to fire up. However, common sense would take over, and I accepted that I was seeing normal cow behavior and there really wasn't anything I could do about it. Or was there?

Since the Bogota herd had been sold, there was an unused feed trough sitting up at the old Bogota pasture. In an effort to provide more trough space for the timid cows, Mom and I retrieved the other feeder with the loader tractor and the hay wagon. The additional trough helped out immediately. Two feed troughs meant that the preppy cows could no longer keep the lower tier cows away from the corn.

The problem was fixed, but I had not yet gotten even with the aggressive preppy cows. Their day of embarrassment was coming. Every day I poured corn in the north trough first and then went to the south trough a few yards away. The cows became quite conditioned to this and started making a mad dash for the north trough whenever they heard the sound of the work truck and the gate opening. The most aggressive cows were always the first to the north trough, while the more timid cows would automatically go to the south trough and wait. The stage was set. One evening I hid a bucket of corn in the feedway of the barn. I planned to feed the cows corn at the trough, but the next morning before I started the truck and opened the gate, I quietly slipped over the fence and retrieved the bucket of corn from the barn. Without being detected by the cows, I dumped the bucket into the south trough.

Now it was time to feed the cows. I made a big production out of calling the cows. This was completely unnecessary because they knew by the sound of the truck and gate latch that it was feeding time. Before any arrived near the troughs, I climbed up into the north feeder with two buckets. One was empty and one was full. When the cows started running for the troughs, I acted as if I was dumping the empty bucket. Then I kept calling them. The preppy cows played right into my hands. They ran right past the south trough full of corn and sprinted up to the empty north trough. The timid cows quickly lined up around the south feeder and started munching away on corn. I continued the ruse by talking with the preppy cows and holding their attention.

Then I poured just a bit of corn into the north trough. This bought the timid cows some more time. Nuisance scarfed down the tiny bit of corn then turned her head toward the south trough. She spotted the timid cows chowing down on corn and swung her head back toward me to deliver a steely glare before backing away from the north trough and dashing for the south feeder. The other preppy cows followed and aggressively butted away the timid cows. However, the timid cows had finished most of the corn already. With the aggressive cows licking the south feeder clean, I dumped the rest of the corn in the north trough. The opportunistic timid cows saw this and dashed over to the north trough. By the time the preppy cows figured out what had happened, the timid cows had cleaned up all the corn. I stood tall in the north trough and relished in the prank. I cackled at Nuisance, "Ha, ha, Nuisance, no corn for you, Bitch!"

Chapter 41: The Phone Call

From May 2008 to 2013, I worked as a civil engineer on a contract basis for a government agency. Civil engineering as a career has some severe drawbacks, but that particular position made me feel like a square peg in a round hole. I sat at my desk all day long, processing data on my computer. From time to time, I expressed to my supervisor that I could do more than just process data. Unfortunately, she insisted that I was working on a contract that she funded; data processing was the work she needed done. While other programs in the agency could have offered me projects that better fit my skills and personality, my role was working for her. It wasn't long before I grew to resent my supervisor and the rest of the agency. In my mind, I was twenty-nine years old going on sixty. I sat in the office all day, hating myself for becoming an engineer. The more I sat and processed data, the more I resented my life's decisions. I was such a fool to follow the American career goals. I never did anything interesting, and without something to be proud of, how would I ever live with myself? I never joined the Marines and fought the Taliban in Afghanistan; I never joined a fire fighting crew and tackled forest fires; I never seemed to make a difference in anything. I sat at my desk processing data as a no-name civil engineer and wallowed in self-pity.

It was a Wednesday morning, which meant that I had a nine o'clock meeting with my boss. I walked down the hall to her office with my notebook and carried along a sense of dread. I didn't know what to expect. Would she be polite today, or would she be snippy and dismissive of my ideas?

I had found some limitations with the software we were using to convert climate data into a form that the watershed model accepted. To address this problem, I had outlined three possible solutions. I sat down across from her desk and described what I had accomplished in the preceding week. She seemed okay with my level of progress. Then I described the software problem I had encountered. She interrupted me mid-sentence by saying, "WHAT? YOU'RE JUST NOW TELLING ME THIS?" Her demeanor and eastern European accent fired out the words like a machine gun. Since the meeting had been going well, I was taken aback.

I stammered, "I-I just found out yester-"

She cut me off mid-sentence and snipped back, "You should have told me as soon as you found out."

I thought to myself, *I was determining the extent of the problem and outlining some solutions BEFORE I came to tell you.* I held by my anger and replied, "Yes, I should have."

When I finally returned to my desk after the meeting, I was fuming. I thought to myself, *Why does she snip away at me before I've finished describing things? Does she think that treating me like that will make me work harder? I don't want to do a god-damned thing for her!* This Wednesday meeting had turned out like so many before. I checked my email then somehow pulled together enough willpower to start working again.

Time seemed to be dragging along that day. When lunchtime came, I was in a self-reflective mood. I kept

327

thinking, *Maybe there is something wrong with me? Maybe I provoke my boss somehow?* After lunch, I returned to working on spreadsheets, and the self-reflection turned into self-loathing. My train of thought was broken when my cellphone started vibrating. I looked down and saw that it was my Dad calling. I answered the phone, and his voice on the other end was a mixture of anger and pain. He shouted, "THAT BITCH GOT ME! SHE GOT ME AGAINST THE DOOR OF MY NEW TRUCK! GOD-DAMMIT! MY NEW TRUCK IS ALL DENTED IN! THAT BITCH!" I could tell that he turned his head away from the phone as he yelled, "I WAS JUST TRYING TO SAVE YOUR CALF, YOU BITCH!"

I didn't have to ask details; I had a pretty good idea of what happened. I asked, "Dad, how bad are you hurt?" His avoidance of the question and insistence that I not call Mom told me that he had no intention of seeing a doctor. Mom and Sarah were away attending a wedding in Virginia. Dad was on the farm by himself, and by the sound of his voice, I expected his anger to subside in an hour or two, and then he would be in a lot of pain. I locked my computer and walked down to my boss's office. I looked her in the eye and said, "My Dad just got attacked by a cow. I don't know how bad he's hurt, but I'm driving down there right now." She simply said, "Okay." As I walked away from her office, I thought to myself, *At least she didn't snip at me. I shouldn't have even told her. Maybe then she would fire me for leaving work. If only I could be so lucky!.*

My Chevy truck was already fueled up, and I made the drive from Champaign to Bogota in less than two hours. I found Dad driving a tractor, applying liquid nitrogen fertilizer in a corn field just south of the curve in the Wakefield-Bogota road. He stopped the tractor at the end of the field and climbed down from the cab slowly. He was hunched over and cradled his right side. By then he wasn't nearly as mad. As I approached him, he said, "Oh, Willy, she got me good." I didn't know what to expect. On the drive down I had plenty of time to think, and I had horrible images of him spitting up blood from internal injuries. He appeared to be in better condition than I had feared.

I spoke up, "Dad, I want you to go home and rest. I'll take over this. I called Sarah's boyfriend, and he's on his way to help, too."

He replied, "No, no. We've got too much work to do. We've got to get the hay cut and baled so we can get that field planted to beans." There was no arguing with him, but at least I could make him do the easiest job that afternoon. I could also check on him periodically. I took over knifing on Nitrogen and he went to cut hay. Sarah's boyfriend arrived in a few hours and took over the job of cutting hay. When I arrived at the farmhouse near dusk, Dad was finally relaxing outside on the bench. He was wearing his shorts and drinking a can of Diet Coke. His whole right side was one giant bruise.

I sat down at the bench across from him, and he told his story. Dad had taken leave from working at the park that afternoon because there was so much that needed to be done on the farm. He got home at twelve-thirty and was concerned that the calf born yesterday had not yet nursed.

329

He was in a hurry to get other jobs done, but he knew the calf needed colostrum. He quickly warmed up a bottle and drove his new Chevy Colorado out to the pasture. He parked the truck right next to the cow and calf. The dumb calf wouldn't nurse the bottle, so he replaced the nipple with the esophageal tube and force-fed it. The cow was growing testy, and at some point the calf let out a bawl with the tube in its throat. The mother cow charged and head-butted my dad into the driver's side door of his truck. She knocked him off his feet and kept smashing him against the truck until she let up and he slid down and away. I cringe to think of how painful and scary it must have been. He had gotten cornered by the cow with her calf under one arm, an esophageal bottle in the other, and nobody there to club the cow into rapid compliance when she charged. Also, nobody had been there to help him take the calf to the barn to avoid giving her the chance to attack. He had been in a hurry, and he had not taken the precautions he should have. The cow had acted motherly and had been more violent than we would have expected. I hate to even consider the worst that could have happened.

I spent the next two days and then the weekend on the farm. Bob came home on Friday. We worked hard and caught up the field work while keeping Dad on the easiest jobs. Luckily, the calf decided to start nursing its mother cow. Dad continued to be in a good deal of pain, and when Mom came home from the wedding, we were all in trouble for keeping the incident a secret. Our fear was that Mom would drive non-stop back from Virginia to get home as soon as possible. Not only would she have missed the wedding, but the continuous drive back would have been dangerous too.

Later the next week, Dad went to the doctor. It was a routine checkup that he had scheduled earlier. The doctor took one look at the widespread bruising and sent my Dad to have an X-ray. Unsurprisingly, the image revealed two broken ribs. He also suffered some internal bleeding. It took about a month for him to regain his strength completely.

On Sunday evening, I drove back to Champaign from the farm. The sun was setting as I cruised up the wide-open two-lane road between the towns of Charleston and Camargo. My attention drifted and I reflected on the past week's events. I was thankful that Dad had not been more severely injured. I thought of the times that cows had charged me. I thought about all the data processing work that I needed to catch up on the next week. A bit of dark humor seeped into my brain as I weighed the pros and cons of facing off with a cow versus meeting with my boss. I let out a sigh of disgust when I decided that I would rather take my chances with a cow.

Chapter 42: Broccoli Cheese Soup

During my first year of college at Southern Illinois University, I happened upon a simple solution to deal with my restlessness and hyperactivity: running. On the farm running was deemed an unnecessary expenditure of energy. Under my parental regime, the approved outdoor activities included working and hunting. The thought of running for fun was considered absolutely absurd by my father. Therefore, I never ran much before I attended college. Once away at college, running became part of my daily routine. I found myself waking up at five-thirty in the morning, running a mile-and-a-half to the gym, working out, and then running back to my dorm to prepare for a day of classes. After class I would run at least two miles around the campus lake. This exercise routine kept me balanced and enabled me to sit through my engineering classes.

After college, and throughout my various jobs, I have always found time to run. Somewhere along the way I started participating in running events. The first was a 10K event, then the River to River Relay, more 10Ks, a few 5Ks, some trail runs, a few biathlons, a few half-marathons, and a triathlon. I enjoyed the company of other runners. When it came to racing, I was usually toward the front of the pack.

As it happened, I signed up for a half-marathon in Olney, Illinois, on the last Saturday of July 2013. Having a half-marathon so close to home was a treat, and I was hoping that I could pull off a first place finish. I had a chance since the event was in a small town, so there would be fewer participants. Also, I had been putting in lots of training miles and felt prepared. The half-marathon started at six-thirty am, which was a blessing, because in July it can get hot pretty quick in the morning. I figured that I could run the race in one-and-a-half hours. Then I could spend some time socializing and return to the farm sometime between nine-thirty and ten. Once back at home, I could eat a good brunch, rest up a bit, pack my truck with tools, and then depart for Cape Girardeau to spend the next couple of days helping my brother with some home improvement projects. If all went well, I would arrive in Cape by five that evening.

Of course, cows can always throw a wrench in the best-laid plans. Marathon Cow was a black cow with no particular distinguishing features except that she was quite rotund. She walked around with a plump roll of fat that hung down under her neck and in front of her brisket. At some point during the summer, she must have walked into a locust thorn or piece of sharp metal because an abscess formed under the skin of her neck. The bump started out as a baseball-sized protrusion. When I signed up for the run, the protrusion was something to check, but not yet serious enough to warrant a veterinarian visit. We checked the cow on a daily basis and from all other outward signs, she was healthy. However, as time went by, the protrusion kept growing until it was nearly as large as a volleyball.

We called our local vet, Joe Rudolphi, to come examine the cow. He was booked to the gills with appointments, but made a point to stop by early one morning to take a look at her. Joe was the best large animal veterinarian in the area. Long after most vets had given up large animals to enjoy the less dangerous work of treating dogs and cats, Joe still made on-farm calls. Because of his skill and willingness to work so hard over the years, his business had blossomed. In fact, Joe traveled so far and wide that he switched from driving a pickup truck, with a refrigeration unit in the back, to driving a diesel Mini Cooper hatchback with coolers squeezed in. From a fuel-economy standpoint, this change makes complete sense. However, Joe is a very tall and large man. Cows tended to have more respect for him due to his size. Somehow, Joe fit into his tiny car, and he drove it all over the countryside like a modern-day James Herriot, treating horses, cows, hogs, sheep, and just about anything else found on a farm.

When Joe examined the cow, he concluded that we needed to lance the abscess. This would require the squeeze chute and enough of our clan to push the unwilling cow into that scary metal contraption. Fortunately, we could round up enough help to do the job at ten o'clock on Saturday morning. I could squeeze the job of treating the cow between running the half-marathon early and traveling to Cape Girardeau, Missouri later. I wouldn't have much time to spare, but at least I would still get to do the event.

On Friday, I moved the cattle squeeze chute from its storage location five miles away to the west barn at the home pasture. I had everything in order, and when Saturday morning rolled around, I was ready for the half-marathon. The event started smoothly at six-thirty. Within the first mile, I was in the lead alongside a local high school track coach. I had run with him before, and the rumor was that he had once

334

missed a spot on the US Olympic marathon team by only twenty seconds. Needless to say, he was faster than me. We ran together for the first few miles. At mile four, he began to pull ahead of me. I found myself running alone in the second place position. I settled into my rhythm of breathing and listened to my footsteps. The sun was still low, but the humidity made the air feel thick. I wished for a dry breeze to cool me down, but the morning just kept warming up. I ran past fields of corn and beans, little farmsteads, and finally, the outskirts of town. At the twelve-mile marker, I knew the finish was just a mile ahead, so I picked up the pace and emptied whatever reserves I had left in my proverbial "gas tank." At twelve-and-a-half miles, the race directors had left off an arrow that I was expecting. I sailed past a turn. Soon I knew that I was going the wrong direction, so after half a mile, I turned around to retrace my steps and see if I could find the missing signage. Back about a quarter mile, I ran into the third-place runner who had also missed the last turn. We decided to head to the finish line by taking a side street. Having run well over 13.1 miles, I was out of fuel. When the finish line came into view, I was running in the third place position. I was disappointed to have run so far and so fast and yet have my rank and time slip because of poor signage. I was exhausted, but after having some snacks and rehydrating, I felt a bit better.

I arrived home just before ten. I barely had enough time to change into my work clothes before Joe the vet arrived. Mom had already driven the cow into the barn. Dad manned the head gate lever located at the front end of the squeeze chute. Mom and I tried to drive the cow into the chute. She balked. Joe took over the head gate while Mom and I moved a pipe gate into position so that the cow had less room to turn around. Dad walked in the backside of the barn to help us. We all tried again. I pushed on the hind end of the cow with all my strength to get her moving forward into the chute. Dad was pushing along with me and Mom was working to keep the cow from raising her head high and jumping the gate. What little strength I had left was fading. Mom started slapping the cow to keep her head down and forward. Then the cow went in reverse. The situation began to deteriorate. At first I could stop her, but my strength gave way. I began to get scared because I was falling down, and I definitely did not want to be trampled on. Fortunately, the cow stopped for a moment, and I got to my feet. Now I was mad. I yelled "Game on!"

Anger fueled my strength, and we all started pushing again. Mom refocused her efforts beating the cow with a stick, I twisted the cow's tail, and Dad kept the gate from swinging wide. Along the way, both the cow and I took a little beating from Mom, until finally Joe said, "Let me come in there. She doesn't know me, and I'm the only one out here that she is seeing." Joe switched places with Mom, and the cow decided that she did not want to be stuck in the barn with that big guy. She walked forward into the chute with minimal coaxing from Joe. Mom quickly shut the head gate around the cow's neck and the cow was trapped.

Next, I held the cow's tail up high, and arched it forward so that she would not buck around inside the chute.

Cows hate this, but we couldn't have her going ballistic in the chute while the vet was lancing the abscess. Mom leaned in hard against the head gate lever. When Dad stepped out of the barn, he traded places with her at the head gate. Mom stepped back and brushed off her clothes, "If you boys are alright, I'm going to head up to the house and start cooking some lunch."

Joe grinned and teased her, "Patty, are you sure that you don't want to stick around? This might get interesting!"

Mom let out a chuckle as she walked away, "I think you boys can handle it."

Joe pulled a scalpel from his kit and made a small incision on the cow's volleyball-sized protrusion. The results were immediate. Liquid that looked like broccoli cheese soup streamed out of the incision. Then the awful smell hit us. Joe chuckled, "Whew, that's a nasty one!" He turned his face away and let out a stream of chewing tobacco spit.

For the next few minutes we were in a holding pattern until the flow of puss stopped. Joe gave the cow an injection of antibiotics. Then he asked, "Jim have you guys got any screw-worm balm?"

Dad, who was still leaning on the head gate lever, wiped some sweat from his brow and replied, "I doubt we do."

Joe continued, "Well, I don't have any in my car, but you guys really outta spray that wound daily until it heals."

I silently laughed to myself and thought; *snowball's chance in hell that cow will ever let us get close enough to spray that wound again!*

Dad adjusted his cap and said what I was thinking, "I'd be surprised if she'll let us catch her again, but you know I could hurry down to Wakefield and pick up a can. That way we could for sure coat that wound once."

As they spoke Mom came walking back up to the barn, "Will, if you guys are done, why don't you head up to the house and get something to eat." Considering that I had already run 13.1 miles and my adrenaline rush from the excitement of pushing a disagreeable cow into the chute was starting to wear off, I was beginning to feel faint. I appreciated Mom's concern. I brushed off my hands and started walking to the house. Mom stood by to watch over the cow in the chute while Dad hurried off to get some screw-worm balm from the farm store. Joe left for his next appointment. Mom was alone with the cow.

Before going in the house, I used the garden hose to wash off the splattered cow manure on my arms and pants. Amazingly, I wasn't too dirty. I took off my boots and I stepped inside the house to the wonderful smell of food. I found that Mom had warmed up some meatloaf and cooked some fresh green beans from the garden. I was greedily filling my plate when Mom came rushing in the house and breathlessly yelled out, "WILL YOU GOTTA HELP, THAT COW'S GONNA DIE!" I ran to the door and gave her a bewildered look. She sensed my confusion, "That damn cow's turned herself sideways in the chute and she's suffocating." Mom tried to catch her breath from running up to the house, "THE RELEASE LEVER IS STUCK. I CAN'T GET IT OPEN. GO QUICK!"

I managed a sprint up to the barn. Just as Mom had described, the cow had turned her head sideways in the head gate and completely cut off her own windpipe. Truthfully, the cow already looked dead. As I rushed across the barnyard, I had snatched an old brick off the ground. I swiftly slammed the brick down on the release lever and jarred it loose. I managed to open the head gate just enough to let the cow fall backwards into the chute. She convulsed violently and gasped for air. I gently reclosed the headgate. The cow was still captured inside the chute, but the headgate wasn't shut around her neck anymore. Mom arrived moments later. The cow managed to stand.

A frantic expression of relief and frustration came across Mom's face. I spoke up, "I think she's going to be OK."

Mom sighed, "Will, that lever was stuck and no matter how hard I pulled I could NOT get it to release."

"Yeah, I know it gets stuck. It just needed jarred loose." I pointed to the broken brick on the ground.

Mom shook her head, "Ugh, why didn't I think of that?"

I replied, "I think she's alright."

Dad pulled his truck alongside the gate and stepped out with a spray can of screw-worm balm. He shook the can and walked over to us, oblivious to what had just transpired. He noticed our concerned looks and asked, "Is everything alright?"

Mom gave him a sideways look, "We just about had a disaster! We almost lost her."

"What?" Dad asked in confusion.

I gave him a quick synopsis of the near disaster and Mom added, "I thought for sure that she was a goner."

Dad frowned, "I didn't even think about that happening." He reached through the bars of the chute and sprayed the wound. The cow stood nearly motionless except for her sides heaving as she breathed. When the wound looked like it had been coated with silver spray-paint, we opened the head gate and released the disgruntled cow into the pasture. She walked away slowly, obviously traumatized.

After my failed lunch attempt, we returned to the house for my second lunch attempt. It was a success, and the good food in my stomach made me drowsy. I postponed the trip to Cape Girardeau for a few hours. I tried to take a nap but despite my heavy eyelids, I really wasn't able to sleep. About two o'clock, I loaded a bunch of tools in my truck, topped off the gas tank and headed south. I wasn't in a hurry, so I took the back roads instead of the interstate. I even made a stop to visit my aunt, uncle, and cousin in Goreville, Illinois. By the time I arrived at my brother's place in Cape, it was after nine, and they had already gone to bed. I quietly took a shower and shuffled into their guest bedroom. I think I fell asleep before my head had even hit the pillow.

I woke slowly. Sunlight was streaming through the bedroom window; it was six in the morning. My eyes adjusted to the light as I sat up in the bed. Yep, my abdominal muscles were sore. I rested my hand on the side of the bed. Yep, the back of my arm was bruised. I swung my feet around to the floor. Yep, my leg muscles were stiff. In addition to my sore muscles, little bruises had manifested overnight, signifying where I had gotten beat around while trying to push that damn cow into the chute. My stomach growled when the smell of cinnamon hit my nose. I wandered into the kitchen. Mylinh was cooking oatmeal. When I sat down at the table, my hunger was severe enough to eat both the oatmeal and the plastic bowl containing the tasty mush before me. Bob, Mylinh, and I ate breakfast and discussed all the things that needed fixed around their place. We made a long list of items needed from the hardware store for all the projects and set off on a shopping run. We visited Ace, Lowes, and Menards. On the way back, the audible rumblings in my stomach could not be ignored. We stopped at a sandwich shop. As I approached the counter, a cheerful cashier chirped, "Would you like to try one of our salads or soups? Today's soup is broccoli cheese." I chuckled to myself and thought; *if you had only seen what I saw yesterday!*

Chapter 43: Displacement Behavior

It was early in the winter, and I was already starting to suffer from cabin fever. The cold, gloomy weather, short days, and long nights meant that I wasn't able to run much during the daylight hours. The Saturday morning before Christmas, the whole family was home on the farm. I was looking forward to their company and telling stories, so I decided to get caught up on my running while they were still asleep. I awoke early, dressed in my running gear, tied on my shoes, and left in the dark for a seven-mile run. It was a pleasantly calm morning, with a cool twenty-degree temperature. My pace started slow but picked up after the first mile. The pre-dawn sky was clear except for a light haze that dimmed the stars. At mile four, the sky started to lighten, and the sun was nearly up as I entered my home stretch. Up the road a distance, I could see my brother walking to the pole barn. This struck me as odd because I figured he would be inside rocking his new baby. I waved to him and he waved back but continued to the pole barn at a fast pace. I ran up the driveway to the house and noticed Mom dashing across the cattle lot toward the west barn. I yelled, "Hey, Mom, what's going on?"

She yelled back, "I've got a cow that's having trouble calving."

I responded, "I'll be right out."

I ran straight into the garage, where I stripped out of my steaming running clothes and pulled on my overalls and a jacket. I was sweating profusely, but if I ended up standing around the barn for a while, I would get really cold. When I got to the barn, Mom and Bob had already lassoed the cow we called Short Round and tied her to a post. Short Round was fighting the rope and flailing about. Two hooves were exposed out of her birth canal. Bob was attempting to attach some twine to the hooves so that we could pull the calf out. It all made sense now—Bob was going to the pole barn to retrieve the lasso when I saw him earlier.

I stepped into the fray and tried to push the cow toward the post so there would be less slack in the rope and she wouldn't have as much freedom to move around and bash us about. She was fighting fiercely. This was unexpected—Short Round always seemed like a mild-mannered cow. However, she was under some intense stress, and when she finally held still, the problem was apparent. The exposed hooves were back legs; the calf was coming backwards, or "breeched."

The term "full breech" indicates that the posterior of the calf is in the birth canal and the legs are folded back inside the uterus. Fortunately, this was a partial breech and the back legs were already present in the birth canal. A small or average-sized calf in this position can be pulled out. In a situation where the calf is too large to be pulled without seriously injuring the cow, only two options remain; remove a dead calf in sections or perform a caesarian that could result in the death of both.

Our lack of tools and expertise meant that we were limited to the pulling the calf; at least until the veterinarian

343

could arrive. Mom had already called Joe when I arrived at the barn. Unfortunately, Joe would not be available for an hour; he was out on another emergency call. We needed to act now.

Bob had twine tied to one back hoof, and I pulled on the other leg so he could tie the twine around that hoof. Short Round started flailing again. She pulled hard against the rope and nearly smashed the exposed hooves of her unborn calf against the barn wall. The cow had about four feet of rope between her and the post. With that extra rein, she was able to keep us from accessing her back end. Bob commanded, "Mom, hold that rope tight!"

Mom responded, "I can't, she's going to choke down."

I jumped away from the cow as she body slammed the wall near me. I was getting frustrated; we were trying to help Short Round, and she insisted on fighting the rope. At that moment I remembered a fundamental rule when dealing with cattle: Always try corn.

I quickly asked, "Mom, do we have any corn?"

She had fed the calves Thunder and Lightning in the barn the day before, and I was hopeful that she stored some nearby.

Mom replied, "I think so."

She reached behind a wall and pulled up a bucket half-full of ground corn. I grabbed a nearby feed pan and set it next to the post. Then I dumped some corn in the bottom of the pan. Immediately, Short Round stepped forward and started eating.

Witnessing a cow in hard labor, who had been fiercely fighting the rope suddenly straighten up and start eating corn made me chuckle. Then I remembered something a former colleague explained to me while he was ranting about some drama at work:

> It's simple displacement behavior. When I was getting my degree in wildlife management, I had this class on animal behavior. One of the things they taught us was that when animals are put in a situation with no clear solution, they will resort to doing something in their comfort zone. It's displacement behavior! Heck, one time I was guiding some hunters on a moose hunt up in British Columbia. The hunters I had weren't much for walking, so I went to look for some moose sign in a nearby bog. It was thick brush, and I instantly happened upon a huge bull moose. This moose was fifteen yards away, just staring at me thinking, "What do I do?" Instead of taking off at a full run, this moose drops its head and pulls up a big mouthful of grass. It chews it for a moment and then saunters off. The moose didn't know what to do, so it just grazed.

Diverting the cow's attention to the corn enabled Mom to take up the slack in the rope. Bob and I got to work. We tied twine on the other foot; then we started pulling in earnest. Short Round strained. She let out a short bawl and started falling over. Mom eased up on the rope. Bob and I kept a constant tension on the twine and followed her right to the ground. I spoke up, "Mom hand us that board! We need to make a lever." A cow's pelvis is shaped such that when pulling a calf, one needs to apply tension at an angle about forty-five degrees toward the ground from straight back. With the cow lying down, we were forced against a wall and had limited room to work. I planted my foot firmly in the dirt behind the cow. We wrapped the twine around the board. Bob shoved the board in the dirt by my foot and then started applying leverage. Mom spoke to Short Round, "Okay, girl, work with us!" A visible contraction pushed the calf back about a half an inch. The next contraction gained more. We were at the hardest part: The pelvis of the breached calf was in the birth canal. The next two contractions were productive, and then the calf's pelvis slipped through. Bob shouted, "Get rid of this board!" I unwrapped the twines from the board and grabbed a leg. Together, we pulled the calf out. I untied the twine from his legs while Mom cleared the placenta away from the calf's nose and mouth. Its chest pumped. This calf was alive!

Still lying on the ground, Short Round started making low "muuuurrrrrh" sounds to her new calf. Bob and I lifted the calf by his back legs and gave him a shake to clear his lungs. Mom grabbed us some flakes of hay, and we rubbed away the placenta. A mother cow licks the placenta off her newborn, and since a cow's tongue is very rough, this action is like an aggressive rubbing— it cleans the calf and provides stimulation to survive. Since Short Round was out of commission for a bit, we were rubbing the calf aggressively to keep it fighting to survive. A few minutes later, Short Round started working to stand up. Bob unclipped the lasso from her. She lurched forward and stood. I caught a little tear in the corner of my Mom's eye as she said, "Good girl. You did good!" Now it was Short Round's turn to get her calf going. We pulled the calf over to a sunny corner of the barn stall and left the pair to recover together.

Walking away from the barn, I looked down to see my overalls soiled more than usual. Truthfully, I was filthy. What was not sweat-soaked had either placenta, dirt, or manure on it. Regardless, I was wearing a smile of triumph. How many people went out and ran seven miles, then joined in with their family to save the life of a calf, all before breakfast?

I washed up and sat down to a breakfast of fresh farm eggs, cereal, and bagels. Right afterward, Mom went out to the barn to check on the new calf. She came back in a hurry to report that the calf was still laying flat and Short Round was ignoring him. Standing in the doorway with her coveralls on, she said, "Hey, Willy, we better get some rags and go get him dry."

I gathered a bag full of old socks and put my overalls back on. Out at the barn, I baited the cow out of the stall with some corn. Mom and I knelt down by the calf and started

347

rubbing him with socks like we were trying to polish his black fur to a high gloss. The calf responded by lifting his head instead of lying flat on the ground like a noodle. We continued for about half an hour until the calf was dry and held his head up. We folded his legs under him so he was lying much like the Sphinx in Egypt. Underneath him, we placed a flake of a straw bale. The next hurdle for this calf was standing, and then nursing would follow. If he could achieve those goals within twenty-four hours, he would likely live. However after being subjected to such a long hard labor, his survival was very uncertain. Breeched calves rarely survive the delivery.

A few hours later, we checked on Short Round and her calf again. He appeared stronger and even tried to stand. He definitely had the will to live, but his legs were weak.

In the afternoon, Dad took vacation time from work and returned home to spend the rest of Saturday with the family. He was glad to see that we had saved the breeched calf. We decided that it would be best to give the calf colostrum with the bottle or the esophageal feeder in order to get him started. He was still too weak to stand and nurse the cow. Giving him a bottle would help him build strength. At about two in the afternoon, Dad and I went out to the barn with a bottle of colostrum. I lifted the calf to his feet. He attempted to stand, but his front hooves folded and he could hardly hold himself up. However the calf was perfectly happy to nurse the bottle lying down. He took three pints of milk. That was enough to tide him over until the next day.

Short Round and her calf spent that night in the barn, sheltered from the elements. The next morning, the calf was able to feebly walk. Dad poured some ground corn into Short Round's feed pan and then gently pushed her calf around to the cow's udder. Her udder must have become sore from not being nursed because she kicked her young calf away whenever he would try to nurse her back nipples. When this happened, Dad calmly pushed the calf back over to her udder and put the nipple back in the calf's mouth. Over the next few days, Dad's persistence paid off, and the young calf started nursing all four of the nipples without our intervention. Slowly, her calf began to gain strength, and around day five, he earned a name. Since the calf was positioned backwards when it was born, his front legs were not straight. His hooves had a tendency to buckle, and we referred to him as Crooked Toes. In a few weeks, his legs grew stronger, and he was able to keep them straight. However, the name Crooked Toes stuck.

Chapter 44: The Cows of Fall

Hauling Grain

It's after sunset when I climb down from the cab of our blue New Holland tractor. My boots crunch the bean stubble left behind by the combine as I walk toward the red CaseIH tractor. Approaching the other rig, I can see a mound of soybeans peaking above the top of the wagon. It looks full. Since seven o'clock this morning, I've been hauling away wagonloads of beans. The first wagons I pulled down to the grain elevator were full of beans, harvested yesterday evening. I had returned the empty wagons and staged them at the field. By ten am, the breezes and sunshine had dried off the morning dew and Dad started cutting beans as fast as our John Deere combine could go. The moisture content of the grain has stayed below thirteen-and-a-half percent; plenty dry enough to get some serious work done. I step behind the large back tire of the tractor, unzip my pants, and take a leak. It's been a busy day. I've had to keep rolling so that Dad would have empty wagons to fill. If I don't keep hauling, we won't have capacity for the beans that the combine is harvesting. That situation means the combine just sits and idles. On a fall day this nice, no farmer wants their combine to sit for very long. I zip up and watch as the giant dust cloud at the other end of the field turns and a green combine emerges. Dad turns the combine back toward the standing beans and drops the header to the ground. He's cutting in my direction now. My cellphone rings and I know its Dad.

I answer, "Hey Dad."

Over the background noise of the combine, I hear, "Yeah, Willy, why don't you go ahead and take that blue wagon to the shed. WCRC is calling for a chance of rain."

I turn to the west and reply, "I heard that. The sky is starting to bank up in the west."

Dad continues, "I'll fill this green wagon and roll the tarp over it."

"Sounds good. Do you need anything? I left you a Diet Coke in the blue tractor."

"Nah, I'm doing fine. I'll grab that drink when I unload my hopper." Looking back toward the combine, I instinctively nod as if he could see it from a quarter mile away.

I respond, "All right, I'll see you at home in about forty-five minutes. Bye-bye."

I flip the phone shut and slide it into the holster on my belt. I take a few moments to observe the beautiful evening. I love the fall season, but it always seems to pass by so quickly. Harvest is the busiest time of year on the farm. As long as the weather is good, we are out there harvesting, hauling grain, planting winter wheat, filling the grain bins, and doing hundreds of other little tasks that keep the equipment running. To the west, the evening sky is colored bright red above the low clouds on the horizon. The sunset is uniquely spectacular because harvesting grain fills the air with dust. I can clearly hear the combine, but it's far enough away that I can enjoy the quiet. I welcome the absence of noise and listen. In the nearby prairie, I hear the gathering call of a bobwhite quail. It's roosting time for them. The covey of quail will circle up in the grass and hide from predators during the night. I see a small flock of doves flying toward me; their wings whistle as they pass.

I climb up in the red tractor and crank the engine. I check the gauges and notice that the tractor will need fueled up tomorrow morning. I turn on the hazard lights and release the parking brake. I shift the tractor in gear and slowly drive out of the field toward the road. I consider, *Hmmm, I didn't check the cows today. Hopefully, they are behaving.* The cows tend to get ignored a bit during harvest. Lucky for us, they are preoccupied with their favorite wild food—acorns.

In Search of Acorns

Between the ages of eleven and fourteen, I was too young to haul grain in the fall but old enough to help out in other areas. During the weekends of harvest season, Dad and Bob would usually head for the fields early in the morning. I would stay around the house with Mom and Sarah. After the boys left for the fields, Mom directed my activities. Since Mom's weekdays were devoted to teaching school, a slew of thankless jobs would always pile up on her. Dirty laundry and floors, old food in the refrigerator, tall grass in the yard; all these things had to be addressed. It was my job to help her with some of the chores. By ten o'clock, Mom would usually release me from duty. This was my chance to escape and head down in the pasture to check the cows.

I'd walked down to the woods at the south end of the pasture. During the summer grazing pattern, the cows slept in the woods mid-day, but during the fall, the situation was quite different. The herd split up into bands of cows in search of acorns. Along my route, I would enjoy walking through the grazed pasture. By fall, the constant grazing and drier weather kept the grass short like a lawn. It was always easy walking.

On this particular afternoon, I crossed the creek down near the south water gap and walked east, into the south woods. There, the majestic white oak trees were dropping their acorns. Fall winds caused the top limbs to sway. With each gust, three or four acorns tumbled from the crown to the ground. The largest group of cows could be found there. They were quietly hanging out with their noses to the ground, searching and sniffing for the freshly fallen acorns. I started counting the cows— one, two, three ... twenty-eight, twenty-nine.

From there, I headed north to find more of the cows. I stopped atop the long hill that terminated as a cliff above the creek. *A-ha, five more cows ... thirty-four.* Then I walked along the creek, checking out each tiny wooded hillside for cows. *Four more cows in the creek branch from our neighbor Elmer's land, that's thirty-eight cows.* I checked under the old burr oak tree. With strong roots anchored into the base of the bluff, its limbs reached out over the bottom. The cows loved the burr oak acorns, and they grazed the area beneath the tree bare, looking for them. *As expected, three more... Forty-one cows.* From there, I walked to the very northeast corner of the pasture and checked our section of pastured woods that butted up against Elmer's woods. Brushy cedar trees lined the west side of the little woods. The cows loved walking under the cedar trees, where the low branches would sweep off flies. I ducked down and followed one of the established paths into the woods. *Just two more. That's only forty-three cows.* Somewhere along the way, I'd missed some cows. Unfortunately, there were plenty of places for them to hide, and it was quite possible that I miscounted. I thought to myself, *I better walk back and check the mysterious hill.* I backtracked and passed by some of the cows that I counted earlier; however, instead of going all the way to the south woods, I headed over to a wooded hillside along the west edge of the pasture. As I approached, I could see the band of cows from the south woods heading for the hill. I hurried up so that I could check the mysterious hill before they would arrive. I crested the top of the hill and found three cows. *Now the count is forty-six cows...Nuts! I needed to count forty-five.* Either I miscounted, or the one of the cows moved to another group and got counted twice. I sat down on a fallen log and watched the cows.

The cow's habit of eating acorns makes them nearly impossible to count in the fall. I knew this, but I still felt silly having walked all around the pasture only to come up with the wrong number. I heard the barking of a fox squirrel and spotted him in a hickory about sixty yards off. I thought to myself, *Maybe Mom will let me take my .410 so I can squirrel hunt while checking the cows.* I'm sure she would let me, but she may impose a two-squirrel limit. A few years prior, I got in trouble when I would go squirrel hunting after school and bring home the legal bag limit of five squirrels repeatedly. I would clean the squirrels out by the chicken house and bring in a plastic bucket full of the meat. Mom would say, "William, I can't keep up cooking all of these squirrels you kill. From now on when you go out, the limit is TWO squirrels."

I walked back to the house knowing that Mom would wonder what took me so long. As I stepped inside the house, Mom asked, "Did you find all the cows?"

I answered, "Well, I think so, but I miscounted because I got forty-six instead."

Mom chuckled and said, "Were they scattered out everywhere eating acorns?"

"Yep! Most were in the south woods, then there were some along Elmer's branch, more under the bur oak tree, a few in the northeast woods, and some on the mysterious hill."

Mom smiled, "How about we take the boys some lunch in the field, then you, me, and Sarah will take a walk to count the cows again this afternoon?"

Return to Hauling Grain

I return to the present from my memories. The tractor gently rocks from side to side as the big back tires are slightly off balance. One hundred yards out from the home barn lot, I clutch the tractor and let it roll. The heavily loaded wagon pushes the tractor along, and after about fifty yards, the rig starts to slow. I turn to the north and coast into the grassy area of the barn lot. To enter the barn, I shift down a
355

couple of gears and pull a wide arc to straighten out the rig. Glancing at the mirrors, I watch the clearance between the wagon and the barn wall. Inside the barn, the tractor is much louder than when running in the open field. When the wagon is completely under-roof, I clutch the tractor and shift to neutral. I set the parking brake and let the engine idle for a few minutes. When I shut off the engine and climb down from the cab, I hear one of the cows bawling at me. It's one of those bawls that says, "Hey, where have you been? I want some corn!" I see the cow. It's Miss Piggy, and she's standing under the post oak tree searching for acorns. I smile and walk up to the house. It's time to relax for the evening.

Chapter 45: Cows by the Numbers

Analysis of any topic would not be complete without a look at the numbers. So let us consider cows by the numbers:

1—Symbolizing the best cow that ever lived on Gillespie Farms, Felini.

2—Subspecies of cattle, *Bos taursus* from Europe and *Bos indicus* from Asia, India, and Africa.[28]

3—Cows first brought to Plymouth, Massachusetts, aboard the ship Anne in 1623. (Also happened to be three years after the Mayflower in 1620. *How did the pilgrims survive for three years without cows?*)[29]

4—The number of nipples found on a cow's udder.

5—The top five beef cattle breeds as reported by American Cowboy magazine: Angus, Hereford, Gelbvieh, Limousin, and Simmental.

6—A cow's large intestine is roughly six times the length of the cow from the base of the tail to nose.

7—The seven top producers of cattle: United States, twenty-five percent of production; Brazil, twenty percent; European Union, seventeen percent; China, twelve percent; Argentina, six percent; India, six percent; and Australia, four percent.

9—Months in a cow's gestation period—more specifically, 283 days.

10—Major cuts of meat: brisket, fore shank, chuck, rib, short loin, sirloin, round, flank, tip, short plate.[30]

44—The average number of cows on a cattle and calf beef operation[31]

---

[28] Thomas, Heather S. *Storey's Guide to Raising Beef Cattle*. North Adams, MA: Storey Publishing, 2009.

[29] http://mayflowerhistory.com/livestock/

[30] http://www.bigbeefbarn.com/images/beef_chart.jpg

[31] http://www.beefusa.org/beefindustrystatistics.aspx

57— Pounds of beef available for consumption per capita in the U.S. for 2010.[32]

800—Roughly eight hundred breeds of cattle recognized world-wide.

89.3—Million is the total cattle inventory for the US in 2013.

915,000—The number of cattle & calf operations in the US. *That means there are a lot more cow stories than just the few contained in this book. Thank you for reading, and I hope you enjoyed, "Cows I Have Known!"*

---

[32] http://www.ers.usda.gov/amber-waves/2012-september/us-consumption-of-chicken.aspx#.UqKR1CesqM0

Guide by Name

Beatrix Butts-a-Lot: *A friendly heifer calf that was taught by my mom to play and butt. As with most calves, once she was moved to the weaning-lot her personality diminished.*

Blacky: *A Holstein steer that was Felini's barn companion while being raised on the bottle.*

Blindy: *A bull calf that was saved from freezing to death. The intense cold damaged his sight.*

Bonga: *A grumpy black cow with white markings on her face. She was believed to be the offspring of Fibbing Face. Bonga always held her head high in contempt of us all.*

Bufoe: *The name given to most recent bull.*

Bullah: *The general name given to the bulls on the farm.*

Calf-Killer: *A coal-black cow that earned her moniker in the scariest event I experienced on the farm.*

City-on-Her-Back: *A large Hereford with an unusually flat and expansive back. We joked that it was large enough to build a city on.*

Corn-Eating Machine: *A very wide Jersey and Angus mix, she was raised on the bottle by my grandpa. She was always tame, but learned to play rough and developed a mean streak in later years.*

Crooked Toes: *He was the calf of Short Round that was breached at birth. We successfully pulled him and saved both Short Round and the calf.*

Falcon: *A pet mallard duck who imprinted me from his birth. He was indeed the greatest duck that ever lived.*

Feedlot Cow: *A very wild cow with tannish-orange fur and a white-patched face. She gave birth to a calf in the feedlot and was transferred to the home herd. Year after year she raised healthy calves. She was a homely cow, and for years we wanted to sell her. She stayed on the farm by giving birth right before we hauled off cull cows.*

Felini: *Herford in appearance, Felini set the bar for all cows before and after. She came into this world as part of a tragedy. Her mother prolapsed her uterus while giving birth and didn't survive. Felini was raised on the bottle and was far and away the gentlest and most loving cow that I have ever known. We will always miss her.*

Fibbing Face: *A yellow and white cow with a terrible attitude problem. She earned her name because of her unexpressive nature.*

Floppiness: *The cow featured on the front cover. She was an absolutely gigantic, cream-colored Charolais. Compare the size of her head to my leg on the front cover. Her name, Floppiness, was given because of her large ears that flopped up and down as she ran toward the trough.*

Good Gray Cow: *A large gray cow that was one of my personal favorites. She had all the good qualities that you could ask for in a cow, and she was tame. She also became the leader of the home herd.*

Horned Cow: *A general name applied to the few cows on Gillespie Farms with horns. For a time, horned cows were present in both herds.*

Hungry: *This bull calf was the offspring of Feedlot Cow. He was all black, bulky and is the calf depicted in Sarah Gillespie's painting titled "Hungry."*

Julia Gulia: *Part of Felini's class, this gray cow was named for having a face that reminded me of Julia Roberts. "Julia Roberts" didn't roll off the tongue, so after I watched the Adam Sandler movie "The Wedding Singer," the character's name, Julia Gulia, stuck.*

Killer Cow: *A coal-black Angus that was normal until she calved. At that point any person within fifty yards of her calf was in the kill-zone.*

Little Red Cow: *A tough, small red cow with a very pleasant personality.*

Miss Piggy: *A tame gray cow with a love for corn and being scratched behind the ears.*

Nuisance (also known as "Black Nuisance"): *Favorite cow of my mother. A coal-black cow with an aggressive* temperament and an attitude that says, "You don't bother me!"

Red Rip: *Large-red Limousin-Charolois mix cow with a gruff personality. She was an ally.*

Snoopy: *A gentle Hereford-Angus mix cow that was always curious about the happenings in the barn.*

Silage Cow: *My favorite cow. She had gray, shaggy fur and kind heart. She was completely tame, and never the slightest bit aggressive to my family.*

Sister: *A coal-black cow that followed in her mother's footsteps by twinning. Unfortunately, sister had an unpleasant attitude. She was aggressive toward us when given the chance. She also ended up at the lowest level of the home herd cattle hierarchy.*

Slimer: *A black heifer raised by the bottle after being abandoned by her mother.*

Slimer's Mom: *A whitish-gray cow that became the first truly negligent mother cow I ever encountered.*

South America: *A gentle Angus-Hereford mix. She was named for the white patch on her face in the shape of South America.*

Square Face: *A large yellow cow in the home herd that was named for her distinctive square face. She narrowly survived a serious illness and later damaged my dad and his truck.*

Swimmer Cow: *A typical-looking Hereford cow with red fur and a white face that was often missing when I would check the cows in the home herd during the summer. Whenever I realized that Swimmer Cow was missing, I knew that she was off taking a dip in the pond.*

Timid Cow: *A Black Angus and Hereford mix that was always shy but never wild. The aggressive cows of the Bogota herd routinely intimidated her away from the feeder. She was a great mother.*

Twinsey's Mom (a.k.a. White Eyes): *A black cow with white patches around her eyes. She perfected twinning excellence with the twin calves, Brother and Sister.*

White-Tailed Cow: *A tan-orange colored cow with white fur on her face and tail. She was part of the Bogota herd and started the lineage of white-tailed cows that were a pain to deal with.*

Works Cited

Amaral-Phillips, D. "Important Steps During the Silage Fermentation Process." *University of Kentucky Dairy Animal and Food Sciences Extension*, 2000: http://afsdairy.ca.uky.edu/extension/nutrition/milkingcows/forages/silagefermentationprocess

Bennett, Pamela J., Et al. "Indiana Territory," *The Indiana Historian,* March 1999: http://www.in.gov/history/files/interritory.pdf

Bolin, Carole. "Leptospirosis in Cattle." *Merck Veterinary Manual*, March 2012: http://www.merckmanuals.com/vet/generalized_conditions/leptospirosis/leptospirosis_in_cattle.html

Borror, Donald J. and Richard E. White. *A Field Guide to the Insects*. Boston, MA: Houghton Mifflin Company, 1970.

Carroll, Sean B. "Tracking the Ancestry of Corn Back 9,000 Years." *New York Times,* May 24, 2010: http://www.nytimes.com/2010/05/25/science/25creature.html?_r=0

Cordoba, Connie. "Understanding Dairy Cattle Behavior to Avoid Animal-Related Accidents on the Farm." *University of Wisconsin-Madison Department of Dairy Science and the Babcock Institute Farm Safety Facts Sheet,* 2005: http://babcock.wisc.edu/sites/default/files/documents/en_behavior.pdf

Curran, William R. "Indian Corn. Genesis of Reid's Yellow Dent," *Journal of the Illinois State Historical Society* XI, January 1919: 576-585. https://archive.org/stream/jstor-40194511/40194511#page/n11/mode/2up

Endres, Bryan A., and Lisa R. Schlessinger. "A Move Towards a More Fair Division: Envisioning a New Illinois Fence Act," *University of Illinois Department of Agricultural and Consumer Economics Agricultural Law and Taxation Briefs*, December 13, 2012: http://farmdoc.illinois.edu/legal/articles/ALTBs/ALTB_12-01/ALTB_12-01.pdf

Hall, J.B., and Susan Silver. "Nutrition and Feeding of the Cow-Calf Herd: Digestive System of the Cow," *Virginia Polytechnic Institute and State University College of Agriculture and Life Sciences Virginia Cooperative Extension*, 2009: http://pubs.ext.vt.edu/400/400-010/400-010_pdf.pdf

Herring, William O. "Calving Difficulty in Beef Cattle: BIF Fact Sheet," *University of Missouri Agriculture Extension*, 1996: http://extension.missouri.edu/p/G2035

Illinois Department of Agriculture. "Facts About Illinois Agriculture," *About the Department of Agriculture*, 2001: http://www.agr.state.il.us/about/agfacts.html

"Illinois Domestic Animals Running At Large Act." *Illinois General Assembly Legislative Information System Illinois Compiled Statutes,* Springfield, IL: http://www.ilga.gov/legislation/ilcs/ilcs3.asp?ActID=1714&ChapterID=41

Illinois, University of. "Ethanol, Food and Fuel Issues." University of Illinois College of Agricultural, Consumer and Environmental Sciences, March 2009: http://web.extension.illinois.edu/ethanol/foodvfuel.cfm

King, Carol. "Dorsal Recumbency: Getting Stuck Upside-Down." *Pygmy Goat World Magazine*, 1994. http://kinne.net/dorsrec.htm

McMahon, Margaret J., Anton M.Kofranek, and Vincent E. Rubatzky. *Hartmann's Plant Science*. Upper Saddle River, NJ: Prentice Hall, 2002.

Mctavish, E. J., J. E. Decker, R. D. Schnabel, J. F. Taylor, and D. M. Hillis. "New World Cattle Show Ancestry from Multiple Independent Domestication Events." *Proceedings of the National Academy of Sciences*, April 9, 2013: E1398-1406. http://www.ncbi.nlm.nih.gov/pubmed/23530234

"Records of the General Land Office, 1800-1908." *National Archives and Records Administration*, http://www.archives.gov/chicago/finding-aids/land.html

Schwartz, Charles W., and Elizabeth R. Schwartz. *The Wild Mammals of Missouri*. Columbia, MO: University of Missouri Press and Missouri Conservation Commission, 1959.

Shamel, A.D. "The Art of Seed Selection and Breeding." *The Yearbook of Agriculture 1907*. Washington D.C.: US Dept. of Agriculture Government Printing Office, 1908. P221-236.

Thomas, Heather S. *Storey's Guide to Raising Beef Cattle*. North Adams, MA: Storey Publishing, 2009.

Thorington, Richard W., John L. Koprowski, Michael A. Steele, and James F. Whatton. *Squirrels of the World*. Baltimore, MD: The Johns Hopkins University Press, 2012.

Umphrey, J.E., and C.R. Staples. "General Anatomy of the Ruminant Digestive System." *Dairy Production Guide Fact Sheet DS31*, Florida Cooperative Extension Service, 1992. http://mysrf.org/pdf/pdf_dairy/cow_handbook/dc15.pdf

Underwood, William H. and Robert A. Halbert. *Statutes of Illinois Construed: Containing the Statutes of 1874 as Amended by the Acts of 1875 and 1877*. St.Louis, MO: W.J. Gilbert Law Book Publisher, 1878. Print. http://books.google.com/books/about/Statutes_of_Illinois_C onstrued.html?id=iEkwAQAAMAAJ

Wetmore, Alexander, and Peter P. Kellogg. *Water, Prey, and Game Birds of North America*. Washington, D.C.: National Geographic Society, 1965.

Epilogue

Picture the perfect pasture: rolling hills covered with lush, green grass, a clear rocky stream, and tree-lined ravines. Unfortunately, cattle are detrimental to the nicest parts of that landscape. Cows don't intentionally damage the land; they simply love it to death. In the woods, cows aggressively feed on tree leaves and create a grazed-out zone from the ground to the limit of their reach, up about five feet. The shade provided by the trees is coveted on hot days. The cows spend so much time lounging under the trees that they compact the soil around the tree roots and destroy the ground cover of leaf litter. The bare soil erodes away and chokes the streams with sediment. The trees' roots become exposed and even more susceptible to damage. In the spring, the cows shed their coarse winter fur. This process must be itchy for the cows because they will rub on trees as well as posts, fences, gates, feeders, barns or any other stationary object. Rubbing on trees causes damage to the bark and to the roots beneath the cows' hooves. In the fall, the cows love to eat acorns. A herd will aggressively search out the fallen nuts by splitting into small bands and wandering about the pasture from oak tree to oak tree. By damaging the existing trees, consuming the seeds, compacting the soil, and causing erosion, cows leave an indelible mark on pastured woods and downstream waterways.

This indelible mark was definitely apparent in woods at the south end of the home pasture. It once provided a spot for the cows to avoid the summer heat. Today, the area is still a woods, but no longer a pasture. A few years after selling the Bogota herd, we downsized the home herd by selling all but 20 of the cows. In 2005, we built fence to exclude the bottomlands and the east side of the pasture. The remaining cows were limited to grazing only in the winter lot and the west side of what had been the summer pasture. The areas outside the fence were enrolled in the CRP program, and we began the process of restoring the land to the native prairie grasses and trees that existed before the area was a cattle pasture. I have always known that cows are destructive to the land and realized their impacts are lasting. Now, more than ten years after the cows last set hoof in the south woods, it's still very evident that this was a pasture woods. New trees are slow to regenerate, and the forest floor lacks sensitive spring flower species like Dutchmen's breeches, jack-in-the-pulpit, and dog-tooth violets. The most noticeable legacy impact is the accelerated demise of the massive oak trees. To the outside observer, the woods is very open and park-like; however, it is not a healthy ecosystem. My family has always felt guilty for its condition and once the cattle were fenced-out, we started a spring ritual of planting trees in the old pasture woods. This year we planted a very special tree.

The Blight

Back in 1904 the chief forester of the Bronx Zoo noticed that the chestnut trees in what was then the New York Zoological Park were dying. The following year scientists determined that the terminal disease was caused by a fungus. This exotic fungus had traveled to New York in wooden shipping crates and spread to the nearby chestnut trees. By

1940 the disease had spread throughout the eastern states, Appalachia, and the Ohio River valley, thus resulting in the loss of nearly every single native chestnut tree. It is believed that prior to the blight, chestnut trees composed twenty-five to thirty percent of the hardwood forests in the eastern woodlands. Chestnut trees that were not killed by the blight were often inadvertently removed during salvage logging operations. The catastrophe had far-reaching effects to the ecosystem since the chestnuts were prolific producers of nuts for the wildlife to eat.

Efforts to restore and protect the American chestnut began not long after the magnitude of the problem was detected. Unfortunately trees grow much more slowly than they die, and only recently have blight resistant chestnut trees become available from nurseries. The trees available are not 100% pure American chestnut; they contain some genes from the blight resistant Chinese chestnut trees, but they are as close to the original trees as one can get. This year we were able to purchase several chestnut trees. Before we even had the trees in hand, Mom and I knew the perfect spot to plant one.

In Honor

As we walked through the former pasture woods, pleasant memories filled my mind. I remembered checking and counting the sleepy cows. When I looked around at their former resting spots, I imagined seeing again the gruff Red Rip, the lovable Silage Cow, the regal Good Gray Cow, the motherly City-on-Her-Back, the ornery Slimer's Mom, the comical Julia Gulia, and Felini. I feel a pleasant sense of nostalgia and reminisce about the cows with Mom. She grins and tells a few of her favorite stories, but her smile fades when we walk to one particular spot in the woods, she quietly shakes her head. It was here that she found Felini. Mom didn't let her children see what had happened, but she told us. A tree fell on Felini. It probably killed her instantly where she rested. Our good Felini was ten years old and likely had many more years ahead of her. She was in her prime. It's sardonic; our herd of cows caused the tree to die, and then the tree caused the death of our best cow, Felini.

I set down the potted tree, and Mom started digging a hole. The soil was mellow and moist, perfect for planting a tree. Apparently nature had loosened up the soil compaction caused by the cows. I pulled the plastic pot off the root ball and placed the tree in the hole. We backfilled around the roots with loose soil and then watered the tree from a nearby pond. Mom stepped back to admire the cheerful young chestnut. I spotted a tear in the corner of her eye. She shook her head and sighed, "You know, Will, I vividly remember the day I found her, but it's all black and white. The sky, the grass, the tree, Felini's body; everything was just gray."

We looked around at the other trees we have planted since the woods has been cattle-free. A few are doing well, but many have been rubbed to death by rutting whitetail deer. In disgust I said, "I brought along some woven wire. Let's put a fence around that chestnut to keep those bucks out." I retrieved the supplies from the truck and thought to myself, *Felini was born in a disaster, enriched our lives, and died before her time. Somehow, it's fitting that we are planting a chestnut tree in her honor.*

Acknowledgements

Since time is the most valuable commodity of all, I am in deep debt to those closest to me for all the time I spent writing "Cows I Have Known." Their support has been unwavering, and for that, I am so thankful. I am especially grateful to my family, who lifted my spirits when the writing got tough and repeatedly assured me, that writing this book was important. They all became characters represented in this book; if they are portrayed as anything less than loving, wonderful people, then I have failed.

Elizabeth Phelps also deserves my gratitude for editing the first version of this book. I chuckle when imagining the look on her face, the first time I called and asked if she would be interested in editing a book of cow stories. Thankfully, she agreed and her efforts vastly improved the manuscript.

Finally, I would also like to express my appreciation for the efforts of this book's focus group. When I submitted the manuscript to them, I was as nervous as a cat on a hot tin roof. They responded with good advice and suggestions that helped me improve the final form.

68222310R00224

Made in the USA
Lexington, KY
09 October 2017